South Africa: The New Revolution

"A book written with passion. It has to be read."
Aggrey Klaaste

"An important work that adds critical insights to the current debate on social transformation."
Saths Cooper

"Controversial and thought-provoking. A must for all interested in the creation of a new, free, just, and nonracial democratic South Africa."
Don Mkhwanazi

"Don Caldwell is an unconventional, original, and lateral thinker."
Frederik van Zyl Slabbert

"Most policy analysis is trapped in too much caution, conventionalism, and precedent. Not Caldwell's. If policymakers read this book, it will transform their agendas."
Lawrence Schlemmer

"The basic principles in this book should be urgently studied by all those who are participating in the debate on constitutional change in South Africa – especially those who are taking part in actual negotiations."
Geert de Wet

South Africa: The New Revolution

"Essential reading for all South Africans yearning to exhume themselves from beneath the dead myths and dying ideologies of both left and right. A revelatory and uplifting vision."
Rian Malan
Author of My Traitor's Heart

"An extraordinary book: entertaining and readable – in parts so witty you laugh out loud – yet thoroughly researched and meticulously argued. It blasts fresh air through the South African debate."
Frances Kendall and Leon Louw
Authors of South Africa: The Solution

"A crisp, insightful, and penetrating analysis of apartheid."
Walter Williams
Author of South Africa's War Against Capitalism

"A remarkably imaginative, incredibly thought-provoking book that shatters political and economic myths and leaves in its wake a refreshing breeze of hope for the future."
Kaizer Nyatsumba
Author of A Vision of Paradise

The Customer is Always Wrong!

"An invaluable aid...inexpensive, brief, and to the point. It could do your employees more good than a month of jargon-filled seminars."
Financial Mail

"Sure to send ripples of discomfort through the business world."
Sunday Star

A book "which every company serving the public should have in its library and every executive on his desk."
Sunday Times

"Seriously funny. A well-deserved swipe at big-name companies."
Femina

" 'n Mens kan nie help om lekker te lag vir die gevallestudies nie. Gelukkig word daar ook oplossings vir al hierdie lastighede in die boek bespreek."
Beeld

"Required reading for all managerial staff."
Sunday Tribune

To my brothers, Rob, Jim, and Tom

Published in March 1992 by:
Conrad Business Books
Box 41469
Craighall 2042
South Africa

Telephone (011) 788-4567
Fax (011) 442-4943

Deliveries to:
11 South Heathrow
Sixth Road
Hyde Park

Contact Conrad Business Books for information on having Don Caldwell address your organisation or for bulk orders of *No More Martyrs Now*, *The Customer is Always Wrong!*, and *South Africa: The New Revolution*.

ISBN 0-620-16518-9

A Bill of Rights for a Democratic South Africa © 1990 by the African National Congress and reprinted with permission ■ *No More Martyrs* © 1990 by Kaizer Mabhilidi Nyatsumba and reprinted with permission

Consultant on book and cover design: Mark Heaton of IntelSet, (011) 444-3100 ■ Typesetting by Theresa Griessel of Conrad Business Services ■ Set in 10/12 Palatino ■ Cover illustration by Mpolokeng Ramphomane ■ Photographs of the author by Robert Tshabalala ■ Printed by The Natal Witness Printing and Publishing Company

No More
Martyrs Now

Conrad Business Books

JOHANNESBURG

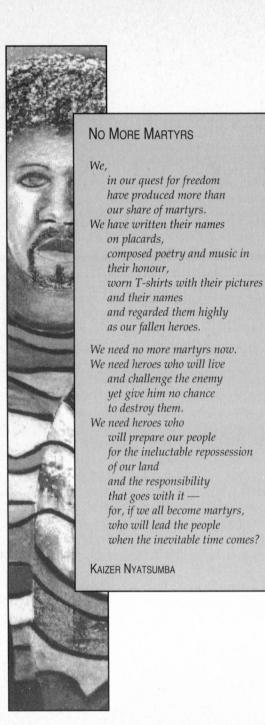

No More Martyrs

We,
    in our quest for freedom
    have produced more than
    our share of martyrs.
We have written their names
    on placards,
    composed poetry and music in
    their honour,
    worn T-shirts with their pictures
    and their names
    and regarded them highly
    as our fallen heroes.

We need no more martyrs now.
We need heroes who will live
    and challenge the enemy
    yet give him no chance
    to destroy them.
We need heroes who
    will prepare our people
    for the ineluctable repossession
    of our land
    and the responsibility
    that goes with it —
    for, if we all become martyrs,
    who will lead the people
    when the inevitable time comes?

Kaizer Nyatsumba

NO MORE MARTYRS NOW

Capitalism,
Democracy,
and Ordinary
People

DON
CALDWELL

Contents

FOREWORD		10
INTRODUCTION		12
1	**CIVIL SOCIETY** The triumph of private life	14
2	**APARTHEID ECONOMICS** Apartheid was socialism	26
3	**TAXES** Bringing taxes under control	38
4	**AFFIRMATIVE ACTION** Look who's racist now	58
5	**FREE SPEECH** No more censors now	76
6	**THE RECALL** Keeping government accountable	88
7	**MAXIMUM DEMOCRACY** Referendums, local choice, and majority rule	104

8 THE ENVIRONMENT 116
The state versus
the environment

9 RIGHTS 128
Making sense of a constitution
and bill of rights

10 THE AFRICAN NATIONAL CONGRESS 150
The ANC's
authoritarian roots

11 AN ANC BILL OF RIGHTS 164
The new
battleground

CONCLUSION 174

DOCUMENTS 176
Freedom Charter ■ ANC Constitutional
Guidelines ■ ANC Constitutional
Principles ■ ANC Draft Bill of Rights ■
SA Law Commission Draft Bill of Rights ■
SA Law Commission Proposed Bill of
Rights ■ NP Constitutional Proposals

NOTES AND READINGS 232

INDEX 262

ABBREVIATIONS 270

ACKNOWLEDGEMENTS 271

ABOUT THE FOREWORD 271

ABOUT THE AUTHOR 272

CONFERENCES AND TRAINING 272

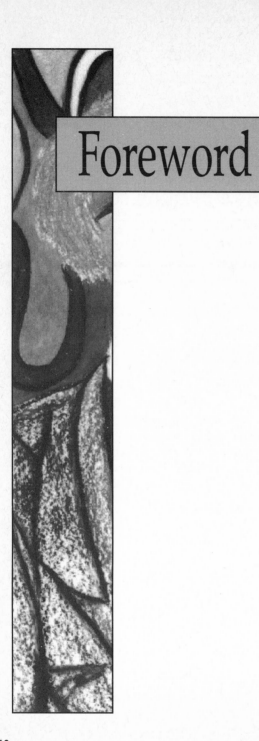

Foreword

'Punchy and penetrating'

Don Caldwell is a prolific writer with an insatiable appetite for debate on current political and economic issues. He explores popular political myths and economic shibboleths from a refreshing perspective that is deeply rooted in the traditions of liberal-democratic capitalism.

This book comes at a propitious time, as leaders in our country are called upon to rise above parochial party political interests for the benefit of a newly emerging democratic, stable, and prosperous society.

It is written in a frank journalistic style, which is punchy and penetrating. This is not a heavy book filled with academic jargon. It is an interesting and intelligible piece of work that forces you to think but doesn't make reading a formidable and painful task.

It presents well-researched arguments that are supported by useful references for those who want to delve further into these contentious subjects. Although some of the arguments too easily brush aside the more constructive ideas that come from the radical left, the book certainly contributes to the current socio-political debate and shines a ray of light on topical issues that are too often clouded by emotion.

It is a thought-provoking and challenging book that should be read by as many people as possible, particularly those who will become responsible citizens of our newly born nonracial democracy.

DON NCUBE

11

Introduction

Ordinary
heroes

Blah, blah, blah, blah, blah, blah, new South Africa, blah, blah, blah, blah, blah, blah, transition, blah, blah, blah, blah, blah, alliances, blah, blah, blah, blah, mandate, blah, blah, blah, blah, blah, blah, blah, blah, blah, blah, domination, blah, blah, blah, blah, blah, blah, equality.

Having trouble following the debate?

A lot of politicians prefer it that way. They love incomprehensible debates that lead to incomprehensible constitutions that enable them to become rich and powerful while everybody else gets screwed.

If there's an overriding message in this book, it's this: show a lot less faith in governments and a lot more faith in ordinary people.

Scattered across the country are great numbers of people who are trying quietly, with enormous energy and goodwill, to make things work. They are South Africa's ordinary heroes. And, if a new government can be prevented from riding roughshod over them, they will help make South Africa a flourishing, dynamic democracy.

What's needed is a constitution that tames power-hungry elites, slashes the size of government, lets diversity flourish, decentralises lawmaking, and unleashes the entrepreneurial spirit of an extraordinary country.

No More Martyrs Now is written from an unashamedly liberal-democratic perspective. It's in favour of capitalism and sceptical of politicians from beginning to end.

You can use the book as a guide to understanding the multiparty negotiations at Codesa, the Convention for a Democratic South Africa. But it won't become obsolete when a new constitution is drawn up. It tackles issues that are going to be around for many years to come. Tough questions about politics, economics, and human rights aren't going to go away just because there's somebody new in the Union Buildings.

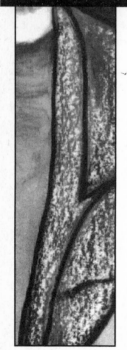

1

CIVIL SOCIETY

The
triumph
of private life

Before his fall and swift execution, Romanian dictator Nicolae Ceausescu treated his subjects like laboratory rats.

His secret police kept meticulous files on people's political opinions, sex lives, friends, and work. They kept samples from every typewriter to identify anonymous letters and manuscripts, and tried to satisfy Ceausescu's ambition to tap every phone in the country.[1] They continually updated a blacklist of people's names that could not be spoken aloud or printed, not even in crossword puzzles.[2] Terrified into submission, a third of all Romanians informed on their neighbours.

Minority cultures were to be eradicated. The country's two million Hungarians were forbidden to teach their language or history. Germans and Jews were allowed to emigrate to West Germany and Israel — but only if somebody paid ransom for them in hard currency.

Ceausescu razed ancient churches and monasteries, historic buildings, and entire villages to build his vision of a socialist society filled with "agro-industrial complexes."[3] He called the programme "systemisation," and a main feature of it was shoddy high-rise housing.[4] No room in any home was allowed more than one 60-watt lightbulb.[5]

Science was just another sphere of life for the government to control and twist. Elena Ceausescu, the dictator's wife, passed herself off as a scientist. Party literature slavishly described her as "a remarkable scientist of world repute, who makes an inestimable contribution to the development of science, education, and culture in our homeland."[6] Mrs Ceausescu, who had studied chemistry briefly, instigated a government decree that nobody should study the subject longer than she had. So for two decades, the study of chemistry was all but eliminated. A defector from the foreign-intelligence service says the esteemed scientist Elena Ceausescu was especially fond of a treatment called *Radu*, in which imprisoned dissidents were bombarded with radiation in the hope that they would die of cancer after being released.[7]

State television, which broadcast just two hours a day, reported largely on the "Hero of the Nation's Heroes" and his wife. Newspapers and radio were also simply mouthpieces of the regime.[8]

Literature, art, film, and law were all eliminated or hijacked by the government. No aspect of life was beyond the reach of the state, not even sex and reproduction. The government outlawed abortion and birth control and decreed that all women should bear five children.[9] Every woman had to submit to a gynaecological examination four times a year, and the police watched pregnant women to make sure they didn't terminate their pregnancies.[10] The Communist Party Central Committee set up Orphanage No. 1, which exported abandoned babies to earn foreign currency.[11]

Society existed for Romania's rulers to shape and control. The party was the state, and the state was everything.

Civil society

Romania's rulers could not tolerate civil society — private life independent of the party and the state. The term *civil society*, which has come to the fore recently as democratic revolutions have multiplied in Europe and Africa, is really another term for the private sector. But it's the private sector broadly defined to include not just businesses but individuals, groups, clubs, associations, cooperatives, and unions. Where free people can associate as they please, there is civil society.[12]

Some of these voluntary organs of civil society get involved in political life by acting as lobbying groups, entering what's called "political society." But many others simply get on with their business. They offer friendship and support, share skills and ideas, and build community life.[13]

But the organisations in civil society do something else, too. Simply by existing, they combat statism. They decentralise power from the state to individuals and their voluntary groups, which allows personal freedom to flourish. And this is exactly what social engineers can't stand. Social engineers dream of a homogeneous, ideal society, whether it be classless, raceless, racist, private-propertyless, or holy. So diversity must be smashed. It's no fun to rule over people who are doing their own thing.

Unfortunately, Ceausescu, for all his infamy, wasn't unique. An odious assortment of leaders — left-wing and right-wing, religious zealots and atheists — have been assaulting civil society in countries around the globe. A few have disappeared in the democratic revolutions in eastern Europe and, more recently, in Africa. But many remain.

The tools of the trade

How do social engineers assault civil society? They pass laws to outlaw organisations, or they order their secret police to harass groups until they disband. Through subsidies, favours, and patronage, they turn once-independent groups into organs of the state or the party. Or they overwhelm civil society with incessant propaganda in schools and the media.

An essential ingredient of their propaganda is self-glorification. They put their faces on money, stamps, TV, and enormous posters. They declare themselves presidents for life, give themselves glorious titles, and surround themselves with sycophants. Ceausescu's party literature called him the "morning star of Romania's national revolution" and "the national hero who with boundless devotion serves the supreme interests of all our people."

A member of Zimbabwe's parliament, Tony Gara, recently called President Robert Mugabe "the only other son of God." ZANU party newspaper advertisements call Mugabe "the most authentic, consistent and revolutionary leader."[14] Zaire's president, Mobutu Sese Seko, calls himself "the one who is and shall always be."[15]

If they rule as a group, they give themselves verbose titles, like the "State Law and Order Restoration Council," the name of the paranoic military junta that rules Myanmar, formerly called Burma. They transcribe their speeches into equally verbose books, such as *The Conspiracy of Treasonous Minions Within Myanmar and Traitorous Cohorts*.[16]

They confidently speak for a whole nation. As Life President Hastings Kamuzu Banda of Malawi explained: "The Malawi style is that Kamuzu says it's that and then it's finished."[17]

Kenyan president Daniel Arap Moi was more loquacious:

I call on all ministers, assistant ministers, and every other person to sing like parrots. During Mzee Kenyatta's period, I persistently sang the Kenyatta tune until people said: This fellow has nothing to say, except to sing for Kenyatta. I said: I did not have ideas of my own. Who was I to have my own ideas? I was in Kenyatta's shoes, and therefore, I had to sing whatever Kenyatta wanted. If I had sung another song, do you think Kenyatta would have left me alone? Therefore, you ought to sing the song I sing. If I put a full stop, you should put a full stop. This is how the country will move forward.[18]

Social engineers are suspicious of ideas in general and foreign ideas in particular. Pol Pot, who led Cambodia's murderous Khmer Rouge, ordered the destruction of all libraries, schools, theatres, and radio and TV stations.[19] A less drastic and more common method of controlling the spread of ideas is to own or control all the media, restrict access to foreign publications, and curb travel and emigration. Albania's rulers, for example, made "flight from the state" a crime.[20]

They label their critics "enemies" and then silence them. Fascists outlaw communists. Communists outlaw fascists. Reactionaries outlaw revolutionaries. Revolutionaries outlaw reactionaries. In Albania, "fascist, antidemocratic, religious, war-mongering, or antisocialist propaganda" was a crime. Cuba imprisons those who spread "enemy propaganda."[21]

To preserve the facade of national unity — a unity that *they* define and impose — social engineers persecute dissenters as enemies of the people or the state. Iran executes members of "atheistic and hypocritical mini-groups."[22] Somalia punishes those declared to be "exploiting religion for creating national disunity or subverting or weakening state authority."[23] Vietnam punishes "subversive activities against the power of the people."[24] Malawi's Forfeiture Act allows the president to seize all possessions of any citizen who has acted in a matter "prejudicial to the State."[25]

This is all in the great tradition of Albania, where back in 1961 the prime minister, Mehmet Shehu, decreed: "For those who stand in the way of unity, a spit in the face, a sock in the jaw, and, if necessary, a bullet in the head."[26]

Propaganda, thought control, and the relentless march toward unity are just the start. Social engineers supplement them with direct attacks on private associations. As in Ceausescu's Romania, any autonomous institution that offers a counterweight to state and party power or encourages independent action or thought must be either abolished or hijacked. This means restricting everything from organised religion (Cuba's dictator banned the Bible)[27] to self-help groups (Poland's dictators outlawed groups for battered women, abused children, and alcoholics).

Groups that aren't crushed are made subservient to the party or state. Consider women's organisations. In civil societies, women's groups fight the status quo from many directions: some lobby for abortion rights and affirmative action, and some call for a return to traditional family values. In socially engineered societies, the whole notion of independent movements is turned on its head. Women's groups become another tool for the rulers, who use them to indoctrinate, mobilise, and persecute. President Hastings Banda of Malawi has established a cult of thousands of women dancers who wear dresses emblazoned with his portrait and sing his praises whenever he appears in public.[28]

The Women's League in Zimbabwe, an arm of the ruling party, sings and dances for President Robert Mugabe. It also tries to solidify his rule. In 1985, the league joined another arm of the party, the Youth Brigade, in widespread assaults on government opponents. In 1990, Women's League representatives appeared on state television to urge the government to fire teachers who supported the opposition Zimbabwe Unity Movement.[29]

Social engineering at home

Of course, you don't have to look far afield to see government control of civil life. The architects of white supremacy in South Africa also controlled or shut down private associations that got in the way of their grand plans.

They strangled the private sector with countless boards and commissions and spun a web of censorship, forced removals, bannings, pass laws, and economic restrictions in an attempt to create a racial version of Romania's "systemisation." Personal choice, markets, and civil society interfere with totalitarian plans, so social engineers of all stripes crush them.

The South African government, however, never completely succeeded in crushing civil society. The National Party rulers lacked the totalitarian will to silence all independent bodies. White institutions, of course, retained more freedom than others. But even blacks were spared the full force of the totalitarian jackboot — or skilfully ducked out of its way.

Through some of the darkest days of apartheid's social engineering, the government left space — and people seized space — for independent-minded churches, universities, private schools, literature, family-planning clinics, research groups, business chambers, human-rights watchdogs, alternative printing presses, street theatre, burial societies, stokvels, and shebeens.

Newspapers — though barred from reporting on much police and army brutality, state secrets, and the utterances of outlawed activists — were allowed scope to express their opinions on the government's political, economic, and human-rights policies. This some did with an intensity and frequency that would be punishable by death in a totalitarian state. The government permitted many foreign magazines to circulate. Typewriters and photocopiers, and later desktop computers, were unrestricted, allowing some independent writing and research. Still, South Africans have to strengthen independent institutions — and add many more — to move from authoritarianism to lasting democracy.

Of course, all governments restrict the institutions of civil society in one way or another. But there are degrees of repression. And the more diverse and independent civil institutions are, the more likely it is that society will be able to resist the authoritarian tendencies of its rulers and preserve freedom.

Free people need space to breathe, away from a suffocating government. South African democrats should fight to make important segments of society off limits to state planners and party functionaries.

The kind of civil institutions that should be kept numerous, diverse, private, and independent include:

■ Churches.
■ TV and radio stations.
■ The press.
■ Universities and schools.
■ Parent-teacher associations.
■ Trade unions.
■ Business and industry and chambers of commerce.
■ Medical and legal associations and other professional bodies.
■ Civic associations.
■ Youth clubs.
■ Women's groups.
■ Service clubs and charities.
■ Human-rights monitors and journals.
■ Sports clubs, cultural organisations, and scientific bodies.
■ Libraries and museums.

These groups should be able to operate on their own property, organised under rules they set for themselves.

The task of building a vibrant civil society will not be easy. Just as the government is easing its control over civil life, some government opponents are gearing up to slap on new controls.

A big stumbling block is the monopoly mentality prevalent among activists, particularly in organisations aligned to the African National Congress. Representatives of these groups forever call for "unity" — a unity that *they* define. It is a false unity, which requires coercion against any who resist it.

A single nonracial teachers' union, a single nonracial cultural body, a single women's league, youth league, trade-union federation, soccer body, lawyers' association, civics association — these belong in a one-party state, not in a tolerant civil society. In its calls for these mass bodies, the hard left shows how little respect it has for independence and diversity.

"Forward to Democratic Working Class Control of Sport," say T-shirts worn at a South African Health Workers' Congress.[30]

"The people shall broadcast!" was the slogan of a march on the SABC, the state TV and radio service. The march was called to oppose the deregulation and privatisation of broadcasting, a move that would, in fact, allow "the people" — many people — to broadcast divergent opinions.

"One Country One Federation," say banners at Cosatu rallies.[31]

Of course, the people who use these slogans confidently assume that *they* will exercise the control or that *they* are "the people." Presumably, Cosatu would not support "one federation" in South Africa if Cosatu were not the federation. And central control of sport by anybody but those calling themselves the working class would be equally unacceptable.

The ANC and its allies also make disturbing calls for political unity — again, a unity that they will define and enforce. At Cosatu's third national congress in 1989, its secretariat complained that imperialists sow disunity by promoting a whole range of different political groupings with different agendas. This, they said, hinders "the process of uniting our people around a programme of fundamental political, economic, and social change" — reminiscent of the monopoly mentality of Ceausescu's Romania.[32]

For years, ANC representatives routinely referred to a two-sided struggle, with the ANC (the democratic forces, the broad democratic movement, the people, the people as a whole) on one side and the government (the regime, the enemy, the collaborators) on the other. This doesn't leave a lot of room for political pluralism. And without political pluralism, civil society is in danger of being destroyed by the ruling party.

Also at odds with civil diversity is the ANC's aim of mobilising an all-embracing national youth organisation. The language surrounding the organisation suggests that the ANC respects freedom of association — as long as you associate with *it*.

At the first national congress of the South African Youth Congress, which merged into the relaunched ANC Youth League in 1991, Peter Mokaba, Sayco's president, welcomed Nelson Mandela, saying: "Comrade Mandela. You are our leader and commander, we are your storm troopers. Give us your orders and we will obey them with the discipline you call for."[33]

In his address, Mandela praised the militant youth and said: "You will, of course, also have to attend to the question of the mobilisation of those sections of the youth who may not wish to be members of the ANC into the broad democratic movement, so that they too can make a contribution to the abolition of the apartheid system and the transformation of our country."[34]

Mobilising the youth into the broad democratic movement? A spokesperson explained that the organisation was following Cuba's example in resolving to set up a Pioneers section to politicise children aged five to 15. It planned to encourage nonracialism, nonsexism, non-competitiveness, caring, and patriotism in these young children. And it wants children's education, literature, music, films, and culture to be controlled by an ANC government to promote these values.[35]

The not-so-civil society

Is it liberal paranoia to see the seeds of totalitarianism in this language? Hardly. The civil society has become a buzz-phrase in ANC and SACP circles, but they've turned the concept on its head. Yes, they say, a wide range of organisations should exist — they most often mention associations of workers, women, and youth. But they should exist to build the *state's* vision of "democracy." The state will assign them a role.

In a formal request for US government financing in 1990, the ANC said it wants to use the money to achieve "a more clear understanding" among South Africans, especially "the women" and "the youth," "on the role which they will have to play in the new democratic order that will be the outcome of the negotiating process."[36]

The ANC's Albie Sachs explained to the journal *Index on Censorship* his interpretation of how to build a nation:

The media have to play a positive role in destroying the racial myths and helping to establish a nonracial quality of life. It is a question of building a nation. That is done not by proclamation, and not by a constitution. The constitution can only help to create the conditions for building a nation.

Agencies such as the unions, the churches, and the media can play an important role, perhaps more important than the government, by helping to create the habits of nonracial thinking and outlook. You can see what TV can do, what news reporting can do.[37]

So for Sachs, such "agencies" are just tools for promoting nonracialism and the ideology of the state and for changing people's habits of thinking. This is neither independent nor civil.

Here's an interchange between Joe Slovo, the ANC-SACP leader, and an interviewer from *Learn and Teach* magazine in 1990:

Learn and Teach: You have said there must be democracy at all levels of society in South Africa. Can you explain this?
Slovo: That's right. Democracy is not only voting in general elections every five years or so. For a society to be truly democratic, democracy must be practised from day to day. It is necessary, for example, for workers to participate in the direction of the factories where they work. Organisations such as trade unions, women's organisations, youth organisations should be given real recognition and participate in the whole process of running society, including civic and local structures and so on and so forth.[39]

But independent groups don't need "real recognition" by the state. They need to be left alone. What's important is to carve out areas of life that are off limits to the state, not to harness groups to "participate in the whole process of running society." Civil society is a reaction *against* people who think they can "run society."

War of position

Since the late 1980s, civil society in South Africa has been subjected to a sophisticated attack by the Mass Democratic Movement, the organisation that fronted for the ANC before it was unbanned in 1990. This attack is based on a communist strategy, called the "war of position," that firmly and unashamedly rejects a liberal society — and twists the concept of civil society.

In an article discussing the South African Communist Party's 1989 policy document *The Path to Power*, *South African Labour Bulletin* managing editor Karl von Holdt explained that the "war of position" was developed in the 1920s by Antonio Gramsci, an Italian communist. Gramsci recognised that churches, schools, trade unions, political parties, culture, sport, and the media could be outside the state and independent of it. But he didn't welcome this. He rejected it — because he (correctly) saw that these autonomous bodies would prevent the state from totally controlling society.

Von Holdt writes:

[Gramsci] argued that civil society was like a system of trenches and forts that protected the [liberal] state from onslaught. Under these conditions a strategy of war of movement, ie insurrection, such as that used by Bolsheviks, could not succeed. What was needed, instead, was a protracted 'war of position,' through which the Communist Party could establish its hegemony in civil society.

The 'war of position' was not a war with physical weapons. It was a strategy for struggling to establish ideological and organisational leadership in institutions of civil society — the trade unions, the media, the co-ops, the schools, cultural and sports clubs, etc.[38]

Gramsci never saw the war of position as a replacement for armed struggle and insurrection. It was a complementary weapon of struggle to achieve socialist victory, or so-called people's power.

Von Holdt writes approvingly that South Africa has become chronically ungovernable because of the success of the Mass Democratic Movement's campaign to control civil society through strikes, boycotts, demonstrations, and marches:

In fact, the MDM has already established a rich practice and tradition of 'war of position,' even if this has not been fully theorised in relation to the question of power. We have here a concrete elaboration, in practice, of Gramsci's schematic concept of war of position. Over the last decade or more the strategy of the MDM has consisted of:
■ Building powerful, militant mass organisations at the workplace and in the communities and schools, with the aim of constantly challenging oppression and exploitation, and building people's power.
■ Establishing a broad multi-class liberation alliance under the hegemony of the ANC.
■ Extending the influence of this movement into many spheres, such as sport, culture, education....
These strategies, taken together, have entrenched the MDM within South Africa's relatively advanced society, and made it impossible to dislodge.[40]

You couldn't ask for a more honest explanation of what many groups on the left have been doing over the past decade. The question, though, is whether this is what ordinary people have been fighting for. Did they know that they were fighting to trade National Party hegemony over civil life for the hegemony of some "democratic" movement?

If it's civil society people want, they are going to have to start calling for individual liberty, the freedom to associate, and the freedom to own property that the state can't trample on. As British journalist Timothy Garton Ash says in his first-hand account of the revolutions in Hungary, Czechoslovakia, and Poland:

1989 was the springtime of societies aspiring to be civil. Ordinary men and women's rudimentary notion of what it meant to build a civil society might not satisfy the political theorist. But some such notion was there, and it contained several basic demands. There should be forms of association, national, regional, local, professional, which would be voluntary, authentic, democratic, and, first and last, not controlled or manipulated by the Party or Party-state. People should be 'civil': that is, polite, tolerant, and, above all, nonviolent. Civil and civilian.[41]

Ed Crane, president of the Cato Institute in Washington, adds:

What we are witnessing in the East is a series of *antigovernment* revolutions. Certainly East Europeans want to be able to vote — who, having lived in a totalitarian state, would not? But they also want to be free to travel, to speak out, to choose their jobs, to accrue wealth, to practice religion, and to engage in a myriad other human pursuits without interference from the state....They want to be free to choose not just more politicians but the course of their lives.[42]

Those who govern will always try to tax, control, or eliminate institutions that conflict with their warped views of how other people's lives should be ordered. And no constitutional clause is guaranteed to stop them. Ordinary people will have to fight nonstop for their individual rights and always be on the lookout for budding social engineers. Glorification of the state and calls to mobilise and unite the people should set alarm bells ringing.

2

APARTHEID ECONOMICS

Apartheid was socialism

partheid wasn't just about race. It was about economics. But what kind of economics?

In left-wing circles, the conventional wisdom is that apartheid was a vicious brand of capitalism.

WOSA, the Workers' Organisation for Socialist Action, says that activists and ordinary workers

know that it is capitalism that built apartheid, that created the ghettoes, that forced the removals, and that oppressed and exploited them for hundreds of years. They know it is capitalism that uses their labour and then throws them out on the street as unemployed. They know it was capitalism that grew rich while they had no hospitals, no clinics, no adequate schools, no housing, no food.[1]

"You cannot separate capitalism and apartheid in South Africa," says the ANC-SACP's Joe Slovo. He told the Communist Party's December 1991 congress: "It is crystal clear that it is capitalism which has failed and brought untold miseries to our people. It is this indisputable fact which, despite socialist distortions elsewhere, unravels the mystery as to why there is such a groundswell of support among our working people for a future of socialism."[2]

ANC information chief Pallo Jordan says: "My starting point is not the success or failure of capitalism or socialism in the abstract, but the failure of capitalism in South Africa. And that is a failure on a massive scale."[3]

The PAC slams "the settler-colonialist capitalist system of De Klerk and Oppenheimer."[4]

Says Cosatu leader Jay Naidoo: "Apartheid, with its institutionalised controls over the lives of workers, is an example of one of the world's most brutal forms of capitalism."[5]

Brutal, yes. But not capitalism. Everything about apartheid smacked of socialism — from the spirit behind it to the laws passed to carry it out.

Apartheid might not be the kind of socialism that the left likes. But, like socialist experiments in eastern Europe and elsewhere in Africa, apartheid was another example of the misery that is created when a strong, centralised government tries to plan an economy and a society.

In a free, capitalist society — under the liberal institutions of private property, contract, and the rule of law — people enjoy a wide range of rights and freedoms:

■ The right to own and exchange private property.
■ The freedom to move within the country in search of better living conditions or jobs.
■ The freedom to work where you choose at wages you negotiate.
■ The right to keep the fruits of your labour.
■ The freedom to travel overseas or emigrate.
■ Diversity and choice in education.
■ Free trade and unrestricted flows of foreign investment.
■ The freedom to start companies and run shops.
■ Equal treatment under the law.

Under apartheid, these and other liberal-capitalist rights were either absent or severely restricted.

The substance of apartheid

The list of socialist-style regulations and controls imposed by the National Party government since 1948 — and by the white governments that preceded it — shows just how far removed from capitalism South Africa's economy has been. Many of the anticapitalist laws were racist, like those that prohibited black ownership of land in vast areas of the country. But many were not particularly racial at all — like today's local-content programme that tells car manufacturers how to build their vehicles. South Africa's rulers have shown both a love of racism and a hatred of the market.

District Labour Control Boards determined whether black farmworkers could get permission to work in town (local white farmers served on the boards). Wage Boards set high minimum wages to prevent blacks from getting jobs by undercutting white wage earners. The

Livestock and Meat Industries Control Board curbed the sale of black farmers' produce. The Publications Control Board censored the country's newspapers, magazines, books, and movies.

The Customs Tariff Commission recommended import protection for companies that hired sufficient numbers of white workers. The Physical Planning Act dictated acceptable ratios of black workers to white.

The Land Acts and Group Areas Act prevented blacks from owning property in most of the country and led to forced removals of families and businesses. Blacks were prevented from managing or controlling businesses in white areas. Even in areas reserved for blacks, such as urban townships, blacks were generally not allowed freehold title to land until 1986.

White property rights were also restricted. The Subdivision of Agricultural Land Act prevented farmers from breaking off pieces of land and selling them, and laws restricted white investments in black homelands.

Pass laws, influx control, and homeland citizenship prevented blacks from moving freely around South Africa, looking for work or shelter. The government withdrew passports from critics.

The central government determined what language students would learn in, who could teach them, and what subjects they would be taught. It shut down private missionary and farm schools. It outlawed television until 1976, when it introduced TV as a state monopoly.

Import controls, tariff barriers, and exchange control severely restricted the movement of goods and capital in and out of the country. Historically, protection was granted to companies that best complied with racist labour legislation.

Assaults on enterprise included: shop-hour laws, licensing laws, a ban on Sunday movies, segregation in movies and restaurants, movie and book censorship, laws preventing blacks from opening businesses in city centres, and liquor-licensing laws. Other statutes prevented entrepreneurs from starting telephone, postal, TV, radio, airline, and electricity services to compete with state-protected monopolies.

The government set up and subsidised the Industrial Development Corporation to finance favoured industrialists. It staffed the state monopolies with political supporters — "jobs for pals." It set up two dozen agricultural control boards to restrict the growing and marketing of food, and it controlled hundreds of consumer prices. It decided which remote areas needed industrial development and then paid decentralisation subsidies to companies that located in them.

Tariffs propped up uncompetitive firms and drove up consumer prices on a wide range of goods. And the government raised taxes to punitive levels and imposed dozens of hidden taxes and duties.[6]

No area of potentially capitalist activity was too minor for the government's economic police to restrict. Anekie Lebese, who grew up in Johannesburg's Alexandra township, had to raise three sons alone when her husband died. Crippled in both legs, she could have begged but didn't want to. So she sold goods on Noord Street in Johannesburg:

I sold fruit and vegetables. This selling took all my three sons to school and made sure they had food and a place to live. But to the police, my working for my children was breaking the law. I slept in jail many times.[7]

Very little was left untouched by the apartheid state: transport, communications, investment, labour, prices, banking, agriculture, energy, construction, travel, movement, housing, arms, education, retailing, entertainment, land, and the hawking of vegetables by crippled widows. This was capitalism?

The government has recently taken long-overdue steps in the direction of freedom by deregulating and legalising backyard and informal business, simplifying licensing laws, and scrapping the Land Acts and Group Areas Act. But the socialist engineering goes on. Exchange control, tariff barriers, state monopolies, industrial subsidies, state-financed development agencies, agricultural boards, censorship, and complicated taxes are among the apartheid-inspired policies that continue today. At recent count, the bloated central government was lorded over by 22 cabinet ministers and 12 deputy cabinet ministers.

Recent anticapitalist highlights include a pledge by Rina Venter, the minister of national health, to prevent the construction of private hospitals because of "an oversupply of beds for private patients"[8]; a projected R5,5 billion cost overrun on the state's Mossel Bay oil-from-gas project, which an official inquiry castigated as "seriously flawed" and undertaken without the necessary planning, costing, or experience[9]; and a court application by state-owned South African Airways opposing an application by a private company to offer flights to Africa and Indian Ocean islands on the grounds that SAA is legally entitled to "absolute protection from competition" on international routes because it provides "satisfactory and proper services." The airline's lawyers complained that granting the private firm a licence to fly would be like giving it a "licence to print money," since it would be able to sell tickets at much lower prices.[10]

The predictable results of all this socialism have been high inflation, environmental decay, pockets of severe poverty and underdevelopment, and low growth, particularly since the state's share of the economy began to soar in the 1970s.

Where the state owns or controls property and industry, freedom is crushed. And in South Africa, successive white governments have waged a long war against private ownership, personal freedom, and a free market.

Blacks suffered most under apartheid socialism because their liberties were the most severely curtailed.[11] As the great liberal economist William Hutt, author of *The Economics of the Colour Bar*, noted as early as 1964: "The African himself is as dependent upon the whim of the politicians and officials as he would be in a totalitarian country."[12]

The spirit of apartheid

The architects of apartheid didn't pretend that apartheid was capitalism. They were quite blunt about their socialist views. Again and again, white politicians — and their cheerleaders in universities, business, and farming — lambasted greedy capitalists and called on the government to straighten things out, all in the spirit of socialism and planning.

Consider these stirring thoughts:

Socialism has done an invaluable service to humanity, and not the least to Christianity itself, by turning its searchlight on the evils of the existing system. We hope and pray that Christianity and socialism may be so guided in their future development that the deep yearning, the widespread movements, and even the passions and the violence of the age may prove to be but the birthpangs of a better social world.[13]

That was Daniel Francois Malan, the first Nationalist prime minister, elected in 1948. Those words capture the spirit of apartheid: sabotage capitalism to promote racism.

The socialist spirit spilled over into all spheres of the economy. On wages, Ben Schoeman, later the minister of labour, said in 1942 that "wage control and fixation should be in the hands of the state...[and] self-government in industry and collective bargaining...should be eliminated from our economic life."[14] On industrial development, the minister of planning in 1969 said that unless business people agreed to invest in decentralisation points, "not another acre" of land would be proclaimed for industrial use in the cities. On banking, the Broederbond in 1933 called for "the nationalisation of finance and planned coordination of economic policy."[15]

Explaining why the government would prevent white businesses from investing in black-designated areas, the minister of Bantu administration in 1963 said, "We will not let the wolves in — those people who simply seek where they can make money in order to fill their own pocket."[16]

The apartheid government's policies were just a watered-down version of the even more extravagant socialism of the extreme right.

The Ossewa Brandwag, founded in 1939 to promote Afrikaner unity through neo-Nazism, said in a 1942 manifesto:

Because the Ossewa Brandwag realises that the Afrikaner currently finds himself in the stranglehold of British-Jewish capitalism, it strives towards neutralising the organised money powers by establishing state control over the key industries, the big banks, the mines, and propaganda organs.[17]

The right's vitriolic attacks on capitalism should come as no surprise. Apartheid socialism may be unique to South Africa, but right-wing socialism isn't. Hitler despised liberals and capitalists, and he crushed private property rights through nationalisation, regulation, and central economic planning. The full name of Hitler's party was the National Socialist German Workers Party, and he correctly called himself a national socialist, or Nazi. Socialists in South Africa mysteriously hold up Hitler's brutal policies as the logical conclusion of capitalism. In fact, like apartheid, they were just one more nasty variation of socialism.

In recent years, the government has reduced its attacks on capitalists and capitalism. Predictably, the far right continues to attack capitalism, recognising that the market will undermine its racial plans. Conservative Party leader Andries Treurnicht — who led the breakaway from the NP in 1982 over plans to bring Indians and coloureds into parliament — opposed the government's stated intention to shift to free-market policies because "an open market and social integration would make apartheid unworkable."[18]

Showing its hatred for integration and capitalism, the small Herstigte Nasionale Party condemned PW Botha's tentative moves toward a freer market, calling the Botha government "not only the biggest Kaffirboetie government, but also the biggest Hoggenheimer government."[19]

Why the myth persists

Arbitrary use of the words *capitalism* and *socialism* perpetuates the myth of apartheid capitalism. Socialism does not mean caring, sharing, and compassion. In the real world, it means state ownership or control. And capitalism does not mean greed and nastiness. It means private ownership and control.[20]

Using these definitions as a guide, we can better judge who's a capitalist and who's not. When people who call themselves capitalists run to the government for subsidies and protection, they are no longer capitalists in any meaningful sense. Call them industrialists or business people or farmers or bankers, but not capitalists. Thus, a sentence like "Capitalists used state power to kick blacks off their land" is a contradiction. It's important to recognise that many of the complaints the left makes about so-called capitalist power are actually complaints — often valid — about state power. Behind apartheid laws was the power of the government, not the power of the market.[21]

And the socialist state was the enemy of black people, just as a competitive market was their potential salvation. William Hutt wrote in 1964:

It is...in the nature of extreme collectivist administrations that they welcome arbitrary powers; and it is perhaps for that reason that the methods adopted by the Government of the Republic have come to resemble so closely those of the countries behind the Iron Curtain....Every repression of the Africans has, at the same time, been a repression of the free market. It is so-called 'central planning' which has caused African labour to become regarded as a mere source of useful, unskilled, muscular strength. And it is profit incentives which have tended powerfully to raise the material standards of Africans, to develop their latent powers, to raise their status and prestige in a multiracial society, and ultimately to win for them equality of respect and consideration.[22]

Hutt's view, while dismissed by the left, was fully understood by the supporters of apartheid, who rallied against the liberalising effects of free enterprise. Piet Meyer, then rector of Rand Afrikaans University and a former head of the Broederbond and the SABC, told a Federation of Afrikaans Cultural Associations meeting in 1980:

The free enterprise system does not differentiate on the basis of different national groups....It forms one integrated economic whole. An integrated economic system tends inevitably towards an integrated society at all levels — political, educational, church and, eventually, in cultural and social spheres....

May the Afrikaners never allow themselves to adapt passively to the tendencies and demands of the free-enterprise system.... [23]

Still, the confusion over capitalism and socialism persists. South African–born economist Merle Lipton occasionally confuses the issue in her exhaustively researched book *Capitalism and Apartheid*. For example, she describes a system of farming that

though capitalist, had features which could usually be called feudal — a tied, serf-like labour force on the white farms and a black agricultural sector that was kept in an undeveloped and precapitalist state, so that it would not compete with white farmers and would instead serve as a source of cheap labour for white farms and mines.[24]

This doesn't sound like a very "capitalist" system at all. Here, Lipton falls into the trap of saying that if there are privately owned farms and machines, the system is capitalist. But that's not so. White South African agriculture, though nominally private, has in fact been largely socialist: a combination of state subsidies and marketing boards on the one hand, and laws that sabotaged black farming and black land ownership on the other. To call such a system capitalist drains all meaning from words.

The economic myths also persist because the government in Pretoria, which in its early days was avowedly socialist, began to call itself capitalist even while it kept racist regulations on the books.

Today, it has dropped most of the racist laws but keeps innumerable controls and taxes in place, while proudly calling its state-socialist system "free enterprise." One of the planks of a recent 12-point government plan to protect minority rights is that "a free market system should be retained." The NP does not understand that you can't retain something that doesn't exist. By spouting such nonsense, the apartheid-socialist government reinforces the apartheid-capitalist myth.

Does it really matter whether we label apartheid as socialism or capitalism? It does. Much of the case for socialism rests on its being the opposite of "apartheid capitalism."

Cosatu general secretary Jay Naidoo tells an SACP congress: "The spectre of apartheid capitalism haunts generations of our working people. The stark ghettoes, row upon row of matchbox houses, the helplessness of the ravages wrought by mass unemployment, the kwashiorkor and malnutrition that eats away the fabric of youth, the crime and violence are witness to our cause."[25]

"Cosatu is committed to changing our capitalist economy and building socialism," says Cosatu's *Campaign Bulletin*.[26]

"Just as socialism eastern European–style failed, so too has capitalism South African–style failed," says the union's economic consultant Stephen Gelb.[27]

"I am...convinced that socialism will eventually work in South Africa," Joe Slovo tells *Learn and Teach* magazine. It's "very odd that people talk about the failure of socialism, but what has failed in South Africa is capitalism, not socialism."[28]

If everyone were more aware that apartheid was a form of socialism, the job of the socialists would become a lot more difficult. They wouldn't be able to discredit capitalism simply by running down apartheid. They would have to make a case for socialism, rather than saying it is the natural alternative to apartheid and capitalism. They would have to explain how their socialism is going to be better than the socialism of the past.

The sham label "apartheid capitalism" also helps to hide the consistent, principled opposition to apartheid by liberal capitalists. The socialists would have us believe that there are only two positions: either you support apartheid/capitalism or you support liberation/socialism. In fact, the most logical position to support is liberation/capitalism — because oppression will continue unless the economy is freed. Capitalism would mark a clean break from the apartheid past, whereas much of what passes for a revolutionary agenda is nothing but warmed-over national socialism. Rather than offering dramatic change, the liberationists offer a conservative solution: the same policies carried out by new people.

If we use principled definitions of capitalism and socialism, we can tackle the important questions. What is the proper role of government in a free society? What was at the root of past problems in South Africa? Is implementing a new variation of state ownership and control what the freedom struggle has been all about?

The interventionists' new line

The new line about apartheid and capitalism is that labels don't matter, because capitalism and socialism are outdated terms. This is the new line mainly of socialists and interventionists, who want to deflect attention from the disastrous track record of socialism and intervention worldwide. But labels *do* matter.

Author and journalist Allister Sparks complains that "dogmatic socialists and theological free marketeers continue to talk past each other in the heat of an increasingly sterile debate." Natal University philosopher James Moulder says: "The debate between capitalists and socialists is sterile and futile."[29] Sparks and Moulder must be going to the wrong debates.

True, the socialist side of the debate is often sterile. The champions of socialism habitually refuse to define, defend, or explain socialism and switch to a new topic whenever the discussion gets too specific. But the capitalist side of the debate — the radical capitalist side — is vibrant. Free-trade zones, choice in education, one-person-one-share privatisation, the ending of government monopolies, the distribution of state-owned land, across-the-board tax cuts: unashamed capitalists do not shy away from debating the specifics of the free, prosperous, democratic society they want. And they don't hesitate to call their policies capitalism — principled, thoroughly debated, anything-but-sterile free-market capitalism. Do those who shy away from labels have something to hide?

The newest line

Now comes the even newer line. It correctly argues that South Africa has never had a free-market system. But it then concludes, perversely, that because there was no free enterprise in the past, it's no big deal that there won't be free enterprise in the future.

The ANC's Albie Sachs says business people and government officials are being hypocritical when, faced with the prospect of majority rule, they are suddenly concerned about private property rights and a free market:

Yet the reality is that enterprise has never been free in South Africa. For the majority of the people (black), it has been totally under (white) state control, totally regulated (by whites), and totally monopolised (by whites). [30]

So Sachs concludes that enterprise should remain unfree, just as it was under the Nationalists. Apartheid's bankrupt economic policies led to a litany of disasters, from uncompetitive industry to a gravy train for bureaucrats. But the ANC doesn't promise to get rid of these policies. Rather, it looks to them for inspiration.

Shortly after his release, ANC leader Nelson Mandela said: "The government has presently nationalised many things in the country, and it should come as no surprise that our policy is that of nationalisation."[31]

After his return to South Africa from exile, Joe Slovo said: "On the question of redistributing wealth, the ANC is acting in a tradition which was actually set by the NP when it first came to power in the 1940s."[32] Slovo said the National Party government used state power and state industries to uplift its followers, but: "Now it appears that the sauce that was good for that goose is not so good for the gander."[33]

Patrick Lekota, an ANC executive member and former UDF publicity secretary, said: "The Afrikaner government maintained the economy with major sectors of the economy nationalised....We won't do anything new, although we may add a bit."[34] And ANC economist Vella Pillay says a new government must reduce inequalities and boost industrial employment through "managed pricing and marketing policies — no different to what is practised now" but "made more extensive."[35]

This is liberation?

Finally, Slovo, explaining the ANC's policy of controls and selective nationalisation, writes:

These economic policies will continue to be criticised as statist and contrasted with free market policies. That is an unnecessary polarisation. The South Africa we have known is not a free market system.

It has been a tightly knit economy dominated by State industries, State regulation, and a few all-powerful conglomerate trusts....[36]

The terms *free enterprise,* a *free market, capitalism,* and *private enterprise* are interchangeable, all describing a liberal market order. So Slovo, in effect, was saying: "The South Africa we have known is not a capitalist system." This is correct. But it puts a leader of the South African Communist Party in the position of supporting the revolutionary overthrow of a capitalist system that by his own admission has never existed.

If enterprise hasn't been free, apartheid hasn't been capitalism. The country's would-be liberators ought to reconsider what they're fighting against.

3

TAXES

Bringing taxes under control

If you thought apartheid was expensive, brace yourself for redistribution. To make up for historical injustices, the country's liberators are proposing drastic tax increases. The ANC's Albie Sachs, in his book *Protecting Human Rights in a New South Africa*, calls for no less than:

■ A 20 percent rate of VAT, rising to 35 percent for luxury goods like cars and minibuses.

■ A roof tax of R500 a month on all houses and flats and a R100-a-month tax on shacks.

■ A top personal-income-tax rate of 90 percent, with a minimum tax of R500 a year on anybody with a job.

■ A R1-a-litre increase in the petrol tax.

■ A R3 surcharge on movie tickets and a host of other luxury taxes.

Sorry, I lied. In fact, Sachs doesn't call for any of these tax increases in his book — at least not explicitly.

What Sachs does call for is a massive increase in government services. He wants the state to provide or finance:

■ Primary health care.

■ School-feeding schemes.

■ A Social and Economic Rights Commission.

■ A Land Commission and land court.

■ An Army and Security Commission.

■ Technical, education, and financial support to farmers, including guaranteed prices, credits, and rural-extension offices.

■ State grants for buying or renting "a decent home" and farmland.
■ Construction of national monuments.
■ Maternity benefits.
■ Child care.
■ Family courts.
■ Education and training for women to gain new skills.
■ An equal-opportunities commission and gender-rights council.
■ Clean piped water and electricity or gas for every home.
■ Family counselling and adoption services.
■ Antenatal, maternity, and postnatal care.
■ Sport-and-recreation facilities.
■ Cultural facilities.
■ Swimming lessons.
■ Mountain-climbing and camping trips.
■ Creches and kindergartens for children of working parents.
■ A children's ombudsman.
■ Legal-services centres.
■ Adult-education and literacy programmes.
■ A national health system.
■ Light, heat, water, communication facilities, and waste disposal.
■ Factory inspectors.
■ Nature parks, green zones, state mountains, state beaches.
■ Pollution controls, protection-of-species laws, and soil-erosion codes.

Now, you might agree with some of what Sachs believes a government should do. Or if you're a sceptic, you might see potential for great waste in things like handouts to farmers and state swimming lessons. But that's not the question here. The question is: who is going to pay for all this?

Socialists and redistributionists sound like such great guys because they promise something for nothing.

How couldn't you like somebody who will give you day care, a house, a farm, playgrounds, legal advice, and electricity? But socialists and redistributionists wouldn't be so popular if they listed all the tax increases they would have to impose to pay for all the goodies.

Nowhere in his 200-page book does Sachs try to estimate how much one of his programmes would cost and nowhere does he specify a single tax rate that he would charge to finance his promises.[1]

Supporters of redistribution quantify the problems with great care: they cite infant-mortality rates and income differentials and give detailed figures of the number of people left homeless by the housing shortage. But when it comes to paying for the solutions, there's hardly a number in sight.

Perhaps the most exhaustive call for state action is made in *Uprooting Poverty*, a book based on the Second Carnegie Inquiry into Poverty and Development, by University of Cape Town economist Francis Wilson and UCT administrator and medical doctor Mamphela Ramphele. In 357 pages, they carefully describe, classify, and condemn the poverty black South Africans live in and offer a wide-ranging list of projects that the government should undertake to "help the poor":

■ Public-works programmes and "massive public investment."
■ A Rural Works Department.
■ Food stamps.
■ Museums.
■ Libraries, study centres, teacher resource centres, and "a massive literacy campaign."
■ Preschools.
■ Parks and playgrounds.
■ A national health service.
■ The training of health workers, with the requirement that doctors work in rural areas after medical school.
■ Subsidised housing loans.
■ The busing of black children into white schools.
■ Solar-energy research.
■ Agricultural land reform, farm subsidies, advisory services, marketing assistance, and the breaking up of large farms.
■ More and larger pensions.
■ Water and sewerage.
■ Road building.
■ Electricity projects.
■ Forestry projects.
■ Housing, jobs, food, water, and energy for all.

The equally long, detailed list of how to pay for these? It's nonexistent.

Throughout most of the book, Wilson and Ramphele don't even mention the word *tax*. When they finally get around to discussing the question of financing — on page 345 — they conclude that cutting the defence budget in half would pay for poverty projects. Cutting the defence budget in half would free some R5 billion a year. That could pay for 200 000 homes worth R25 000 each — a tiny dent in the single promise of "housing for all." The price tag on the whole lot would be astronomical.

We're not debating *intentions*. The pockets of poverty in South Africa are horrific. But repeating the poor's needs over and over again doesn't satisfy those needs.

Worse, programmes with good intentions but no grounding in economics could backfire on the very poor in whose names they're carried out. Editor and columnist Ken Owen condemned the massive state intervention proposed in *Uprooting Poverty*, saying it is "a kind of upper-class deathwish, rooted in guilt, and it would condemn South Africans to another century of tin shacks and mud huts."[2]

In my review of *Uprooting Poverty* in the *Financial Mail*, I questioned the cost of the recommendations:

If R5 bn is not enough, how much do Wilson and Ramphele suggest: R10 bn, R30 bn? Where will *that* come from and how will it be distributed? The last thing SA needs is higher taxes and more government.[3]

A year after *Uprooting Poverty* came out, Wilson responded to critics in a chapter on redistribution in the book *The Political Economy of South Africa*. Wilson welcomed the robust debate:

Virtually all the criticism of the economic track record of the present government made by the most ardent 'free marketeers' [is] beyond dispute. Indeed the degree of waste, of corruption, and of misallocation of scarce resources is a legacy which will haunt South Africa for years to come.

But then the catch:

But whilst there are areas of the economy that clearly require the bracing medicine of privatisation and removal of government restrictions, it is just as apparent that the government has a central role to play (not least by means of allocating public funds) in reshaping the pattern of growth in such a way that resources are channelled to the poor.[4]

So we're back to the same problem. Where are these "public funds" going to come from? Wilson's chapter is 11 pages long. In it, he does not recommend a single tax or a specific tax rate to pay for the redistribution that he continues to say is needed. Instead, he writes:

In arguing, as the Carnegie report did, that any new government must aim both for growth and for a redistribution of wealth and income, it was saying no more than seemed perfectly obvious. However, use of the word 'redistribution' seems to have touched off a reaction by some critics which suggests that they feared some sort of Stalinist liquidation of kulaks was being recommended.[5]

Cute remarks, but irrelevant. Critics of redistribution don't fear a murderous purge. We fear that he and Ramphele don't understand economics. The fear is that blind, sweeping plans for government action will lead to a steady destruction of the economy. In the name of redistribution, a new government will be tempted to raise taxes and institute corrupt, overstaffed programmes and deadening controls — as happened, for example, in Zimbabwe. This would curb local enterprise, encourage skilled workers to flee, multiply unproductive bureaucracies, scare off foreign investors, and stifle growth. The hardest-hit victims? The very poor people in whose name upliftment is carried out. As the economy grinds down, they would remain rooted in poverty.

Numbers that make sense

You can ask people how much their plans would cost, but then a new problem arises. The huge numbers don't have any meaning. You might hear calls for a R20 billion education programme, a R450 million legal-aid plan, or a R3 billion housing project. But how are they going to affect you?

You can see the answer more clearly if you translate the numbers into common taxes. Consider two: VAT and the petrol tax.

When value-added tax was introduced at 10 percent in 1991, it was expected to cost consumers just under R18 billion a year. Call it R20 billion. So, roughly speaking, a R2 billion government project could be financed by increasing VAT by one percentage point.[6]

Now look at the taxes hidden in the petrol price. The government today imposes a 50-cent tax on every litre of petrol. This costs drivers about R5 billion in a year.[7] So if the government wanted to embark on a new R1 billion project, it could finance it by pushing up the petrol price 10 cents a litre for one year.

In short:

■ 1 percent VAT = R2 billion.
■ 10-cent petrol tax = R1 billion.

Armed with these figures, we can take a fresh look at the interminable calls for government spending.

A *Business Day* headline trumpeted:

**R4 bn plan to replace
hostels with houses**

The story was about a joint proposal by the ANC and the trade-union federation Cosatu to convert barracks-style worker housing into single-family homes. A call like that makes them sound as if they're concerned about the average downtrodden person. But have they thought through their concerns?[8]

Consider the cost. To pay for such a project, the government could increase VAT by two percentage points — from, say, 10 percent to 12 percent. This would mean cutting the living standards of 39 million consumers to improve the living standards of tens of thousands of people living in hostels. Put that way, it's less clear who is most concerned about the downtrodden, the people who support the plan or the people who oppose it. Imagine the outcry that would be caused by a headline saying:[9]

**ANC, unions
call for 2% VAT hike
to convert hostels**

And if the government financed a R4 billion hostel-renovation plan through a petrol-tax increase:

**Unions, ANC call for
40-cent petrol price hike
to convert hostels**

That's the side of socialism you never read about. Check out this actual headline from *Business Day*:

**Call for R10 bn rise
in welfare budget**

The story began: "SA should increase its welfare budget by R10 bn to R12 bn a year, the SA National Council for Child and Family Welfare argues in a discussion document released yesterday."[10] Who can oppose a plan to make children better off? But imagine how much more interesting the story would have been had the council said how the R10 billion would be raised. It could come from a five percentage point increase in VAT or a one-rand increase in the petrol tax:

**Call for 5% VAT increase
to fund welfare budget**

Or:

**Call for R1-a-litre
'welfare tax'
on petrol**

The Building Industries Federation recently called for R9 billion to be spent on a mass housing programme.

The headline you saw in *The Star*[11]:

**Bifsa looks at R9 bn
low-cost housing plan**

The headline you'll probably never see:

**Builders look at 5% VAT rise
to fund home building**

If price tags were put on politicians' promises and people's demands, we could have a real debate on welfare, redistribution, government spending, and taxes.

But put these figures to the supporters of redistribution and they'll tell you that they don't plan to get the money from VAT, the petrol tax, or any other tax that hits ordinary people. No, they are going to get the money from somewhere else. Two favourite targets: rich people and companies. Don't be fooled.

Albie Sachs has complained that "in a country where tens of thousands of whites have private swimming pools, millions of blacks do not even have piped water."[12] Emotive descriptions like this are often true. It's just not clear what we're supposed to conclude from them. If thousands of whites *didn't* have swimming pools, would millions of blacks then have piped water?

There are 351 000 individually owned swimming pools in South Africa, according to the National Spa and Pool Institute. What would be a reasonable pool tax? Suppose it's R1 000 a year. That would cost (enraged) pool owners R350 million a year. How much is the government going to be able to accomplish with this sum of money?

There are several things it could do. Since there are 30 million black people in South Africa, it could divide the money and give each R12 a year to put toward piped water. Or it could pinpoint a few areas and spend R350 million a year on water-and-sewerage systems for them (after paying modest overhead expenses to its friends, the contractors). This would benefit a very small number of blacks; many millions of them would see none of the money.

Either way, it would still be true that while "tens of thousands of whites have swimming pools, millions of blacks do not even have piped water."

The sad truth is that there aren't enough rich people to go around in South Africa. It is delusion to believe that the tiny minority of South Africa's population who are rich could uplift the millions of people who aren't. Even if all their wealth were ruthlessly confiscated, the money would pay for only a small fraction of the programmes that redistributionists promise.

But the story doesn't end there. There is a false notion that taxing people — particularly rich people — has no costs. You just do it, and suddenly you've got money to spend. But consider the ill effects of the pool tax.

Pool owners are typically managers and skilled workers, and there is a limit to how much punitive taxation they will accept before they simply pack up and go. There are other places where they can live, places where their skills and energy are welcome. A R1 000 pool tax — particularly if it formed part of a broader tax increase and drop in living standards — would encourage a flight of skills. This would reduce the economic growth that the downtrodden desperately need.

Similarly, the tax would discourage an inflow of foreign skills and investment. It would announce that South Africa is a land of envy, where people who make enough money to buy a pool are clobbered by the government. Foreign investors would recognise that they can invest their money here only if they are prepared to gamble on what "luxury" will be taxed next.

The divider effect

Then there is what I term the "divider effect." Government spending is popularly thought to have a "multiplier effect" that gives the economy a kick-start. For example, the government spends money building homes, which gives jobs to homebuilders, who spend their wages at shops, which gives income and jobs to other people, and so on.

But the multiplier effect is deceitful, because it is only half the story. The government must tax to get the money to begin with. This sets off an equal-and-opposite "divider effect," which gives the economy a kick-stop. The divider effect is a measure of how much wealth the government *destroys* as the effects of its tax collection ripple their way through the economy. The millions of rands that pay for, say, a water project are drained from taxpayers, who then have less money to spend on such things as clothes, cars, food, and shoes. So the companies that make those things retrench workers and cut production, and so on.[13]

In the case of the pool tax, the divider effect would obviously be felt by the pool industry. The cost of owning a pool would rise by R1 000 a year, so fewer people would buy one. Pool builders and their employees would be thrown out of work, which would also hurt their suppliers.

The divider effect would be felt by yet another group: the companies and individuals who would have received the R350 million that pool owners were forced to give to the government. The pool owners wouldn't have just thrown away their R1 000 each. They would have spent it on goods and services throughout the economy. So shops and restaurants in pool-owning areas would lose business. The taxed pool owners might also cut costs at home by firing their gardeners and maids, or paying them less, or not hiring help in the first place. On and on the ill effects go.

It would be helpful if people who call for soaking the rich would consider how much tax rich people already pay, how much more they could pay, how they would react to higher taxes, and what unintended effects the tax increase would have.

OK. If we aren't going to soak the rich, we'll soak big business. That's the approach of an ANC-Cosatu economic discussion paper, drafted at a conference in Harare, Zimbabwe, and released in 1990. But first the paper's wish list. In addition to supporting the continuation of the National Party's banking regulation, exchange control, small-business subsidies, and export incentives, it recommended that the state carry out or finance:

- The breaking up of large corporations.
- The renationalisation of privatised firms.
- Child care.
- Industrial and strategic planning.
- Investments in mining.
- A State Minerals Marketing Authority cartel.
- Research and development, tax incentives, import tariffs, and cheap loans for mining-related industry.
- A Minerals Policy Research Commission.
- A land-claims commission.
- Support services and training for new farmers.
- Land credit and training for women farmers.
- Environmental protection of land.
- State commissions on housing, transport, and unemployment.
- Public-works programmes, including home building and the provision of serviced stands.
- Youth-training schemes.
- A national compulsory retirement scheme.
- Water reticulation.
- Sewerage.
- Electricity.
- Stormwater drains.
- Tarred roads.
- A national state housing company.

In this 13-page document, there is just one passage in which the ANC-

Cosatu economic advisers explain how they propose to pay for all this:

> The new state would also undertake tax reform to make taxation more equitable and
> effective in many areas. Over time, the expected expansion of income and employment
> will widen the tax base. At present the tax burden is carried disproportionately by
> individuals through both direct taxation and indirect taxation. The new state would begin
> the process of shifting the burden of taxation, especially towards the corporations.[14]

You can hardly quibble with the first half. If employment and incomes increase, the same tax rates will bring in much more revenue.

But the last two sentences reflect one of today's most pernicious economic myths — that you can shift taxes away from "individuals" to someone or something else, like "corporations." But *all* taxes are paid by individuals. Politicians like to pretend that "corporations" can pay taxes. But corporations are nothing but collectives of individuals: workers, managers, and owners. Shift the burden of tax to corporations and some combination of those individuals — plus their customers — will pay. When the government in 1991 imposed a new tax on the capital bases of banks, major banks announced they would hike lending rates by 0,25 of a percentage point and consider reducing the interest paid to savers. Notice that the government announced a new tax on "banks." It did not announce a new tax on "bank customers" — though that's what the levy amounts to. Where else are banks — or any other business — supposed to get the money?[15]

Taxes such as personal income tax and VAT are fairly visible, so people have an idea of how much they pay. But corporate tax is completely hidden. In supporting a shift to hidden taxes, the ANC and Cosatu are endorsing a tax system that prevents people from seeing how much they're paying for government services. The National Party government also favours such a tax system, with its stiff tax on corporate profits and its Regional Services Council levies, paid by companies based on their turnovers and wage bills.

But who really pays? An increase in company taxes must be paid either by the owners of the companies (through lower dividends for a few people or millions of shareholders), the employees (through lower wages), or consumers (through higher prices).

You can see this more clearly if you consider the reverse situation. Suppose all company taxes were abolished. Companies could then charge less for cars, houses, furniture, and everything else, and they could pay the workers who build cars, houses, furniture, and everything else more. People who want to increase taxes on corporations are really endorsing a tax on workers and consumers — the masses.

They make the call because they can get away with it. It's almost impossible for an individual to determine the exact effects of such hidden taxes on his own wallet. People simply ignore the taxes that they don't pay directly — but many would have a stroke if they determined the total.

The call to shift taxes away from "individuals" to "corporations" is hardly unique to South Africa: it's popular around the world and across the political spectrum. But wherever it's carried out, the result is the same: people are led to call for far more government than they're actually willing to pay for.

And, as with those who plan to soak the rich, those who plan to soak the bosses never consider the practical problems and the ill effects. How much money can the government raise by pushing up company taxes? Some people seem to believe that "capital" has a bottomless pit of wealth. But this is obviously nonsense. Like a household, a company that's forced to pay higher taxes has to spend less on something else. So one likely response by companies to a tax increase would be simply to stop reinvesting in the economy — to stop building new factories. So higher company tax means fewer new factories and jobs.

How much money and effort will be spent avoiding the taxes? The time spent with lawyers and accountants is time that could be spent actually producing goods for consumers. So the masses suffer because the most clever brains are busy coping with tax. What happens to struggling companies, like mines, when their taxes are raised? If they're subsidised, the government must raise taxes further. This creates more struggling companies, which require more subsidies, which require higher taxes, which create more struggling companies.

Will everybody continue to work hard under higher taxation? Company owners might show less enthusiasm for innovation, research, development, and long hours. Workers might not work as hard for lower salaries, so productivity would fall. Potential foreign investors might shy away from investing in a country where business is seen to be a milch cow.

Shortly after the joint ANC-Cosatu document was released, the ANC's department of economic policy released its own recommendations, which included endless promises about what a new ANC government would do. Here are the taxes it proposed to pay for the massive spending increase:
- Capital gains tax.
- Capital transfer tax.
- Land tax.
- Progressive property tax.
- Minimum business tax.

Note the burning desire to tax inanimate objects. Note also that inanimate objects don't have any money. A government can say it's taxing capital, land, property, buildings, and businesses, but it's really taxing the *owners* of capital, land, property, buildings, and businesses. Similarly, a government taxes smokers, not cigarettes; drinkers, not booze; and consumers, not imports.

Most people will try to pass the cost of any new tax on to other people. The owner of a shopping mall, for example, will raise the rent on tenants, who will then try to pass on the cost to their customers. In the end, every cent of tax is paid by South Africa's 39 million people.

What to do with a windfall

But let's say I'm wrong. Assume that a new government could painlessly raise huge amounts of tax from rich people, corporations, or dirt. Or maybe it would get the money from foreign governments, by selling stockpiles of oil, or by picking crisp banknotes off money trees.

For the moment, the source doesn't matter. The government has raised billions of rands. What is it going to do with the money? The left claims to oppose VAT. If so, a left-wing government should cut or eliminate VAT at the first opportunity. Would it?

If it collected billions of new rands, would an ANC-led government earmark the revenues to offset a decrease in VAT? Or would it spend the new money and keep VAT at the same rate — thus implicitly endorsing VAT?

If the government raises R6 billion from a capital gains tax (or from foreign aid), it could build low-income housing. Or it could cut VAT by 3 percentage points for a year. Or it could cut the petrol price by 60 cents a litre for a year. By choosing the housing project, it supports VAT and expensive petrol.

The logic is straightforward: if (a) an unpopular tax like VAT exists and (b) you recommend that the government spend money, then (c) you endorse the unpopular tax. This is true even if you try to argue that VAT has nothing to do with your plan.

If you truly oppose VAT, you have to get rid of it. The first R20 billion that you collect in new revenue — from whatever source — must first go toward eliminating VAT. Or you must recommend that R20 billion of current programmes be scrapped along with VAT.

An example illustrates. Go back to the R4 billion plan to renovate hostels. Suppose the government somehow got its hands on R4 billion. If it embarks on the hostel-renovation plan, it implicitly opposes cuts in VAT or the petrol price:

**Supporters of hostel plan
reject 2% cut in VAT**

**Supporters of hostel plan
oppose 40-cent cut in petrol price**

Suppose the government somehow raised R10 billion for welfare and gave the money to an independent trust. If the charity spent the money, it would then be endorsing VAT — because it could turn down the money and tell the government to cut VAT by 5 percentage points instead.

**Welfare trust,
to help poor,
opposes 5% cut in VAT**

Or it could turn down the money and tell the government to cut the petrol price by 50 cents a litre for two years.

**Welfare trust
rejects two years
of cheap petrol**

The government falls into the same trap with its transparent attempts to finance redistribution from "good" sources like the sale of oil from its strategic stockpiles. In 1991, the government announced that it had sold R1 billion of oil and that the money would go toward so-called development projects. Again, you have to look at what else the government *could* have done with the money. With a billion rands, it could have reduced VAT by a half percentage point or cut the petrol price by 10 cents a litre. But, by earmarking the money for redistribution, it implicitly opposed these tax cuts.

**Government rejects
0,5% reduction in VAT rate**

**Government opposes
10-cent cut
in petrol price**

In December 1991, the ANC announced plans for a postapartheid development bank — the South African Trust for Equity and Development — that would be financed by $5 billion, or about R15 billion, in foreign aid.[16] The month before, the ANC endorsed a two-day strike against the implementation of VAT. So what would an ANC-led government do if it got its hands on R15 billion? If it sets up the bank, it would be endorsing a 10 percent VAT — because it could use the R15 billion to virtually eliminate VAT for a year.

**ANC rejects 8% drop in VAT rate,
establishes development bank**

You decide which would help the masses more: the near elimination of VAT, or the establishment of a multibillion-rand bureaucratic bank staffed with political cronies. Supporters of more government spending say they're looking after the masses. But they are implicitly opposing tax cuts. And few seem to realise that one of the biggest burdens the masses face is a confiscatory level of taxation.

How to democratise taxes

High, hidden, complicated, distant taxes undermine a free society. They hide the cost of government. They undermine the capacity of the economy to grow. And they're good for the state and not so good for the people — a sure sign of authoritarianism, not democracy.

A standard assumption is that "democratising the economy" means bigger, more expensive government (bigger and more meddling than even the colonial and apartheid governments of the past). This would benefit a new elite of politicians and vested interests and would do little to benefit everybody else, a perverse notion of democratisation.

Here is a seven-point liberal-democratic programme for democratising the economy and taxes in a way that should leave ordinary people better off.[17]

1. Require a price tag on all government proposals. Any law that proposes a new programme or that would expand an old one should have to carry a detailed explanation of how the programme will be financed — no more vague references to getting money from "the state" or "the general fund." Taxpayers shouldn't have to listen to any more calls for more health services, hostel-renovation plans, tourism promotions, or farmer subsidies without hearing which tax is going to be increased to pay for them.

The price tag should also explain how many — and which — people will benefit from the programme. This would remind voters that most redistribution programmes redistribute wealth from the masses (consumers, workers) to an elite (the government's friends).[18]

2. Require a referendum on all tax increases. All elected bodies — from parliament to city councils to neighbourhood boards — should be able to draft and propose tax increases, but not institute them. This should be done only with the majority approval of area voters through a referendum on each tax. Compulsory referendums would prevent elected bodies from sneaking taxes onto the books. Instead, taxes would reflect the broad wishes of the people who suffer them. Taxpayers would get only as much government as most are willing to pay for, and no more.

3. Require a referendum on all spending proposals. Elected bodies should investigate and draft spending proposals, but the voters should have the final say on every rand that's spent.[19]

This would allow voters to pass judgment on the hundreds of controversial programmes on which elected officials spend their money. Recent government spending included R68 million for a jet to be used by the president, cabinet ministers, "and other dignitaries" for local and overseas travel[20]; R1 million to the Bible Society's *Bibliathon '91* to buy bibles[21]; R1,2 million to two national sports bodies[22]; and R11 000 to airfreight two cheetahs to Cuba.[23] You might agree with some of these programmes and oppose others. But you had no say on any of them. Where at all possible, everybody should have the chance to vote on all such plans directly.

All governments would like you to believe that they spend money only on roads, schools, the elderly, the homeless, and malnourished children. As soon as politicians start talking about the "need" to raise taxes, they mention poor people — as if welfare is the only thing they spend money on. Before VAT was introduced in 1991, the government ran a radio advertising campaign to sell the tax. One ad in the series said:

Today's fact on VAT.
  Find yourself asking where all the money coming from VAT will go? OK, it'll go into schools, roads, housing, health services, and community services.
  VAT. A better tax for a better South Africa.

Who is the government fooling? The ad could have said:

OK, it'll go into secret police, censorship committees, civil-servant pensions, handouts to farmers, overseas junkets, and political slush funds.

Requiring referendums on spending would bring this all out into the open. There, right before the eyes of every voter, would be a list of every project the government wants to finance. And if the voters say "No," the project would have to be scrapped.

American humour columnist Dave Barry recommended a similar proposal to combat rampant spending by the US government, though he modestly hid it behind a veil of silliness:

I would eliminate all giant federal departments — Transportation, Commerce, Interior, Exterior, etc. — and replace them with a single entity, called the Department of Louise. This would consist of a woman named Louise, selected on the basis of being a regular taxpaying individual with children and occasional car trouble and zero experience in government. The Department of Louise would have total veto power over everything. Before government officials could spend any money, they'd have to explain the reason to Louise and get her approval.

"Louise," they'd say, "We want to take several billion dollars from the taxpayers and build a giant contraption in Texas so we can cause tiny invisible particles to whiz around and smash into each other and break into even tinier particles."

And Louise would say: "No."

Or the officials would say: "Louise, we want to use a half million taxpayer dollars to restore the childhood home of Lawrence Welk."

And Louise would say: "No."

Or the officials would say: "Louise, we'd like to give the Syrians a couple million dollars to reward them for going almost a week without harbouring a terrorist."

And Louise would say: "No."

Or the officials might say: "Louise, we want to..."

And Louise would say: "No."[24]

The referendum would have the same effect as the Department of Louise: people could finally say "No" to billions of rands of wasteful projects that benefit nobody but politicians and small groups with vested interests.

4. Prohibit government borrowing without voter approval. All levels of government should be required to balance their budgets with current revenue, unless voters specifically approve borrowing in a referendum. This would prevent politicians from embarking on more and grander programmes without a visible and immediate rise in taxes to pay for them.

5. Decentralise taxing and spending powers. The central government's power to tax should be severely curtailed. And regional, local, and neighbourhood governments should be free to determine their own tax rates, with the approval of voters. Sales tax, income tax, petrol tax: all could vary from place to place. At local levels, taxing and spending can be more easily monitored and controlled. Also, with different tax rates in different parts of the country, voters could see which policies work best. Cape Town might opt to become a tax-free enterprise zone, while Pietersburg combines high taxes with high services. Some areas will tax personal incomes, while others won't. Over time, residents will see what mix of taxes, at what levels, works best. People, investment, and wealth will flow to the best-run areas, putting pressure on mismanaged areas to shape up. When nationwide tax rates set by Pretoria are a disaster, there's nowhere to hide. Everybody suffers.

6. Discourage complicated taxes and outlaw invisible taxes. All levels of government should be prohibited from collecting taxes that people don't know they are paying.

People continue to be lured by promises made by politicians and socialist policymakers because they have no idea how much tax they pay. They grumble about VAT and steep income-tax rates. But they can think of several services they receive in exchange, so there is anger and protest, but not revolt.

However, VAT and personal income tax account for only about 60 percent of Pretoria's revenues. The rest comes from a web of hidden taxes — on companies, mines, estates, cigarettes, alcohol, tyres, soft drinks, perfume, imports, rents, banking transactions, investments, shares trading, home buying, petrol, meat, milk, licences — that most people probably don't even know exist. If you're aware only of VAT and income tax, you're aware of only about half your actual tax burden. That's the way the politicians like it. And those are just central-government taxes.

To bring it into the open, the 50-cent-a-litre petrol tax should be tacked onto the price of petrol at the end of the sale, not hidden in the pump price. If, for convenience, the pump price continues to include all taxes (thus hiding the huge tax), the law should at least require that signs be posted at each pump informing customers how much tax they pay on each litre.[25]

Similarly, VAT should be made a visible tax at the final stage of collection, like the GST that it replaced. Rather than being hidden in the cost of goods, VAT should be added to retail prices at the till. This is not what the government wants.

Another radio ad preceding the implementation of VAT:

Today's fact on VAT.
  With GST, you often ended up getting a bit of a shock when you got to the till. With VAT, the price you see is the price you pay.

Here the government tries to turn hidden taxes into a virtue, so that people won't notice as the tax rate is increased to 15 percent or 20 percent. But people *should* get a bit of a shock every time they go shopping — it will remind them who pays for every new government programme.

7. Abolish the words *duty, tariff, surcharge, levy,* and *fee.* All money collected by the government should be called what it is — *tax*. Stamp duties, excise duties, import duties, import tariffs, import surcharges, milk levy, petrol levy, airport fees, licence fees: they should be called stamp taxes, excise taxes, import taxes, milk tax, petrol tax, airport taxes, licence taxes.

This will act as a constant reminder of how much of the economy the government already owns and controls. And it might temper calls for yet more intervention. Expect loud objections from the politicians, who have come up with the whole vocabulary of innocent-sounding words to replace *tax*. They'll object because they know that if their subjects kept reading every day about taxes, taxes, taxes, and more taxes, they might revolt.

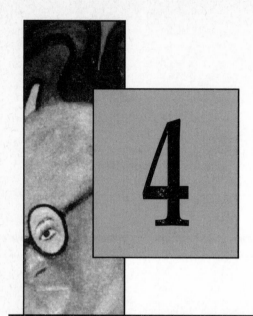

4

AFFIRMATIVE ACTION

Look who's racist now

The Population Registration Act of 1950 was a particularly vile apartheid law that classified every South African by race. This made it easy for the government to implement legislation that pitted one race group against another. Government committees across the country, called Race Classification Boards, had the honour of judging people's race. The boards took into account language skills, hair type, nose shape, and testimony from neighbours to determine who was black, white, or one of several categories in between.

From 1983 to 1990, the government's scientific classifiers reclassified 7 127 South Africans:

- 86 from white to Cape coloured.
- 3 455 from Cape coloured to white.
- 50 from Cape coloured to Chinese.
- Eight from white to Chinese.
- 35 from Chinese to white.
- 11 from white to Malay.
- 54 from Malay to white.
- 18 from white to Indian.
- 385 from Indian to Cape coloured.
- 340 from Cape coloured to Indian.
- 107 from Indian to Malay.
- 117 from Malay to Indian.

- Four from other Asian to Cape coloured.
- 1 827 from black to Cape coloured.
- 100 from Cape coloured to black.
- 15 from black to other Asian.
- 27 from black to Indian.
- 29 from black to Griqua.
- 79 from Cape coloured to Malay.
- Seven from Chinese to Cape coloured.
- 16 from Indian to white.
- 92 from Malay to Cape coloured.
- Five from black to Malay.
- Two from Griqua to black.
- Nine from Cape coloured to Griqua.
- Two from Indian to black.
- Two from Indian to other Asian.
- One from Griqua to white.
- Five from Griqua to Cape coloured.
- Two from other coloured to Indian.
- One from other coloured to black.
- Three from Malay to Chinese.
- One from Chinese to Malay.
- One from Chinese to Indian.
- One from other Asian to Indian. [1]

"I don't even want to talk about it now, it was awful," a former race classifier told a reporter after the government announced the scrapping of the act in 1991. "Thank goodness it will never happen again."[2]

Was race classification appalling? Offensive? An insult to civilised values? Nazi-esque? Yes.

But don't believe it can never happen again. Race classification is exactly what affirmative action will require. Otherwise, how will we tell who qualifies for special treatment, or which companies are meeting their government-set racial quotas?

Suppose a law is passed saying that 30 percent of all company directors must be black. First question: what's black? Does somebody who was classified "coloured" under apartheid pass for "black" under affirmative action? How about a previously classified "Indian"? Does hiring a coloured or Indian (or Malay or Chinese or Griqua) give a company full credit or half credit toward the 30 percent quota? How about hiring the child of a white/coloured marriage? A black/coloured marriage?

Second question: suppose a bunch of fairly white-looking directors simply declare themselves to be black, thus beating the 30 percent quota by a landslide? Will a reconvened Race Classification Board be called in to test their hair?

If the spirit of the Population Registration Act lives on in postapartheid South Africa, it won't be the only country to have institutionalised racism. Wherever you find affirmative-action policies, you'll find official or unofficial population registration. This includes the United States, which made the scrapping of the Population Registration Act one of the conditions for lifting sanctions against South Africa.

"I feel like we're back to the Nuremberg laws," said a professor of English at the University of California at Berkeley, commenting on the race classifications the university uses for admissions and promotions. According to Berkeley comparative-literature professor Robert Alter, "The numerical quotas have institutionalised racism here."[3]

These statements are heresy to the supporters of affirmative action. They will deny the existence of race classification, even as it appears in neon lights all over their policies. So Berkeley, whose law school reserves 23 percent of the places in each entering class for blacks, Hispanics, and other certified minorities, continues to maintain in its university catalogue that "the university does not discriminate on the basis of race, colour, national origin, sex, handicap, or age in any of its policies."[4]

Some affirmative-action supporters realise that a government cannot be colourblind and colour-conscious at the same time. But they don't like to admit this. So they resort to verbal gymnastics.

For example, in *Protecting Human Rights in a New South Africa*, Albie Sachs flips and flops his way through nonracialism, group rights, and affirmative action.

"Just as race classification and group areas will disappear from legislation," he writes, "so will they vanish from citizenship and the electoral system. There will be a common voters' roll, made up of and speaking in the name of the whole nation. In this sense, the constitution will be completely colourblind and totally race-free. There will be no special privileges for racial or ethnic groups, no vetoes, no areas of special competence, or 'own affairs.'" So there will be no mention of race in the constitution.

Flip.

"Race will only enter the constitution as a negative principle, that is, to the extent that the constitution is not only nonracial but antiracist. The antiracist character will be guaranteed by provisions, expressly referring to race, which: outlaw racial discrimination, prevent the dissemination of racial hostility, and ensure that measures are taken to overcome the effects of past racial discrimination." So the constitution will expressly refer to race.

Flop.

"There just cannot be coexistence between racial group rights and nonracial democracy. It would be like saying that just a little bit of slavery would be allowed, not too much...." So there can be no group rights.

Flip.

"It is not just individuals who will be looking to the Bill of Rights as a means of enlarging their freedom and improving the quality of their lives, but whole communities...." There can be some group rights.

Flop.

"What we do know for sure is that attempting to defend minority privileges by force of arms, whether through the present system, or by means of a constitution based on group rights, can only result in continuing strife and violation of human rights. The only system that has a chance is one based on nonracial democracy." There can be no group rights, just a nonracial constitution.

Flip.

"The constitution is a special document that should speak to the whole nation without fear or favour (except, possibly, favour to the oppressed)." Flip-flop in the same sentence.

Sachs sums up: "Affirmative action could be constitutionally recognised as a legitimate complement to the general principle of nonracialism."[5]

A valiant try. But affirmative action is the *opposite* of nonracialism, not its complement. Not that Sachs is the first to try to reconcile the irreconcilable. US Supreme Court justice Harry Blackmun tried the same thing. "In order to get beyond racism, we must first take account of race," Blackmun wrote in an affirmative-action ruling. "There is no other way. And in order to treat some persons equally, we must treat them differently."[6] Or as a 1990 ANC economic document stated: "A future democratic, nonracial and nonsexist state would give top priority to applying affirmative action principles to black women."[7]

The term *affirmative action* describes policies that promote people based on the group that they're in, not on their individual qualities. American economist and author Thomas Sowell, who has studied affirmative-action policies around the world, prefers the term *preferential policies*— policies that offer benefits, or preferences, based on group membership.[8]

But whether it's called preferential policies or compensatory preferences or positive discrimination or reverse discrimination or just plain discrimination, affirmative action — *in practice* — boils down to government-mandated preferences for government-defined groups.[9]

But the supporters of affirmative action detest specific definitions. My experience in debates is that if I offer a realistic definition that encompasses group privileges and racial quotas, my opponent will simply deny that that's what affirmative action means. Yet, in the real world, that is always and inevitably what affirmative action means.

Why do its proponents have such a hard time defining the policy? Why all the flip-flopping? It seems that few want to admit that affirmative action means forcing people into groups to meet quotas and accepting lower standards for the "preferred group." Thomas Sowell notes that "just as American preferential policies are seldom called preferential policies, so a lowering of admission standards in American institutions has almost never been called a lowering of admission standards."[10] Nobody likes to call their policy "racist group promotions" or "special rules for blacks," so the verbal gymnastics continue.

At Duke University, the Committee on Black Faculty proposed that all departments at the university be required to hire at least one minority professor during the next five years. Erdman Palmore, a sociology professor and chairperson of the committee, expected opposition.

"We knew that this sort of programme would carry a stigma in some people's eyes," Palmore said. "We tried fooling around with the name. We used to call it the add-on policy, but that didn't sound so good. Now we call it the opportunity appointments."[11]

Camille Holmes, president of Harvard's Black Students Association, said affirmative action should not be defined as preferential treatment. "That definition sounds like you're holding a gun to someone's head and saying: hire these incompetent black people."[12]

Unfortunately, changing the words doesn't change the reality.

Affirmative action is couched in fine words — diversity, talent, merit, opportunity, tolerance, development. But when carried out, it is always punitive. In fact, affirmative action *must* be punitive. It requires the government to target one group for help because of its race or ethnicity. This means it must target all other groups for punishment. To benefit blacks with quotas, a government must hold down whites. To benefit whites with quotas, it must restrict blacks. This is the logical flipside of affirmative action, but it is widely ignored. And so affirmative action leads to unintended (but easily predictable) consequences. It increases group conflict, as resentment by the punished groups grows and the demands of the beneficiaries increase. It emphasises group differences, rather than eliminating them. It discourages effort by the beneficiaries, who come to expect special privileges. And it destroys equality at law.

Affirmative action has been repeated around the world, over the decades, again and again. Sometimes it is carried out by majorities against minorities, and sometimes it's carried out by minorities against majorities. But it's always a set of punitive racist policies.

In Indonesia, the government wanted to help the indigenous Indonesians. So to expand opportunities for them, it restricted opportunities for the immigrant Chinese. A 1959 law prevented the Chinese from running stores in villages. The government also confiscated Chinese-owned rice mills and restricted where Chinese could work and live.[13]

In Canada in the 1920s, the government sought to help whites. So it passed a minimum-wage law to prevent Japanese immigrants from undercutting the wages of white workers and taking their jobs.[14]

In Malaysia, the government tries to benefit majority Malays at the expense of the more successful minority Chinese. It has made Malay language instruction compulsory in schools that used to teach in English, so many Chinese students have left to study in Singapore. The country has also imposed quotas aimed at "racial balance" in universities, government employment, and foreign-owned enterprises. Public criticism of these racial policies is a federal crime.[15]

In Sri Lanka, laws pit the Sinhalese against the Tamils. The government reserved the leading teaching-training college for Sinhalese. To prevent the perceived anti-Sinhalese influence of Christian missionary schools, the government took control of 2 623 private schools "to ensure equality of educational opportunity to all children regardless of race, religion, economic condition, or social status" and to provide an education "which is national in its scope, aims, and objects."[16] And it restricted the number of Tamils allowed to attend university, initially by arbitrarily downgrading their entrance examinations and later by setting quotas.

In the United States in the late 1880s, Chinese workers were the dominant employees at California vineyards, shrimp-fishing firms, cigar companies, shirtmakers, and canneries. To promote whites, Chinese vineyard workers were driven out by discriminatory taxes (as well as violence, an advanced form of affirmative action). Today in the US, racial laws prevent "too many" whites from gaining university admission, jobs, and government contracts.[17]

In South Africa, the government imposed racial quotas on companies, schools, and universities. It forcibly shut down Indian stores to protect whites from competition. It reserved work in the western Cape for coloureds. It prohibited blacks from forming companies. It reserved jobs in government, mining, and industry for whites.

Apartheid was just another case of destructive affirmative action —

not significantly different from preferential policies around the world.

Those seeking salvation for South Africa's racial woes in *more* affirmative action might consider a few questions first.[18]

■ **Are there hard-and-fast rules about who is black and who is white, or do the definitions change to fit the immediate purpose?** Are South African coloureds black or white? Are American Hispanics black or white? Are Chinese and Japanese and Vietnamese repressed minorities or honorary whites? Where do you have to come from to be black? Well, it all depends.

The head of a major South African bank says black consultants and union officials have complained that too many of his nonwhite staff are Indians and coloureds.[19] They have told him that affirmative action must mean hiring more black people, not more brown people. That might come as a surprise to brown people, who were welcomed as fellow blacks in the struggle against white oppressors. But watch how quickly coloureds and Indians are moved out of the "black" group when it comes to dishing out affirmative-action favours.

In fact, shuffling around brown and yellow people is a favourite pastime of affirmative-action supporters.

When riots swept Miami in 1989, some black leaders categorised the Hispanic police officers as "white" to prove that their response to the rioting was racial.[20] At other times, of course, Hispanics are brown and beautiful and part of a "rainbow coalition." It all depends on what fleeting point is being made.[21]

Some US universities, under pressure to hire more black professors, are hiring black academics from overseas. But Reginald Wilson of the American Council on Education said hiring West Indian and Caribbean blacks should not count because "Africans who may be educated in England cannot understand the experiences of black Americans."[22] So not even black-blacks can necessarily fill a quota for blacks.

Williams College in Massachusetts tried to use Spaniards to fill its teaching slots reserved for Hispanics. But minority activists stopped the practice with the allegation that "what the college considers 'Hispanic' are really white Europeans who don't have a clue what it's like to be Chicano or Puerto Rican."[23]

■ **Is affirmative action fundamentally different from apartheid?** Cut through the muddled rhetoric, and affirmative action boils down to institutionalised racism, the pitting of one government-defined group against another. In frank moments, supporters acknowledge this.

"You guys have been practising discrimination for years," US Supreme Court justice Thurgood Marshall told a white friend. "Now it's our turn."[24]

Said the ANC-SACP's Joe Slovo: "In our own country, the very people in authority who extol the virtues of the unregulated free market used every possible state device to upgrade and uplift their own disadvantaged people, including sheltered employment and massive land handouts based on black dispossession. Now with majority power looming, they engage in privatisation and other devices in order to prevent the boot from being worn on the other foot."[25]

So much for the moral high ground.

■ **In the absence of discrimination, would all groups be proportionally represented in all spheres of human life, such as education and jobs?** Supporters of affirmative action assume that any statistical differences between groups must be the result of discrimination — and can, therefore, be cured by affirmative action. What they fail to see is that statistical group differences are the *norm* in life.

Just consider some of the group differences historically, and around the world, that Thomas Sowell has exhaustively compiled.

■ Irish women newly arrived in the United States worked disproportionately as domestic servants — 99 percent of all domestic servants in New York City in 1855 were Irish women.

■ At the beginning of the twentieth century, 50 out of 110 presidents of the American Federation of Labour unions were of Irish ancestry — but the Irish rarely ran businesses.

■ In the US, during the wave of immigration from Europe a hundred years ago, the rate of alcoholism among Italians was less than one-fifth the rate among the Irish.

■ In 1937, Italians constituted 40 percent of the membership of the International Ladies Garment Workers Union.

■ By the middle of the twentieth century in Brazil, Italians owned nearly half the industrial enterprises in the Sao Paulo metropolitan area, while less than one-sixth were owned by people of Portuguese ancestry.

■ In 1890 in Buenos Aires, Italians owned more than twice as many restaurants and bars as native Argentines, more than three times as many shoe stores, and more than ten times as many barbershops, but they were largely absent from politics.

■ Germans, just 4 percent of the more than four million immigrants to Brazil from 1884 to 1939, made economic contributions out of all proportion to their numbers, introducing tobacco, potato, rye, and wheat farming and establishing the dairy industry and the first textile mill.

■ In the US, beer, piano-manufacturing, and optical companies were created and dominated by German immigrants. In the early 1900s, 90 percent of the lithography firms in the US were owned by individuals of German ancestry. In the 1800s, more than half the cabinet makers in New York were German.

■ In 1938, Jews constituted 8 percent of the population of Cleveland, Ohio, but were 18 percent of the city's dentists, 21 percent of its doctors, and 23 percent of its lawyers. Jews were about 25 percent of the population of New York at the time, but were 55 percent of the doctors, 64 percent of the dentists, and 65 percent of the lawyers.

■ By 1969, Jewish family income was 72 percent above the US national average.

■ In the same year, black West Indians in the United States earned 94 percent of the average income of Americans, while native US blacks earned 62 percent.

■ In the US, Hispanics with doctoral degrees in history outnumber Asians with doctoral degrees in history by 2 to 1, but Asians outnumber Hispanics 7 to 1 in mathematics and 10 to 1 in chemistry.[36] Black doctorates in history outnumber Asian by 3 to 1.

■ In Malaysia, where there are about equal numbers of Malay and Chinese college students, the Malays outnumber the Chinese in liberal arts by 3 to 1, while the Chinese outnumber the Malays in medicine by 2 to 1, in science by 8 to 1, and in engineering by 15 to 1.

■ In Thailand, where 9 percent of the population is of Chinese ancestry, 79 percent of the students at the country's two most prestigious universities are of Chinese descent.[26]

How can discrimination explain all this? And the list goes on of traits, skills, and preferences that are not proportionately represented in groups: alcohol consumption, immigration patterns, performance in sports, performance on tests, shoemaking. Even in activities in which discrimination is completely irrelevant, there are widely different patterns among racial, ethnic, and national groups: choices of TV programmes and card games, average age of marriage, the naming of children.[27]

"The point here is not to praise, blame, or rank whole races and cultures," says Sowell. "The point is simply to recognise that economic performance differences are quite real and quite large. Simple and obvious as this point may be, it goes counter to many prevailing approaches, doctrines, and conclusions."[28]

These aggregate differences among groups can stem from cultural values, traditions, language, education, skills, age, number of children, geography, isolation, urbanisation, weather, the number of generations in one place, savings patterns, discipline, peer pressure, property rights, literacy, the availability of books and magazines, religious beliefs, views of other groups, and attitudes to the sexes, marriage, drink, individual achievement, trade, and leisure. But the supporters of affirmative action would have us believe that group differences are solely the result of institutionalised discrimination. This stretches the imagination, especially when some universally persecuted groups — like Jews and immigrant Indians — regularly outperform those who discriminate against them. Yet these supporters argue that there is a "correct" — and easy calculable — number of people who should be represented in every job or walk of life. That distribution, they say, is what *would* have resulted in the absence of discrimination. This premise of equal group performance is baseless. As Sowell says: "The idea that large statistical disparities between groups are unusual — and therefore suspicious — is commonplace, but only among those who have not bothered to study the history of racial, ethnic, and other groups in countries around the world."[29]

Governments can best respond to this by treating *all* people as equal citizens before the law — and then allowing any group or cultural differences to emerge naturally and, perhaps, diminish over time. This is preferable to having the state embark on a futile attempt to engineer a racially and culturally "proportional" society.

A simple local example. South Africa has few black-black accountants. Of the 11 000 registered chartered accountants, only 42 are black Africans.[30] It is easy to say this is unnatural and unacceptably low. It is less easy to say just how many black accountants there *should* be. The trouble will begin when an affirmative-action bureaucrat decides on the correct number — somewhere between 42 and 11 000 — and proceeds to harass companies and schools with lawsuits until that magical number is reached.

■ **What kind of role models does affirmative action create?** To induce black students to maintain minimum grades and graduate, Pennsylvania State University pays them $580 if they maintain a grade average of C to C+. For anything better than that, they get $1 160. The cash awards are granted regardless of economic need, and white and other minority students are ineligible for them.[31]

Shelby Steele, a professor of English at San Jose State University in California and author of *The Content of Our Character*, writes: "Here is the sort of guilty kindness that kills. What kind of self-respect is a black student going to have as he or she reaches out to take [money] for C work when many white students would be embarrassed by so average a performance? What better way to drive home the nail of inferiority?"[32]

It's not just the self-respect of blacks that suffers. Other people's respect for blacks can also suffer. Each programme acts to confirm the worst prejudices about the supposed superiority of whites.

Affirmative-action supporter Randall Kennedy, a Harvard Law School professor, claims that preferential treatment reduces racism because it "teaches whites that blacks, too, are capable of handling responsibility, dispensing knowledge, and applying valued skills." A fine sentiment. But — in practice — does preferential treatment expose whites to black achievement and black skills? Or does it expose whites to blacks who can't handle the task given them?

At Berkeley, admission standards are far lower for blacks than for Asians and whites. So, predictably, the average black student — who may have flourished at another university — struggles at Berkeley. Bud Travers, a senior Berkeley official in charge of minority admissions, conceded that Asians consistently finish with the highest grades in the university and blacks with the lowest — even though Asian students are disproportionately enrolled in engineering and other hard sciences.[33] Black and Hispanic undergraduates, admitted with lower qualifications, drop out of Berkeley at far higher rates than whites and Asians. About 25 to 30 percent of whites and Asians drop out before graduation, compared to more than half of Hispanics and more than 60 percent of blacks. And an internal university report, noting that huge numbers of Hispanics and blacks drop out before the end of their first year, says they seem to stay "only long enough to enhance the admissions statistics."[34] Keep in mind that these students are supposed to be role models.

The University of North Carolina at Chapel Hill sponsors "3.0 Minority Recognition Ceremonies" each year to honour black and Hispanic students who score a B average. "No such celebrations are considered necessary for white and Asian students," Dinesh D'Souza drily observes in his book *Illiberal Education*, which looks at the new racism on US campuses.[35]

At the University of Michigan, black students formed the United Coalition Against Racism and demanded that all black professors be given tenure immediately.[36] What, then, are we all supposed to think of black professors? For whom are they a role model?

Some of the intended beneficiaries — the new "role models" — are also wondering what kind of message preferential treatment sends out. "I want to be accepted on the basis of merit," said Kenny Williams, a black female English professor at Duke who complains that she is frequently treated as if hired solely on the basis of her race and sex. Williams is an unwitting victim of affirmative action, shunted into what South African journalist Denis Beckett calls "the mental category 'Second Class — Artificially Assisted.'"[37]

D'Souza writes:

Black students interviewed by the *Indianapolis Star* for a series of articles on college life said that professors have such low expectations that they "express amazement" when blacks do well in class. Dwayne Warren, a black political science major at the University of Massachusetts at Amherst, told the *Washington Post*, "Some whites don't expect you to excel, and when you do, it's a shock to them." In order to build black confidence, three students at Iowa State University have produced a video documentary, "Black By Popular Demand," which begins by warning black students what many whites think of them: "A lot of times they assume that just because you're black, you can't read, you can't write, you can't speak." Dayna Matthew, the first black student to [have an article accepted in] the *Virginia Law Review* on academic merit, told columnist William Raspberry that by calling into question the achievements of minorities, the University of Virginia's new preferential treatment plan for the law journal "hurts us more than helps us."[38]

All this from a policy that supposedly "teaches whites that blacks too are capable of handling responsibility, dispensing knowledge and applying valued skills."
■ **Does affirmative action operate from the premise that blacks are, always and predictably, failures and victims?** Consider the story of Stephen Carter, a graduate of Stanford, who applied to the Harvard Law School and received a letter of rejection. A few days after Carter received the rejection, two Harvard officials telephoned Carter to apologise for their error. As one explained: "We assumed from your record that you were white." The other noted that the school had recently obtained "additional information that should have been counted in your favour" — namely the fact that Carter is black.
Carter recalled:

Naturally I was insulted by this. Stephen Carter, the white male, was not good enough for the Harvard Law School. Stephen Carter, the black male, not only was good enough, but rated agonised phone calls urging him to attend. And Stephen Carter, colour unknown, must have been white: how else could he have achieved what he did in college?[39]

Said Rafael Olmeda, who turned down a chance to go to an Ivy League school, choosing instead the City College of the City University of New York:

When I was a senior at Bronx Science [high school], I sent for Harvard's admission materials. The package came to my house, and out came this Minority Student Information Request Card for me to send in, and a leaflet saying, "Here are some of the things minority students experience at Harvard." And I thought: What is this....I want to know, what do *students* experience at Harvard? Like, what am I to them? Well, I knew what I was. I was the fulfilment of a quota. And I have no intention of being that.[40]

Harvard University gives full financial aid to all minority graduate students, *regardless of need*. Richard Blow, a white doctoral candidate at Harvard, commented: "This breeds cynicism, even among those who benefit from it. A black student told a friend of mine that he was about to reapply for his annual scholarship. "Oh, do you have to maintain a certain GPA [grade point average]?" my friend asked. "No," the student laughed. "I have to prove I'm still black."[41]

The view of blacks as perpetual failures and victims spills into popular culture. As South African writer Kaizer Nyatsumba said at a seminar on culture and censorship: "Now I for one, as a black person, am tired of being forever portrayed as a victim in works of art, and would like to be presented as an all-round human being for a change."[42]

■ **If blacks do not receive education and training, is it any wonder that they are "underrepresented" in positions that require education and training?** Take the case of black university professors in the United States. Charging American universities with "institutionalised racism," supporters of affirmative action have successfully demanded racial hiring quotas. But where are the universities going to find these professors? The US Department of Education reports that although blacks constitute about 12 percent of the US population, they receive just over 2 percent of PhD degrees. And in recent years, about half those degrees have been in a single field: education.[43] In 1987, across America, one black received a PhD in computer science, three in chemical engineering, and two in philosophy. In 1988, there were no new black PhDs in a wide range of subjects, including astronomy, immunology, comparative literature, and German. So universities are fighting over the tiny number of blacks qualified to become professors. They hope to poach blacks from other universities faster than their black staff is poached from them. Many universities simply hire available black professors even though none of them fills a specific opening in a department.

"There just aren't many minority professors out there," said Jay Strauss, affirmative-action officer for the University of Arizona. "We'll be lucky to break even," said Varro Tyler, executive vice president of Purdue University. "We're just bidding against each other. It's a kind of academic musical chairs."[44]

That blacks in America have suffered from discrimination is not debatable. But at some point, shouldn't blacks themselves be held responsible for not grasping opportunities and getting the education they need to stop being the object of musical chairs? Affirmative-action supporters in South Africa, while demanding more black accountants/professors/managers, tend to ignore the *supply* of blacks qualified to hold these positions. If I believed there were thousands of qualified South African blacks running around unable to get jobs because of racism, I would be sympathetic to calls for affirmative action. But where exactly are these qualified blacks?

The tough truth is, if South African blacks want to be represented in greater numbers in top posts, they must acquire the skills they need to hold those posts. No amount of number crunching or quota setting — or excuses — can change that basic fact.

There is outrage and anguish each year when fewer than half of black matric students pass their exams. Where is the outrage and anguish when black ringleaders boycott classes and physically prevent their classmates from studying; when thugs take over schools and kick out the headmasters; and when students ransack schools or shout foolish slogans like "Pass one, pass all" when principals refuse to promote those who failed? Another generation of students is being lost. But are black students themselves in no way responsible? Why do so many blacks who actually attend classes — even at second-rate, segregated government schools — manage to succeed?

As Nokwanda Sithole, editor of *Tribune* magazine, wrote at the beginning of 1992:

Yes, there will always be forces militating against our survival as a people, but our history is full of shining examples of people falling back on their own resources when they ran out of choices....

We have the power to restore the social structures we so desperately need for a stable future. We can each recognise the potential in ourselves and get up and do something about it. We can stop waiting in the wings for someone else to map out our political, economic, and social future and add our voices to the working out of this future.

White people and their policies may have contributed to the erosion of our self-esteem. They may have contributed to the self-hatred we suffer from. Yet at this moment, there is no white man holding a gun over anybody's head, forcing him to sell drugs in the townships. No one is being forced to be mediocre, or to generally do as little as possible, particularly in work situations. There is a huge crisis of ethics in the black community at the moment, and Verwoerd is not its architect.[45]

The message is clear: even as discrimination lingers, the disgruntled can look at what they can do to better their own lives. Thuy Nguyen, a student at the University of California at Davis and a Vietnamese boat person, arrived in the United States in 1980 knowing only a smattering of English she picked up in a Thai refugee camp. She says: "I have faced some discrimination, but I don't worry about it." Nguyen plans to become an architect. Her philosophy? "You just have to be persistent in what you are doing. Don't worry about how much racism there is in society. The main thing is to focus on what you can do yourself. The future is more important than the past, and you can change the future."[46]

Chia-Wei Woo, former president of San Francisco State University, says Asians in America work extra hard to combat outside forces that might hold them back. "There is no time to lament," he says. "We've got work to do." Critics of the Scholastic Aptitude Test — a private test taken by high-school students across the United States and used by many universities in admission policies — say it discriminates against the underprivileged. But a Stanford University sociologist was puzzled by the success of poor San Francisco–area Asian Americans on the SAT. So he conducted a study and found a simple answer: Asian Americans "work a heck of a lot harder" to raise their scores.[47]

"Working hard" is not in the vocabulary of affirmative-action supporters. They relish failure because it proves the goodness of their cause. A hopeful sign in South Africa is that many blacks are rejecting the permanent victim status that affirmative-action supporters wallow in. Ironically, South Africa's publicly militant black-consciousness groups are often far more nonracial than the supposedly nonracial groups allied to the ANC. While the nonracialists portray blacks as underprivileged incompetents in perpetual need of help, many in the BC movement applaud black successes — and accept responsibility for black failures. Many prominent black lawyers, hawkers, managers, journalists, teachers and entrepreneurs dismiss the patronising attitude of the nonracialists: they take pride not only in their heritage but in their achievements.

"I destroy the myth of black inferiority," said Don Ncube, after being appointed an alternate director at the huge Anglo American Corporation in 1991 at the age of 44. "Apartheid was directed at all blacks. It was not meant to be selective. But I do not revel in the glories of victimology."

Ncube, a graduate of the University of Fort Hare in South Africa and Strathclyde University and Manchester University in Britain, is also a director of several Anglo American metals and manufacturing subsidiaries. "Black Consciousness taught you self-reliance and self-respect," he said. "It's not the colour of your skin but your state of mind that counts."[48]

Echoes South African–born writer Mark Mathabane, author of *Kaffir Boy* and *Kaffir Boy in America*: "To dwell on racism and to somehow have the attitude that white people are in a conspiracy against you and that they are therefore omnipotent and that whatever you do, you can't fight this power — it leads to a fatalism."[49]

■ **How will antiapartheid activists react when race classification is brought back for affirmative action?** South African writers on the left have mocked the government's "black, coloured, Indian, and white" groupings for decades. Refusing to implicitly endorse the categories, they have referred to "so-called Coloureds" or "Indian-classified" and "black-classified" people. Understandably, books ran disclaimers about race. In a typical disclaimer, the editors of the 1991 book *Towards Justice? Crime and State Control in South Africa* wrote: "Like many commentators in South Africa, we abhor ethnic classifications which carry connotations of racial discrimination. In South Africa, however, it is impossible to avoid such classifications when describing official practices, one of the central themes of this book. Accordingly, we have used, without quotation marks, the official terms white, coloured, and Asian/Indian."[50] Merle Lipton, in her book *Capitalism and Apartheid*, similarly wrote: "Many people understandably resent the arbitrary and compulsory racial classification of the population by the 1950 Population Registration Act. Unfortunately, as all authors discover, it is impossible to analyse government policy without using these categories. The use of the terms does not, however, imply that they provide any justification for discriminating against people, or for fostering differentiation among them."[51]

That was fine when race classification was being used by the enemy. But what happens when the antiapartheid left wants to use the same classifications for affirmative action?

A 1990 ANC economic policy document, complaining that power is concentrated in the hands of 1 000 white males who sit on the boards of the country's top companies, called for affirmative action to address the racial imbalance. What exactly is meant by "1 000 white males"? Should we not rather talk about the "1 000 white-classified males" or "the 1 000 'so-called white' males" who dominate corporate boards? The nonracialists can then explain how their nonracial government will guarantee a more balanced mix of nonexistent races.

Nafcoc, the long-established black business association, has proposed that companies listed on the Johannesburg Stock Exchange achieve the following targets within 10 years:
■ The boards of directors should be at least 30 percent black.
■ Blacks should control at least 40 percent of shareholdings.
■ At least 50 percent of outside purchases should come from black suppliers and contractors.
■ At least 60 percent of top managerial staff and personnel should be black.[52]

Will antiapartheid writers in the future refer to this as a plan for 30 percent of directors to be "so-called black" or "black-classified"? Will they ask if a shares registry is to group shareholders by colour? And will they ask whether black includes brown-blacks or only black-blacks?

Offensive questions? Don't be offended by them. Be offended by the supporters of affirmative action, who want to revive official race classi-fication and keep blacks a permanent class of second-class citizens.

Or is statutory racism only objectionable — and to be disclaimed — when carried out by the National Party?

5

FREE SPEECH

No more
censors
now

t an Idasa conference on press freedom in Johannesburg
in November 1990, I sat in a workshop with a range of
alternative left-wing editors, activists, lawyers, and journalists. Before long, the discussion turned to what forms
of expression a new, democratic government should outlaw.

A member of the ANC's national executive argued for a ban on
fascist and Nazi expression, including the suppression of the militant
Afrikaner Weerstandsbeweging. He said banning the AWB could not
be seen as equivalent to banning the ANC and SACP because the
ANC's struggle is correct while the AWB's views are backward and
reactionary.

His view was echoed by an embattled Afrikaans journalist, a long-
suffering subject of government harassment. He pointed out (with no
apparent irony) that just as the Nationalists had successfully banned
the hammer and sickle, so a new government should ban the swastika.

Then a delegate argued that sexist language and symbols should be
banned. The state, she said, needed to protect women collectively from
slurs. She was adamant that provisions for free speech could not
include speech that women find offensive.

Intrigued, I asked her at the tea break what organisation she was
with.

Her reply? "The Anti-Censorship Action Group."

And that about sums up the new threat to free speech. It turns out that many of the government's left-wing opponents don't really oppose censorship. What they oppose is somebody else's censorship. For them, the opposite of apartheid censorship isn't no censorship; it's "good" censorship. In fact, South Africa's liberation movements and left-wing commentators are surprisingly open about their calls for censorship and political bannings.

The ANC's Albie Sachs says that under a democratic bill of rights "there would be no freedom to call for the maintenance or restoration of apartheid."[1]

Nicholas Haysom, a member of the ANC's constitutional committee, explains that the movement's draft bill of rights would make "offensive" views on racism, fascism, ethnicity, and regionalism a crime. It would also allow the state to prohibit materials that "insult, degrade, or encourage abuse of any ethnic, religious, racial, gender, or linguistic group."[2]

Sachs and Haysom are simply restating the censorship clauses of the ANC's 1955 Freedom Charter, which stated that the preaching of "national, race, or colour discrimination" shall be a crime and that "all national groups shall be protected by law against insults to their race and national pride."

At a press-freedom seminar at Soweto's Vista University, journalist Denis Beckett found representatives of black political groups taking turns making glowing statements about press freedom — and then listing what speech they would censor.

The PAC's Philemon Tefu applauded free expression and political diversity: "We must vanquish our opponents with facts and not with knuckle-dusters." He then said the PAC "recognises only one race, the human race, and it is from this premise that we recognise freedom," so a PAC government would "definitely not have exponents of racism expressing" their contrary view.

Azapo's Pandelani Nefolovhodwe called for prohibitions on expressions of racism, regionalism, fascism, sexism, or tribalism. Also, he said, promoting antisocial behaviour and failing to present a "proper range" of views "must not be allowed."

For the ANC's Mathole Mothsekga, racist speech was on the hit list. It is not, he explained, "that we want to restrict freedom, but that we don't want to allow dangerous freedom."[3]

Already, the left is tackling the problem of how to turn the bad old censorship of the past into the enlightened, politically correct censorship of the future. For example, the government bans pictures of naked white women for the old-fashioned reason that such pictures promote lust. It instructs magazines to put stars over pictures of female nipples.

A recent *Weekly Mail* article suggests that left-wing censors would also ban pictures of naked women, but for progressive reasons:

Can you legislate against [sex] discrimination without legislating morality? Perhaps the answer is to be found not by doing away with state control, but by putting into place an enlightened control board that looks at not whether an image is sinful or immoral, but whether it is degrading and offensive to women.[4]

Along with making censorship boards more enlightened, the left is weighing up the pros and cons of political reeducation. A 1989 Idasa study of the views of white university students concluded that they were "uninformed," "racist," and "politically unsophisticated." But this can be corrected by a little "conscientising" — in the words of Susan Booysen, an international-politics lecturer at Rand Afrikaans University who helped set up the study. Booysen explains:

A process of systematic political socialisation would be essential to effect far-reaching resocialisation....A process of resocialisation would start with the widespread dissemination of information on political worlds hitherto unknown and feared....An essential supplement would be political education in education institutions, from the primary to the tertiary level.[5]

The response by human-rights watchdogs to these regular calls for censorship and thought policing? Very muted. The old liberation mythology is still strong. Apartheid is the only enemy, the myth says, and there is no threat to freedom from the left.

The new censors pledge to outlaw only "bad" things like racism, fascism, Nazism, regionalism, tribalism, ethnicity, sexism, misogyny, and divisiveness. Then we will all live happily ever after — democratic, united, nonracial, nonsexist, and free of hate propaganda. But since when has censorship brought about contentment?

The left has a bizarre sense of history or a short memory. Allowing the apartheid thought police to determine correct expression — in movies, books, newspapers — led to untold government abuse behind a veil of secrecy. Yet journalists and organisations that were silenced or harassed then are the very people who are now drawing up their own lists of things they'd like to censor in the future.

They have a rich tradition of censorship to draw on. The Publications Act authorises anonymous censorship committees, deliberating in closed sessions, to find a publication undesirable — and, therefore, to outlaw it — if it:

(a) is indecent or obscene or is offensive or harmful to public morals;
(b) is blasphemous or is offensive to the religious convictions or feelings of any section of the inhabitants of the Republic;

(c) brings any section of the inhabitants of the Republic into ridicule or contempt;
(d) is harmful to the relations between any sections of the inhabitants of the Republic;
(e) is prejudicial to the safety of the State, the general welfare, or the peace and good order.[6]

With its sweeping, ill-defined categories, the act is a censor's dream. And it's not clear which, if any, of these categories tomorrow's censors would scrap. Clearly, they could learn a lot from old National Party techniques.

One rule for the new censors to keep in mind: lump your enemies together and give them a catchy label. Like rightist regimes around the world, the Nationalists preferred "communist" and so passed the Suppression of Communism Act of 1950 (replaced by the Internal Security Act in 1982), in addition to other security and secrecy laws.

The government's censors then scrupulously hunted for subversive — "communist" — expression to outlaw. Other favoured targets have been sex, violence, blasphemy, swear words, and the stirring up of racial hatred. Typical of the countless rulings of the Publications Appeal Board was one in 1981 outlawing the book *Chiang and Mao — China 1919-1949*. The board found that it created the impression "of the invincibility of Communism. It is calculated to seize young hearts and to win them over to Communism."[7]

The left's preferred label for the enemy is "fascist" or "racist" (or, more recently, "sexist"). So a left-wing government could just dust off old laws and rename them — the "Suppression of Fascism Act" — and drag out old censorship rulings and replace the necessary words. So a book on Verwoerd or Hitler (or Thatcher?) could be banned for being "calculated to seize young hearts and to win them over to Fascism."

To prohibit racial political parties, it could revitalise the Prohibition of Political Interference Act of 1968. A clause of that act, removed in 1985, outlawed parties that are multiracial; a new clause could outlaw parties that aren't.

And just as Matthews Ntshiwa was jailed in 1983 for possessing a coffee mug engraved with pro-ANC slogans, so a troublesome rightwinger could be jailed for possessing pro-AWB crockery.[8]

Supporters of the jailed and silenced fascists could then reprint anticensorship posters of the 1980s. "Stop the police state. We want a free press," said a poster issued by the South African Students Press Union in 1989. "Hands off the media," said one published a year earlier by the Association of Democratic Journalists. "Defend the *New Nation*. Make your mark against censorship," said a poster printed by that harassed weekly in 1988.[9]

In defence of their actions, the new censors can say that, by silencing racists and fascists, they are promoting freedom. As Raymond Suttner, the ANC's political-education officer, put it: "Racism and fascism fall out of the definition of freedom. If we suppress apartheid views and organisations with fascist views, we will be acting for freedom, not limiting freedom."[10] He contrasts this with the *unjust* suppression of democratic organisations:

Applying this to South Africa, democrats have justly attacked the banning of popular organisations, of democratic individuals and publications. The restrictions on expression of legitimate antiapartheid views has likewise been condemned. There is a right, claimed, to propagate democratic antiapartheid convictions, in accordance with universally held principles of human rights.

Does 'logic' require that the same freedom be extended to opponents of democracy, even if their views foster social divisions, animosity, racism, and threats to democracy? By no means! It is not 'intolerance' to suppress such views.[11]

So we can ban any view that fosters animosity. This is "democratic"?[12]

A handful of academics are encouraging the left to rethink its intolerance of opposing views. One is University of Cape Town philosopher Denise Meyerson, who abhors racist views but slams as "reactionary" calls by Albie Sachs and others for a new government to silence racists. It is, in effect, a call for the police to clamp down on "false" views. Meyerson says:

[T]hose on the left should not be quick to betray the values of the tradition from which their views derive. It is conservatives, not progressives, who appeal to revealed truth and the infallibility of authority, and who want the state to save us from false beliefs. Those on the left have...always and rightly asked for truth by demonstration, not revelation, and they have always celebrated, not distrusted, thought. It can only be a backward step to switch allegiances now, enlarging the powers of the state in what is essentially a reactionary way.[13]

Defining the enemy

It's easy to say you're going to outlaw racism and fascism. But what is a fascist? a racist? And do you want postapartheid censors to do the defining?

Beware of loose definitions. Is the outspoken journalist Denis Beckett a racist? He believes the next government should be colourblind and race-classification-free. An ardent and early supporter of democracy in South Africa, he thinks that every adult should have the vote, regardless of colour, and that the next government should not carry out apartheid-style head-counting. But he believes that affirmative-action racial quotas for jobs and university places constitute institutionalised racism and should be opposed by democrats. For this, ANC-supporting students have called him a racist.[14]

So if you support government-mandated race classification (apartheid), you are a racist. And if you oppose government-mandated race classification (affirmative action), you are a racist. You can't win — unless you're the censor.

Those who call for restrictions on speech invariably refer only to *other people's* speech. Their own speech is never unacceptable. The ANC's Albie Sachs supports a ban on racist speech. Sachs also says that "just as land was taken from blacks because they were black, so in future must land be taken from whites because they are white."[15] This is *not* racist speech?

Perhaps the new censors believe they have some scientific way of sorting all this out. The National Party, at the height of its emergency censorship in the 1980s, thought it did. Shortly after the government imposed extensive new press controls in August 1987, home-affairs minister Stoffel Botha announced a system of "scientific evaluation" to determine whether newspapers were promoting violent revolution. A panel of expert political scientists, psychologists, sociologists, journalists, and lawyers would help with the scientific evaluation. These would not, the minister said, be "fly-by-night and prejudiced experts."[16] Of course not.

Even some journalists seem to believe that censorship can be made objective and good — blissfully ignoring the fact that all governments inevitably turn "good" censorship laws against troublemaking journalists and political opponents.

Mia Doornaert, a Belgian journalist and the president of the International Federation of Journalists, told a University of the Witwatersrand audience in 1991 that she favours laws that make the advocacy of racism and the incitement of racial hatred a punishable offence:

It is not advocating or fomenting racism to report, for instance, an attack by a group of Belgian or French or German racists on immigrant workers, and to comment on that. It would be incitement to racism and violence to applaud this kind of crime as a way to "solve" the problem of immigrant labour from other cultures.[17]

Note the self-confidence with which Doornaert defines what is and isn't racist speech. It is reminiscent of the confidence with which Louis Pienaar, chairperson of the Publications Appeal Board in 1990, ruled on blasphemy:

Blasphemy is out...it's not something to which I'm prepared to apply the test of prevailing tolerance levels...it's just out.[18]

This confidence in defining the exact point at which speech becomes unacceptable is shared by some former victims of apartheid censorship. Donald Woods, the newspaper editor who befriended black-consciousness leader Steve Biko and was banned, wrote after his return from exile in 1990:

By all means pass laws forbidding the media to commit flagrant crimes such as defamatory attack; by all means define statutorily the crime of racial incitement or even promotion of racism in application to our particular postapartheid national needs. But do not resort to the old totalitarian trap of defining such crimes so loosely that an authoritarian politician can arrogate the role of judge and jury in such matters.[19]

Here we go again with calls for watertight, scientific definitions of thought crimes. Do some people never learn? We can't predict how "tightly" a government would define the crime of promoting racial hatred. We *can* predict that a government will always find a way to twist the definition to suit its political agenda.

In 1988, a Directorate of Publications censorship committee prohibited distribution of *A World Apart*, Shawn Slovo's autobiographical movie about her slain activist mother, Ruth First. Among its reasons: "It will be detrimental to the safety of the state as well as causing friction and distrust between white and black sections of the South African community."[20] If new, postapartheid censorship committees outlaw "racially inciting" speech, they will be able to use the same reasoning for *their* rulings. A Conservative Party newspaper, for example, could be banned for "causing friction and distrust between white and black sections of the South African community."

But irony is typically lost on censors. Communists censor fascists and fascists censor communists, but they don't see that their methods are their opponents' methods. The Internal Security Act of 1982 made it illegal to promote any doctrine that aimed to establish "any form of socialism or collective ownership." All the while, the Nationalist government proudly owned or controlled its own socialist collection of assets: TV and radio, the post office, the phone company, an airline, harbours, the railway, the central bank, an iron-and-steel company, the electricity company, the arms company, abbatoirs, nuclear research facilities, an oil-from-coal plant. By its own definition of undesirable socialist behaviour, the government should have outlawed itself. But censorship doesn't work that way.[21]

Censorship has little to do with fascism or racism or civilised values and a great deal to do with controlling your enemies. Banning fascists — or communists — means banning anybody you don't like, particularly those who criticise cabinet ministers.

Often, the censors don't have to shut you up — you'll shut yourself up. The threat of prosecution insidiously curbs debate on controversial issues: race, sex, conscription, state security, human-rights violations, taxation, corruption, inefficiency. George Washington University law professor Mary Cheh, arguing for the total scrapping of South Africa's publications controls in the *South African Journal on Human Rights*, explains:

Speech is fragile and is easily chilled by restriction — any restriction. When people have to take account of restrictions they begin to think carefully about what they say, where they say it, and to whom. They tend to self-censor and overcensor in order to steer clear of real and imagined prohibitions....Suppression, by its nature, is insidious. It proceeds by small encroachments passed in the name of worthy objectives like national security, good order, or the public welfare. It chips away at freedom and feeds on our natural tendency to see danger in all opinions we do not share.[22]

The liberation movements and antiapartheid journalists in South Africa issue high-sounding calls for censorship as if they've discovered something new. But promoting "democratic" control of the media, curbing false doctrines, and banning fascism, racism, and tribalism are not new tactics. They have been used by tyrants around the world.

Albania censored "fascist, antidemocratic" propaganda. Mozambique's government justifies censorship "in the national interest." Angola's censors ensure that only "correct" news reaches the public.[23] Censors under Mikhail Gorbachev ensured the "objectivity" of news.[24] Kenya's Daniel arap Moi blamed "tribalists" for promoting unrest and banned the prodemocracy *Nairobi Law Monthly* for contributing to the chaos.[25] Tanzania's president can detain and silence anyone deemed to be "dangerous to peace and good order."[26] Former Zambian president Kenneth Kaunda clamped down on newspapers that reported "lies." So did former Philippines president Ferdinand Marcos, whose other targets included "disparaging remarks" about the government, "deliberately slanted" news, and "false, vile, foul, and scurrilous statements."[27]

So-called right-of-reply laws and requirements for "balance" also pave the way for government abuse, by inviting the state to judge the quality of news. Singapore's government insists on a right of reply to coverage; it restricted *Time* magazine's circulation because it wasn't prompt enough in printing a letter citing errors in a story about an opposition leader. It also restricted circulation of *The Wall Street Journal* because the newspaper refused to print in full a lengthy government letter about a report on a proposed stock exchange.

Finally, governments cite "confusion" caused by too much information as a reason to gag the press. Mozambican information minister Teodato Hunguana, who directed journalists in March 1989 to suspend their coverage of a strike by university students, justified his action by saying:

We are at a critical phase in these transformations that are taking place in Mozambique, and it's a time when all the various tendencies are in a dialectic in which things are still unclear. There are many forces in play and information can sometimes have a negative influence. In the case of the student disturbances, they did not arise as a safety valve to let off frustrations, it was a case of ideological confrontation. The reporting of the strike generated a situation of confusion.[28]

Note that the strike didn't cause confusion, and the government's totalitarian laws that prompted the strike didn't cause confusion. The *reporting* of the strike caused confusion.[29] So behind all the verbal smokescreens is a simple message: the press should prop up the state, the party, and the reigning ideology and not show any disturbing signs of independent thought.

As President PW Botha said in a dispute with business leaders over the state of emergency in June 1986: "Instead of criticising the government in the most irresponsible fashion, you should be helping it. That is your duty as a South African."[30]

An outrageous view? Unfortunately, it's shared by a lot of leaders and thugs in the liberation struggle. Thami Mazwai, a senior editor of the *Sowetan*, explains:

Little has been said about a new type of censorship that is around in the townships and poses the most powerful threat to press freedom in this country. We have a situation in which journalists are far less exposed to arrest, detention and incarceration by the government than they used to be, but are being threatened and manhandled by political activists in the townships, in the towns and everywhere, and are being told to toe the line 'or else.' Now when you are told to toe the line, you must make your stories convey a particular meaning, in other words you must be a propagandist....
  We have now reached a point where the journalist is told, 'You are either for us or against us.'[31]

Mazwai and other black journalists told an Institute of Race Relations seminar that pressure comes from all liberation organisations to take sides, to stop "dividing the oppressed," or to lie about the number of people who show up at a rally.

"Reporters in Natal," reports Mazwai, "say they are having difficulty practising their profession: one night Inkatha people will come to them saying, 'Look, we don't like what you are writing,' and then the next night people from the ANC or UDF will come and say, 'Look, we don't like what you are writing,' and in the end they feel like saying, 'I have had enough,' and getting out."[32]

Kaizer Nyatsumba, a political journalist on *The Star*, says he has been manhandled by Inkatha supporters at a protest, threatened with death by PAC members for critical coverage of an economic document, and threatened on other occasions by members of the ANC and Azapo. "No single group on the left is innocent," he says.[33]

And *City Press* journalist Connie Molusi says the country is doomed if South Africa's liberators continue to mimic the intolerance of the old regime:

It is interesting that for some time people couldn't put on their political T-shirts because they feared the state, but currently putting on an organisation's T-shirt puts you at risk of becoming a panga victim, a tyre victim, or having your house petrol-bombed. I find it interesting that people have resorted to the very tactics they so strenuously criticised when it was the state that used them.[34]

6

THE RECALL

Keeping government accountable

When Archie Simonson, a state judge in Madison, Wisconsin, made an outrageous ruling in a rape case, he didn't remain state judge for long.

Simonson suggested that the 16-year-old victim had been dressed in such a way that she had invited sexual assault, and he placed the offending 15-year-old youth on probation. Irate Wisconsin citizens didn't just write letters to the press complaining about what they perceived to be a gross injustice. They acted. Entitled by law to recall all elected state officials, citizens successfully petitioned for a snap election and voted Simonson out of his job — less than four months after his rape ruling.

The voters were carrying out a proud tradition of local politics in America: kicking incompetent, corrupt, lying, plundering, or unpopular officials out of office before their terms have expired.

The procedure that gives voters this power — the recall — involves a petition drive followed by a special election. Thirty-six states permit the recall of some local officials, particularly city councillors and school-board members, and 15 of those provide for the recall of all elected statewide officials.[1]

The idea is that when government officials start to abuse their power, voters shouldn't have to suffer in silence until the next election. In recent years, American voters have recalled various state and local officials for a wide range of reasons. Two Idaho state legislators were recalled for supporting legislative pay increases. The president of the

Los Angeles school board was recalled for supporting a forced school-desegregation plan that required apartheid-style racial headcounts. Two Michigan state legislators were recalled after voting for a big tax increase. Voters in Omaha, Nebraska, recalled their mayor for being arrogant. Voters in Medford, Oregon, recalled a state senator after he pleaded guilty to sexually abusing a 13-year-old girl, despite his pleas for forgiveness. Arizona's governor was made the target of a recall campaign after making demeaning statements about women and minorities, but was kicked out of office by the state legislature before voters had their chance.[2]

Contrast this with the utter powerlessness of South Africans — even "privileged" whites — to do anything about those who rule them.

Even when faced with widely publicised scandals, like the death squads run by the army's Orwellian-named Civilian Cooperation Bureau, concerned South Africans can do little more than "demand" over and over again that politicians fire themselves:

■ **November 1989.** The Afrikaans weekly newspaper *Vrye Weekblad* publishes allegations by a former police officer, Dirk Coetzee, that the CCB runs police hit squads involved in political assassinations, poison drinks, letter bombs, and attacks on neighbouring states.[3] The outrage is immediate. A wide range of people — human-rights lawyers, newspaper editors, opposition politicians, and activists — demand that politicians' heads roll. The government seems in no particular hurry to punish the offenders.

■ **January 1990.** The government appoints judge Louis Harms to conduct a one-person judicial commission of inquiry into alleged atrocities committed inside the borders of South Africa.

■ **February 1990.** South African Defence Force chief Jannie Geldenhuys, responding to reports that spending on the CCB had "snowballed into a free-for-all," discloses that funding for the army's clandestine unit totalled R28 million a year.[4] Reports say CCB agents were paid in cash in brown envelopes. Activities of the CCB are "suspended." A *Sunday Times* front-page story says: "The Government and Opposition parties were preparing for a snap debate this week which, parliamentarians believe, could place the career of Minister of Defence Magnus Malan on the line."[5]

■ **March 1990.** An SADF major-general tells the Harms Commission that the CCB had been in operation since April 7, 1986 — more than three years before Malan says he knew about the unit. A front-page story in *The Star* says: "There is open speculation in political circles now that General Malan's admission last night — that he knew nothing of the existence of the CCB until November last year, in spite of the

CCB being in existence since the mid-80s — will be a nail in the coffin of his political career."[6]

■ **July 1990.** The CCB is "operationally disbanded" on the last day of the month.

■ **September 1990.** The Human Rights Commission releases a report on the CCB urging that it be genuinely disbanded.[7]

■ **November 1990.** Justice Harms releases his 200-page report, which implicates the CCB in murders, conspiracy to murder, a school bombing, car theft, arson, and perjury and says the unit "arrogated to itself the powers to try, to sentence, and to punish persons" outside the law. Complaining that CCB operatives had destroyed or concealed records, Harms observes that their conduct suggests "they have been involved in more crimes of violence than the evidence shows." Harms adds: "The Minister of Defence is of course politically responsible for his department and that includes the CCB."

Malan comments: "This is clearly a case of employees or officials who, in the course of their service, committed crimes for which I or anyone else cannot be held responsible."

President de Klerk, after studying the commission report, says he can find "no reason to condemn the politicians in charge for the way in which they carried out their duties and responsibilities."[8]

Lawyers for Human Rights director Brian Currin says Malan's failure to assist the commission in tracking down missing documents "is reason enough why General Malan should resign."[9]

Sunday Star columnist Jon Qwelane writes: "I believe General Malan got off scot-free in so far as hit squads are concerned. I think he must resign — and this is being very, very nice to him."[10]

The Weekly Mail comments: "If South Africa were indeed run on the same democratic standards as, say, Holland or Canada or Britain, Malan would have been fired [the day after the report was released], if not long before."[11]

Activists under the banner of the "Campaign for a Judicial Enquiry into Hit Squads," joined by members of the Democratic Party, march in Cape Town demanding Malan's dismissal.[12]

■ **February 1991.** Malan says more than 80 percent of the CCB's administrative structures, including front companies, have been disposed of but that the CCB could not simply be disbanded "by the sweep of a pen."[13]

Auditor-general Peter Wronsley reports to parliament that the CCB spent R12 million without proper authorisation over two years and that he has a "strong suspicion that virtually everything my audit team sought was/is, in fact, available in writing somewhere, but the archives have been selectively and purposely withheld or destroyed."[14]

The *Pretoria News*, commenting on the millions of rands of improper spending, says: "Once again, the onus is on General Malan to explain how this happened."[15]

Colin Eglin, a Democratic Party MP, speaking in parliament after the auditor-general's report, says Malan must take responsibility for the control of secret funds and projects: "If he has any sensitivity and sense of accountability and concern for the integrity of the government and president, this afternoon was the time to hand in his resignation. But he does not have the sensitivity or the guts to do that."[16] A Conservative Party MP, Frank le Roux, says Malan has no option but to resign.[17]

The Star, describing the CCB as "a mad-dog organisation running out of control," says: "Surely the Minister of Defence, Magnus Malan, will now have the integrity to resign — or President de Klerk will find the courage to dismiss him."[18]

Business Day comments: "Magnus Malan has patently outstayed his welcome at the Defence Department."[19]

The Weekly Mail shouts on its cover: "Fire This Man! Five reasons why FW should sack Malan." The story asks: "Why does President FW de Klerk tolerate this man in his cabinet?"[20]

■ **March 1991.** The National Party–supporting newspaper *Beeld*, under a front-page headline "CCB: Magnus did know," claims that a document signed by Malan and dated December 5, 1988, shows that the general knew of the CCB a year before he says he did. Calls for his resignation are expected to increase following the *Beeld* story.[21]

■ **April 1991.** The ANC issues an ultimatum to the government to take seven steps before May 9 to curb the violence sweeping the country. Among the demands is one calling for the dismissal of Malan and law-and-order minister Adriaan Vlok along with all army and police officers responsible for "the setting up, management, the crimes and misdemeanours of the CCB and other hit squads." ANC information chief Pallo Jordan says Malan "has been caught either deliberately deceiving the public in his accounts of the CCB, or confessing to signing away public funds without bothering to ascertain the purpose they were being put to." Either way, Jordan says, it's "a shocking dereliction of duty."[22]

In parliament, De Klerk defends Malan, saying he has confidence in him.[23] Democratic Party law-and-order spokesperson Tian van der Merwe says the CCB affair has "proved beyond doubt that it's impossible to get fired from a National Party cabinet."[24]

Malan fires the director of the CCB and 27 other operatives who refuse the retrenchment packages the army offers them. Malan tells SABC-TV news that he is prepared to resign if it is to the advantage of the president, the National Party, or the SADF. "No mention of the interests of the country as a whole, or the taxpayers," complains a *Business Day* editorial.[25]

Azapo publicity secretary Strini Moodley says the ANC's call for the resignations of Vlok and Malan is meaningless because, even if they were to quit, violence would continue to form part of the government's strategy. "Azapo has always demanded that the entire regime resign," Moodley says.[26]

■ **July 1991.** Following newspaper reports, the dirty-tricks scandal takes on a new angle and explodes into Inkathagate. The government confirms that it secretly paid R250 000 to finance two Inkatha rallies and R1,5 million to finance the Inkatha-aligned trade union Uwusa, which, investigative reporters charge, is run jointly by Inkatha and the South African Police. Foreign-affairs minister Pik Botha also reveals that the government gave "well over R100 million" to parties that opposed Swapo in the Namibian elections.

The CP calls for the immediate resignation of De Klerk and his government and demands a general election.[27]

"Should De Klerk fire himself?" the *Sunday Star* asks. Replies vary. Anglican Archbishop Desmond Tutu says he shouldn't — but only if he fires Vlok and Malan, opens government records to independent auditors, appoints a commission of inquiry into the police and army, brings those implicated in violence to court, and sets up a joint mechanism to control the security forces. Columnist Jon Qwelane, saying "our political overlords are a discredited, nasty bunch," argues that De Klerk and the entire cabinet must go. "Unless we are saying we shall be content with even more horrifying scandals in the future, and unless we wish to set precedents for the government of the 'New South Africa' — whoever it will be — Mr de Klerk and his men must pack up and leave. Today."[28]

De Klerk announces a cabinet reshuffle. Malan is to be demoted to minister of water affairs and forestry, and Vlok to minister of correctional services. Roelf Meyer is named to replace Malan, and Hernus Kriel to replace Vlok. Pik Botha, who authorised the payment to Inkatha, is left untouched.

Vrye Weekblad editor Max du Preez responds: "It is certainly not what I would have wanted to see — I would like both men out of the Cabinet — but it was a much more imaginative step than anyone would have thought President de Klerk capable of."[29]

ANC deputy president Walter Sisulu says: "The removal of guilty parties from the cabinet is what we demanded, and that does not mean shifting them around from pillar to post."[30]

Says Barney Desai, information secretary of the PAC: "Had this been a democratic government, in the accepted sense, this entire government, starting from the president downwards, would have had to resign because of the appalling scandals that they have been engaged in. They have been guilty of deception and gross misuse of taxpayers' money."[31]

■ **December 1991.** *The Weekly Mail* reports that Inkatha has received paramilitary training for "an elite hit-squad unit" and more than R7 million from front organisations of the army's Department of Military Intelligence. The report alleges that the army paid for training and salaries of the hit squad at Mkhuze, in northern Natal. It also charges that the army trained Inkatha members in Namibia in 1987 "in urban and guerrilla warfare, demolition [and] using mortar-bombs, limpet mines, antipersonnel mines, and hand grenades."[32]

The South African Police confirms that it funded a third rally addressed by Inkatha leaders, this one an Inkatha Youth Brigade rally in January 1991 — ten months after state financing of Inkatha was said by De Klerk to have stopped. Police commissioner-general Johan van der Merwe defends the spending, saying: "The aim of the rally was to motivate youths to counter crime and violence in the area." ANC spokesperson Gill Marcus says: "All secret state funding must be completely exposed."[33]

A former CCB leader, Joe Verster, warns that former agents are dissatisfied with the retrenchment packages offered by the army. "Some have already begun compiling material for videos about CCB operations which they plan to release to the international media if their financial demands are not met," he says.[34]

■ **January 1992.** *The Weekly Mail* reports that the SADF used religious and educational front companies to train vigilantes to fight the UDF and ANC in black townships. "How army sponsored township violence," the newspaper's front-page headline cries. The paper alleges that the army's dirty-tricks network — run like the CCB — was set up in the mid-1980s and still exists. The newspaper calls on De Klerk to "come clean and tell, once and for all, the full story of covert SADF activities."[35] The government names a commission under judge Richard Goldstone to investigate the charges.

Other reports say the National Intelligence Service has been instructed to "persuade" right-wing groups to take part in negotiations and to discredit them if they refuse. If true, the Conservative Party says,

"President De Klerk should not only resign, but should be pilloried."[36]

The neverending story

On and on it went, the scandal growing bigger every month with new exposés of hit-squad activity, slush funds, police and army abuse, and state-sponsored violence. And on and on went the calls for the president and his appointees to be held accountable.

But when De Klerk opened the 1992 session of parliament — calling for "the elimination of domination and abuse of power" — Malan and Vlok and the rest of the gang were still sitting in the cabinet, more than two years after the CCB scandal began to unfold.[37]

The protests have been understandable, given the seriousness of the charges and the government's half-hearted responses to them. But the outrage was a bit naive. How do people expect governments to behave? Governments always abuse power, whether they're elected or not. The only surprising thing is that they don't do it more often.

The pressing question: what's the best way to combat it?

If South Africa's marching protesters, crusading newspapers, and outraged parliamentarians want government brutality stopped, they should demand the right of recall. The recall would have allowed them to start a petition drive against Malan as soon as the scandal erupted, force a recall vote — and give him the chance to persuade the public that he is fit to run the army. Then they could have used the recall on anybody else in government who refused to take the scandal seriously. More importantly, the recall could be used in the future, as new hit-squad operators, embezzlers, incompetents, hypocrites, and liars take office.

"The police can't police the police," thundered a *Sunday Star* headline over a story on the shooting of protesters, the deaths of activists in detention, and questionable internal police investigations.[38] "The guards appear to be unguarded," proclaimed a headline a month earlier.[39] The old question of who can guard the guardians isn't difficult to answer with a little imagination. Voters can, through the recall.

Cut your losses

The recall is very simple. It is nothing but a quick election, called by the people, to "de-elect" a politician before his term expires. It allows voters to cut their losses.

Suppose a cabinet minister or your member of parliament, just one month into a five-year term of office, begins to abuse his position — votes to soak you with higher taxes, awards government contracts to his friends, treats the public with disdain, or embarks on an important fact-finding mission to the south of France. Rather than suffering under him for another four years and eleven months, you can start the recall procedure. No protests, no marches, no pleading newspaper headlines, no unsightly begging. The voters are in control, not the politicians. Aggrieved citizens start a petition drive. If they collect signatures from, say, 10 percent of the registered voters in the city, region, province, or country, depending on the delinquent official's job, a special election is held within 30 days. If 51 percent of the voters vote against the politician, he immediately loses his job and another election is called to replace him.[40]

It doesn't matter whether the politician has actually done what he's accused of. He could be thrown out just because voters are suspicious. This will keep officials on their toes. Unfair? No. People can elect a politician for any reason they want. They should be able to depose politicians, at any time, for equally personal reasons.

Of course, politicians generally don't like the recall, so it hasn't been instituted in some US states and doesn't apply at all to the central government. But why restrict it to some levels of government? And why stop at elected representatives? South Africa's new constitution should take the recall procedure further.

Everybody in government or in state corporations, whether elected or appointed, should be made accountable to the electorate.[41] And the recall should apply to every level of government: local, regional, and central.

After decades of arbitrary government, South Africans need all the protection from politicians and civil servants that they can get. The power of recall will be particularly important if, in the transition to democracy, the government refuses to dismantle and deregulate to-day's huge state structure.

Offensive postal clerks, vindictive vehicle-licensing officers, traffic cops, school principals, development officials, broadcasting administrators, Banana Board functionaries, cabinet ministers, the state president: all should know that if they abuse their positions, they could swiftly lose their jobs.[42]

Some civil servants arguably require greater independence from the electorate to do their jobs — for example, judges or professors at state universities. No problem. Subject them to petition and recall as well, but require a 75 percent vote to fire them, rather than a simple 51 percent majority. A case can be made for protecting judges from the public's passing whims and prejudices, as a counterweight to majority rule. But no case can be made for keeping them completely unaccountable to the people who pay their salaries.

The recall would dramatically transform South Africa's political landscape. Consider just a few of the benefits:

1. The recall prevents government agencies from becoming unaccountable mini-dictatorships. In September 1990, traffic departments across the country began giving drivers the new "K53" driving test, a long, complicated procedure that gives examiners lots of reasons to fail you. A writer in the *Saturday Star* complained that he had failed the test because he didn't look over his shoulder every five to eight seconds.[43]

The new rules were met with general outrage by the driving public, but also general impotence. The K53 test remains. But it's nothing that a little recall campaign couldn't sort out. Identify the Department of Transport official who dreamed up the rules. Start collecting signatures. Watch how quickly officials consult the public on a new driving test.

2. The recall provides a peaceful alternative to thuggery. In the dying days of apartheid, militant activists and hooligans have got into the habit of setting opponents on fire, burning their houses down, or terrorising their families. A new government might not hesitate to crush such violence and intimidation. Yet many grievances that evoke the violence today — against town councillors, police officers, or corrupt officials — will remain. The recall empowers activists to control the government without petrol bombs.

3. The recall allows a small group to send a message of dissatisfaction. The majority rules in a democracy, but dissidents shouldn't be ignored or persecuted. A recall drive would allow small groups to draw attention to their causes. For example, an environmental group could petition for the recall of pollution-loving planning officials. Cattle farmers could take on the Meat Board. Proabortion activists could target antiabortion members of parliament or the minister of health.[44] These groups might never win a single recall campaign. But through their recall drives, they would win in other ways. They'd force issues into the public eye, so that decisions could no longer be made behind closed doors. They'd force officials to speak coherently on issues and to seek consensus to avoid de-election. And by highlighting the differences in opinion in society, they'd undermine the dangerous notion that "the people" speak unanimously on every matter.

4. The recall quells police brutality, promotes justice, and encourages evenhanded law enforcement.

"'Tools of torture' found inside police station" was a recent headline in the *Sunday Times*. Armed with a court order, Durban lawyers searched a police station in Mooi River, Natal, and found items that two men

claim were used to shock and suffocate them.[45] Dozens of variations of
this story appear in the press each month.

Many people are fighting a valiant struggle to bring the current
government's police to task for torture and murder. Even if they succeed, how will they prevent it from happening again? There is a broader
issue involved here than what to do about the CCB and police abuse
today, and that is how to prevent such abuse in the future. Subjecting
all law-enforcement officials, from the law-and-order minister to local
traffic cops, to potential recall would bring them under popular control.

**5. The recall prevents top officials from washing their hands of
departmental scandals.** The people at the top should be accountable
for the graft at the bottom. If they refuse to take responsibility, the
electorate should be able to throw them out.

The newspapers are filled with reports of misdeeds in government
ranging from petty rulemaking to allegations of official favouritism in
government contracts to outright multimillion-rand scandals. Most of
them fade from memory before taxpayers see an official punished.
Police and home-affairs officials identified R4,6 million in false claims
for movie-making subsidies.[46] The *Sunday Times* reported a row over a
R50 million contract for the transport of mail, which was allegedly
awarded to a company in which the brother of the postmaster-general
is a senior executive.[47] A parliamentary committee, believing that at
least R50 million had been lost in corrupt deals between officials and
outside contractors, recommended a judicial inquiry into the Department of Development Aid, which funded black homelands.[48] A report
compiled by a Johannesburg chief magistrate found that more than
R24 million earmarked to buy books for schoolchildren in the homeland of Lebowa had gone missing.[49] Auditor-general Peter Wronsley,
in a 1991 report, found that finances in state departments were "still
not in all respects as desired." He identified R40 million in unauthorised spending, including R17,2 million by the Department of Education
and Training, R14,9 million by the Department of Transport, and R1,5
million by the Prisons Department. He said the finances of the country's 259 black local authorities were "chaotic" and reported that only
five had presented proper accounts for the year.

Who is to blame for these "irregularities" and abuses? And is anybody losing his job over them? Voters should have the power to recall
government ministers and department officials who they believe do
not investigate scandals seriously — or who actually benefit from
them.

6. The recall minimises pay and pension abuses. Is it any wonder
that government officials award themselves huge pay increases? You

would, too, if you could set your own salary and then forcibly collect the money to pay for it from the 39 million people around you. Members of parliament gave themselves a 26 percent pay increase in 1990 and almost doubled their allowances to run their constituency offices. They already get large car allowances and free air travel. David Breier, political writer for *The Star*, wrote that most members of parliament were "coy about going public on their own pay increases, but they generally regarded the increases as justified in view of the high expenses they incurred."[50] A good way to make parliamentarians less coy would be to threaten to recall, say, the finance spokesperson of each major party.

Meanwhile, the Democratic Party estimates that the lavish pension schemes for the country's civil servants will cost future taxpayers R50 billion. In 1991 alone, the government said it would pay in an additional R1 billion to cover pension costs. DP finance spokesperson Ken Andrew said: "The extent of the pensions deficit dramatically demonstrates the way in which the ineptitude of the Government has mortgaged our financial futures. The profligacy over decades and its pandering to the bureaucracy has meant that future generations are now saddled with this massive debt. Taxpayers are now being penalised for the Government's sins of the past." Conservative Party finance spokesperson Willie Botha called for the firing of finance minister Barend du Plessis over the pension fiasco. The recall would allow voters to fire finance officials, one by one, until they were replaced by officials who would overhaul the state pension scheme.

7. The recall shifts the balance of power from politicians to the people. Inner-city shopowners in Johannesburg, complaining that the city is becoming a crime-ridden pigsty, want the city council to act. Maurice Reznick, the owner of 15 stores who is leading Operation Clean-Up, told the *Sunday Times*: "We have had enough. This must be the most dreary, drab and dangerous urban area in the world." Shopowners want the council to crack down on muggers, provide more refuse bins, prevent hawkers from completely blocking pavements, and provide ranks for black taxis. "Council officials are doing nothing about this mess," said a jeweller. "They should resign." Under threat of recall, officials might take business complaints seriously.[51]

8. The recall prevents unbecoming grovelling by the citizenry. People shouldn't have to beg government officials to act. Officials should jump when told.

Consider the case of Nkululeko "Squeejee" Skweyiya. Back in February 1987, the school board of Pretoria's Afrikaans-medium Menlo Park High School prevented the young Durban long-jumper from competing in a high-school athletics meeting because he's black. The decision made headlines across the country. It was a dreary time in South Africa's history, but Menlo Park's parents were galvanised into a stirring display of goodwill and outrage. Tired of being pushed around by petty officials, a parents' action committee called for a vote of no confidence in the school board. Parents crammed the school's auditorium, where they voted overwhelmingly — 755 to 155 — to ask the board to resign. The board went into hiding, ignored the parents' vote, and refused to comment. It even refused to resign after being asked to do so by both the minister of education and the Transvaal director of education.

Stroebel Hofmeyr, an agricultural official who headed the parents' committee, told *Leadership* magazine that parents were embracing change: "This school is going to do what the parents see as being reasonable. We want to see sport being practised in a normal way. As a community we are certainly ready for it. From all over the country our committee is receiving encouragement and support. People are telling us, please go on, we are right behind you. At Menlo Park we feel that the time is ripe. If we had not taken the lead someone else would have. To put it clearly, we are ready to play soccer against Mamelodi High. Hoërskool Menlo Park will compete with its peers in future."[52] But the system was stacked against the parents. They shouldn't have had to request the board's resignation. They should have had the recall power to fire the entire board on the spot. That would put an end to grovelling.

9. The recall promotes open, accountable government. Officials who want to keep their jobs will have to avoid any appearance of impropriety, which means, among other things, no more secret meetings on controversial issues. The recall also improves attitude.

Some Edenvale town councillors held secret meetings about merging with neighbouring local authorities. Councillor Matthew Tulip slammed his colleagues for the clandestine talks. "This is the most important thing that has happened in the history of Edenvale, and I am furious that it has been done behind closed doors," Tulip said. "This council has no mandate from ratepayers to explore the possibility of amalgamating with any other local authority. Coming on top of serious allegations of overspending, these secret talks must be seen in an extremely serious light."

Replied management committee chairman Karel Jankowitz: "If we had to get a mandate every time we wanted to discuss something, we would never get anything done." That's an attitude that deserves an electoral test.[53]

10. The recall curbs wanderlust. What fun it is to travel when some-body else has to pay for your plane tickets and accommodation. Various Johannesburg city councillors in 1990 proposed trips to Moscow to study libraries (rejected), to the Far East to study solutions to traffic problems (approved), and to Cape Town and Durban to study their festive decorations (approved). If some of these itinerant councillors had been greeted at the airport on their return with a recall petition, their colleagues might see more clearly the benefits of staying at home.[54]

11. The recall restrains the desire to go on building sprees with other people's money. The cost to taxpayers of renovating Johannes-burg's civic theatre, initially put at R24 million, soared to nearly R150 million. "I wish people would stop criticising the theatre and start supporting it," said Cecil Bass, a city councillor overseeing the long-delayed project.[55] Support it with even more money, perhaps?

12. The recall discourages weak excuses. The post office's opulent new 13-storey building near Joubert Park in Johannesburg has been called a palace because it has, among other things, polished granite ceilings in the entrance hall. John McLachlan, a Witwatersrand regional manager of the post office's telecommunications division, defended the building to *The Weekly Mail* in 1990: "The planning and the alloca-tion of contracts for the erection of the building was initiated in a totally different socio-political era, eight years ago. If the planning were to be undertaken today, different finishes would probably be used." He also said that the hub of the country's telecommunications network "warrants a certain amount of prestige and cannot be consid-ered extravagant in its present state."[56] A rather lame argument. One wonders whether, given the chance to express themselves in a recall election, voters would agree with the official's view that the different "socio-political era" of 1982 justified a granite post office.

Nice try

Politicians hate the recall. They see it as a nuisance that prevents them from lording over other people's lives. That's all the more reason to demand that it be entrenched in the new constitution.

Politicians and civil servants committed to serving the public have nothing to fear from the recall. In fact, they should welcome it as a way to get rid of their corrupt colleagues.

Left-wing activists — perhaps because they are beginning to realise that "good" politicians can abuse power, too — are showing signs of support for the recall. The constitution of the ANC Women's League provides for the recall of league leaders. A 1991 report on restructuring local government in the Ciskei, prepared by the UDF, ANC, and the

Border Civics Congress, says local councillors should be subject to recall by a majority vote at an adequately advertised meeting.

The government's constitutional advisers, on the other hand, are unenthusiastic. A 1990 President's Council report on constitutional mechanisms recognises that "the mere existence of such a [recall procedure] will ensure that, from the outset, a representative will take care to serve the interests of his constituents properly."[57] But the report then takes the position — unsurprising coming from politicians — that the electorate should not be given the power of recall because the leaders generally know best. It says the recall "could easily be abused, prevent decision making and the necessary stability in government" and warns that it "may create a reluctance on the part of the legislature to make decisions which initially appear to be unpopular but may in the long term prove to be acceptable."[58]

Wrong on all counts:

■ The recall cannot be "abused" any more than an election can. Remember, no government employee can be kicked out of a job unless 51 percent of the electorate agrees.

■ The recall doesn't "prevent decision making." It prevents bad decision making by forcing arrogant officials to think before they decide.

■ The recall doesn't make a government unstable. That is accomplished quite well by stupid laws passed by unaccountable politicians. On the contrary, the recall encourages government officials to go out of their way to ensure justice and stability, rather than ploughing ahead with ridiculous plans.

■ The recall doesn't prevent a legislature from making tough decisions. If a legislature believes a difficult decision is in the long-term interest of the people, it should be obliged to persuade the people of this.

Democratic legislatures around the world continually burden people with "unpopular" laws and taxes that are supposed to pay off some day. The excuse is wearing thin. South Africans have suffered for too long under unaccountable politicians and officials who think they know best. The recall will remind politicians that they are there to serve the people, not the other way around.

7

MAXIMUM DEMOCRACY

Referendums, local choice, and majority rule

Suppose you heard a proposal for a single world government elected, very democratically, by all five billion people on earth. Whatever government 51 percent of the voters chose would be the government everybody would live under. The majority-rule world parliament would make decisions affecting everybody, everywhere, on a wide range of issues: shop hours, the school curriculum, gambling, taxes, language, religious rights, the press, company law, labour relations, traffic lights, road building, you name it.[1]

The capital of the world would be Phnom Penh, where the parliament would meet to determine things like abortion policy in Sri Lanka and farm subsidies in Albania.

Supporters would say: "We believe in a democratic system in which people elected on the basis of one person, one vote administer the world in the interests of the people as a whole."

Would you say the world's people would be living in a democracy?

Hardly. The mind reels at the mischief such a centralised world parliament could make under the banner of "democracy." Suppose representatives from China and India dominate and vote for compulsory one-child families and male sterilisation. The whole notion is absurd.

Why should a person in Sydney have a say, through the central parliament, in the shopping hours in Timbuktu? Worse, who wants homogenisation on a world scale — reminiscent of Ceausescu's systemisation lunacy in Romania? There is no reason for the history curriculum in Honolulu to be the same as that in Addis Ababa.

And how excited should we be that 51 percent of the world's population is living under the government of its choice, when 49 percent isn't? What becomes of them? Do they just become, very democratically, slaves of the 51 percent?

And what if the 2 500 000 001 people who form the majority have questionable notions of press freedom, religion, property ownership, trade, money, morality, sex, race, and justice? Must the other 2 499 999 999 just toe the line?[2]

Do we ignore huge cultural differences and animosities because, after all, we are all human beings — united, equal citizens of the world? Would unity be strength?

What's lacking in this centralised model are guarantees of accountable government and good old-fashioned freedom.

Start with this model of a single world government. What could you change to counter abuse of state power, promote greater freedom, and increase the number of people who actually like the government they're living under?

Devolution of power

The obvious step would be to abolish the centralised government and replace it with far smaller, independent units of government.[3] Just cutting the earth in half, so to speak, would be a good first step. Say there are two independent governments instead of one — one for the western hemisphere and one for the eastern hemisphere. If the world's ideologies and values were exactly evenly spread, the same party that won the world election would win the two half-world elections. So, *at worst*, the exact same number of people, 51 percent, would be living under the government of their choice. But it's far more likely that different parties and policies would dominate in each half, better reflecting the views of each hemisphere's citizens.

Now cut the world in half again at the equator and set up four independent governments. At worst, the same party gets 51 percent of the vote in each quarter, so there are still almost 2,5 billion unhappy people. But, of course, such a result is less and less likely as government power is further decentralised — into 8 or 16 or 32 or 64 or 128 or 256 regions. Different parties would win in different places and at different times; people who would have been swamped as insignificant minorities at the world level could become self-ruling majorities in a region.

Something else happens as governments become smaller and more localised. The laws tend to reflect the norms of the people living in that area, so they are less likely to be completely unacceptable. Even if your party loses a particular election, you aren't miserable living under the winning party because it typically offers a variation of policies that are generally acceptable to you, not something radically different. The more state power is decentralised, the greater the number of people who will be living under a government that they have chosen or at least find tolerable. In many areas, close to 100 percent of the people will accept their government even though they do not agree with all its policies. They will support the general thrust of the rules they live under. The smaller the area, the more likely it is that a 100 percent acceptance will arise. Contrast that to the discontent (and armed rebellion) that would exist if people were ruled by a distant world parliament.

Note that the fundamental principle of majority rule doesn't change. Majorities still rule. But if you add up the people who say they are in the majority, you get far more than 51 percent of the world's population. There is more consent of the governed, so there is more democracy.

Another benefit of devolution of power is that if you're disgruntled with the government you're living under, you can easily move to another jurisdiction. In other words, you can vote with your feet. Under one centralised world parliament, you'd just have to suffer. If there were two parliaments, one for each hemisphere, you'd have to move halfway around the globe to escape bad government or to switch to the less bad one. But if power were devolved right down to your community, you could move just a few kilometres, or even a few blocks, in search of better government. You could probably change your government without changing your friends or your job.

Devolution would allow diversity rather than forcing conformity. It would end the destructive (and ultimately insoluble) fight over which coalition of the world's diverse people is going to rule everybody else. It would allow thousands of education systems, language policies, tax regimes, and codes of morality, rather than one. And if these smaller governments allowed free trade and travel, the world would be no more fragmented than it would be under a centralised parliament. There can be unity, but a unity brought about voluntarily, among free people — people who are generally happy with the regime they live under. Strength lies in diversity, not in enforced unity.

At home

Now suppose you heard a proposal for a single South African government elected, very democratically, by all 39 million in the country.[4] Whatever government 51 percent of the people voted for would be the government everybody lives under. The majority-rule central parliament would make decisions affecting everybody, everywhere, on a wide range of issues: shop hours, the school curriculum, gambling, taxes, language, religious rights, the press, company law, labour relations, traffic lights, road building, you name it.

Parliament would meet in Cape Town to determine things like the history curriculum in Pietermaritzburg and the official language of the Karoo.

As ANC veteran Walter Sisulu put it: "We believe in a democratic system in which people elected on the basis of one man, one vote administer the country in the interests of the people as a whole."[5]

Would you say South Africa's people would be living in a democracy?

Hardly. As with a centralised world parliament, the mind reels at the mischief such a centralised South African parliament could make.

People in Durban would be meddling in the lives of people in Oudtshoorn. The majority's notions of press freedom, religion, property ownership, trade, money, morality, sex, race, and justice would be shoved down everybody else's throats. And even if the parliament is voted in by a majority, how excited should we be that 51 percent of the country's population is living under the government of its choice, when 49 percent isn't?

Just as centralised power would be undemocratic for the world, so it would be undemocratic for South Africa. The same friction, fights, resentment, corruption, and abuses of power would result.

With devolution, different parties could win in different places and at different times; people who would have been swamped as insignificant minorities at the national level could form majorities in a region. The number of South Africans happy with the laws they live under would soar.

Devolution would allow diversity rather than forcing conformity. It would end the destructive fight over which coalition of the country's people is going to rule everybody else. It would allow a wide range of education systems, languages, tax regimes, and codes of morality, rather than one. And if the constitution guaranteed free trade and travel among these lower tiers of government, the country would be no more fragmented than it would be under centralised rule. There would be unity among free people.[6]

The 1991 proposal by the Democratic Party to devolve power to eight to twelve state governments doesn't go far enough. Though clearly preferable to a single centralised government, it would not provide the diversity that's needed. There would still be some four million people living in each state, so millions of people could be left unhappy. How far could devolution go in South Africa? A lot farther than people think.

Consider the now-famous devolved system of Switzerland — the basis of proposals by Leon Louw and Frances Kendall in *South Africa: The Solution*, parts of which seem to have influenced the government's latest constitutional plans. Seven million people — speaking German, French, Italian, and Romansch — live in a tiny country. At 41 000 square kilometres, Switzerland is half the size of Scotland; it's one-tenth the size of California; it's about the same size as Lesotho, the tiny mountain kingdom that South Africa surrounds; and it would fit fully three times into the Orange Free State. So, what for some people is the outer limit of devolution — a third of the Orange Free State — is just the starting point for Switzerland. It devolves real lawmaking power to 26 second-tier states, called cantons, and 3 000 communities.[7] Seen in this light, the DP's call for devolution of a few powers to just 12 states in all of South Africa looks almost Stalinist.

While other ethnically diverse countries experience regular constitutional conflict (Canada, Belgium, Fiji) or degenerate into violence (Yugoslavia, the former Soviet Union, and countless African countries), the liberal model of Switzerland carries on as a multilingual but united nation. Yet left-wing politicians in ethnically diverse South Africa still argue that only *centralised* power will unite the nation, against all evidence to the contrary.

A glance through the newspapers shows how many contentious issues in South Africa could be settled at regional or, preferably, local level: abortion, capital punishment, policing, education, health, language, culture, recreation, housing, roads, town planning, business regulation, industrial development, liquor laws, shop hours, gambling, prostitution, monument building, pollution control, conservation, tax. There is very little that could *not* be settled locally. Nobody would be happy with all the decisions made across the country, and nobody would be happy with every decision made in their area. But it's the socialists who promise utopia, not democrats; one person's ideal South Africa is not what devolved democracy delivers. Dramatic devolution of wide-ranging legislative powers to hundreds of areas would simply allow many South Africans to be satisfied with the rules that govern them and virtually everybody to at least accept them. In a divided country as potentially explosive as South Africa, that would be no small feat.

The policies of your choice

Going back to the proposal for one centralised world parliament, what else could be done to democratise the government besides devolving power?

To see the answer, consider the problem. Suppose that in the election for a world parliament, you vote for the party that promises not to persecute or slaughter minority cultures. That's your only concern. With any luck, that party wins. Then suppose this elected world government — *the government you voted for* — doubles your taxes, decrees that all education be carried out in Mandarin or Urdu, and bulldozes your neighbourhood. Who's actually doing the ruling, the majority of people (including you, who voted for the winning party) or the handful of elected politicians?

Obviously, the politicians. This problem is not unique to a world government. It's inherent in representative democracy — that is, democracy by an elected parliament, congress, or council. And it occurs at all levels of government.

You can cast your vote on one issue, only to find that your winning candidate disagrees with you on almost everything else.

Your dilemma is clear: in a two-person contest, you support one candidate's stance on tax, education, and conscription and another candidate's stance on everything but tax, education, and conscription. Who do you vote for? You are forced to decide which issues are more important to you. Even if the candidate you select wins, you lose. Standard political analysis holds that in a representative democracy, 51 percent of the people have the government of their choice — the much-vaunted majority rule. But that analysis is misleading. The majority could find that they strongly oppose dozens of laws passed by the parliament *that they elected*. In a representative democracy, you can easily get the government of your choice without getting the policies of your choice.

The solution is to have people vote directly on each issue in referendums. The issues appear on the ballot and voters choose "yes" or "no" — whether it is a proposal to subsidise farmers, raise the petrol tax, or increase education spending. That way, voters can mix and match policies in a way that no single party's platform can ever do. At all levels of government, everybody can vote directly on taxes, education policy, minority protection, traffic problems, and so on. That can still lead to majority tyranny, of course. But at least on every issue, a majority is happy, something that doesn't happen when a majority-rule government makes the laws.

Basic mathematics explains why voting on each issue is more democratic than voting for a representative to represent your views. Suppose there are two candidates standing for parliament in your area. There is just one issue, issue A. You select the candidate who agrees with you on this issue, and so does everybody else. The winning candidate will exactly represent the will of the majority on issue A in parliament.

Now suppose there are two issues. Issue A, for example, is whether to legalise abortion in South Africa or keep it illegal. And issue B is whether to privatise the post office or keep it a state monopoly. When there are two issues, there are four possible positions:
■ yes to both,
■ yes to A and no to B,
■ no to A and yes to B,
■ and no to both.

If there are just two candidates, two of the combinations *cannot* be represented. If you're lucky, one of the candidates will support your combination. If not, you must decide what is more important to you — in this example, getting the abortion law you want or the postal service you think is best. Even if your candidate wins, you lose on one issue.

This is not a ridiculous example. Suppose 51 percent of the people in South Africa implacably oppose abortion and 49 percent vehemently favour abortion on demand. Meanwhile, 98 percent (everybody but the politicians) agree that the post office should be privatised immediately, if not destroyed by a nuclear bomb. But suppose everybody cares more about abortion. Passions rage, and everybody makes the decision on the abortion issue. The antiabortion party wins. The majority rules. But, because the winning antiabortion politicians oppose privatisation, the post office remains a nationalised nightmare — even though every single citizen wants it nuked. This is "the triumph of democracy" that we learn about in school.

With three issues, A, B, and C, there are eight possible combinations:
■ yes to all three,
■ yes to A and no to B and C,
■ yes to A and B and no to C,
■ yes to A and C and no to B,
■ no to A and yes to B and C,
■ no to A and B and yes to C,
■ no to A and C and yes to B, and
■ no to all three.

It is unlikely that the winning candidate will exactly reflect the will of the majority on these issues.

And so it goes. Suppose there are ten issues — which is reasonable even in a local election — for example, street lights, schools, Sunday movies, a proposed road, property taxes, petrol tax, liquor licensing, abortion, topless bars, town planning. Then there are fully 1 024 combinations of yes and no.[8]

If your choice is between two candidates, it is virtually impossible for your views to be properly represented in the parliament or city council.

This is not theoretical philosophising and number crunching. In South Africa, virtually all national elections for whites over the past five decades have been decided on ethnicity and nationalism (the broad package of black rights and white survival). In recent elections, crudely put, the racists (or the very nervous) voted for the CP, the half-hearted racists voted for the NP, and the antiracists voted for the DP. And, on the race issue, the parties in recent elections were a fairly good reflection of the three strains of public opinion.

But beyond that, white representative democracy was a monumental failure. What is the will of the majority of the white electorate on sales tax? conscription? press censorship? privatisation? capital punishment? the Banana Board? None of these issues was ever seriously debated at election time. It was just race, race, race. But even if other issues had been debated, what party would you have voted for if you were, say, a racist who was opposed to handouts for farmers? or a half-hearted racist who supported massive privatisation? Those positions were nonexistent.

No modification of representative democracy can solve this mathematical problem. The only solution is to introduce direct democracy — referendums that allow the electorate to vote on every important issue directly. This way, the will of the majority will always prevail on every single issue. And this can be instituted at all levels of government. Voters would no longer have to put up with a tradeoff between abortion, postal service, and tax policy.

Though the term *referendum* is widely used for both referendums and initiatives, the two are traditionally different:

■ An *initiative* is a law proposed, or initiated, by the people. Supporters collect signatures on petitions for their proposal. If they get, say, 5 000 voters locally or 1 percent of the electorate nationally to sign a petition, the issue is put to a vote. If 51 percent of voters approve, the initiative becomes law, *no matter what the parliament or local council thinks of it*. For example, the people might initiate a law demanding that the post office be disbanded. If approved, the post office would go — no matter how much lobbying the post office carried out. The famous 1978 tax revolt in California, Proposition 13, was an initiative.

■ A *referendum* gives people the power to reject a law that has been approved by the government. For example, if the government voted to raise the petrol tax 10 cents a litre, as it did in late 1991, opponents could collect signatures on petitions to veto the petrol-price increase. If they got 1 percent of the electorate to sign, the issue would be put to a vote. If 51 percent rejected the tax increase, it would be rescinded, even though the elected parliament or council passed it.[9] Had even just white voters had this veto power in past decades, it would probably have been widely used against such infuriating laws as pay increases for government officials, sales-tax increases, the cordless-telephone ban, and the TV licence fee.

Referendums offer many other benefits besides that of solving the mathematical problem of regular representative democracy. Four of them:

1. **The referendum undermines the power of vested interests and small lobby groups.** Under representative democracy, it is easy for a small group (say, dairy farmers) to get a law passed giving them privileges and money. It is not worth anybody else's time and effort to fight the law. A R39 million handout to farmers would cost each South African one rand. Who can bother to lobby against a programme that costs them one rand? It would be madness. But it makes sense for the people who receive the R39 million to lobby like mad. Under direct democracy, the time and effort required to combat these special-interest handouts and favours would be minimal — particularly if *all* government spending proposals had to be tested in referendums, not just those for which a successful petition drive has been held. The people would simply go to the polls every few weeks and vote no on all costly proposals that benefit vested interests. Most liberal critics of government abuse these days don't criticise mob rule, or the tyranny of the majority. They criticise the rule of lobbies and vested interests, powerful minorities with friends in parliament or congress. In a typical, and accurate, attack on America's pork-barrel politics, Emory University public-choice economist Peter Aranson writes: "The problem is that of minorities — cohesive interest groups — exacting benefits from the public sector at collective cost."[10] With regular referendums, particularly on tax issues, programmes that benefit a few powerful interests at the collective expense of the masses can simply be rejected by the average voter at the ballot box. Few of the politicians' pet projects — public works, lavish grants to hometown industrialists and farmers, monopoly franchises to favoured business people — would be approved in referendums. The people who are forced to pay would finally have the power to say no.

2. The referendum prevents government from getting bigger and bigger out of institutional momentum. Parliaments and city councils, since they are spending other people's money, tend to embark on grander and grander schemes as the voters get used to the existing level of grandeur. Through the referendum, people can say no to creeping government bureaucracy.

3. The referendum makes everybody responsible for government tyranny. If they have voted directly, everyone will have to recognise that the laws and taxes they approved curb people's rights and plunder their wealth.

When distant politicians increase income taxes, outlaw textbooks, or soak the middle class to subsidise wealthy farmers, voters just shrug their shoulders. They didn't make the decisions. But if the voters themselves had to vote to increase income taxes, outlaw textbooks, or subsidise farmers, they would be more likely to consider whether it is really the moral thing to do. If the politicians outlaw abortion, voters can ignore the plight of teenagers who try to terminate their pregnancies with coat hangers. That's more difficult to do if they're the ones who personally voted to outlaw abortion. When politicians build a new highway and expropriate several dozen homes in the process, people can shrug and blame it on "progress." But if individuals had to vote on confiscation of property, it might happen far less often.[12]

4. The referendum ends the debate over who speaks for "the people." Many contentious issues in South Africa could be resolved with referendums, which would shut up the self-appointed voices of the people. Should South Africa join the United Nations? the Commonwealth? the Frontline states? the Organisation of African Unity? Should the government subsidise the teams South Africa sends to the Olympics? What should the mascot be for national sporting teams? What should South Africa's national anthem and flag be? Should the names of roads and airports and dams be changed to break from the apartheid past, or are there better things to do with taxpayers' money than put up new signs? One can predict that the natural caution of ordinary people will generally lead to better decisions on these issues than those reached by power-hungry and point-scoring politicians.

Direct democracy is best combined with decentralisation of political power to regions and cities. After all, a referendum at the national level can still leave millions of people (in South Africa, 19 499 999) unhappy on every issue.

Such a combination could win wide support. University of the Western Cape economist Pieter le Roux, for example, supports a social-democratic welfare state but is wary of the way state power has inexorably grown in his favourite social democracies. To prevent such creeping authoritarianism in South Africa, he also calls for a combination of referendums and local decision making. He warns correctly: "Statism is always a danger when government is not directly responsible to the people."[11]

Morality versus practicality

A final note on the mathematics of majority rule. Everybody talks about the "right" to vote for a democratic government, as if there is some intrinsically moral case for majority rule. There isn't. I have yet to hear a convincing explanation of why 51 percent of the people around me should have the power to conscript me, force me to pay for somebody else's education, prevent me from watching the films of my choice, or do anything else to me. The majority has no moral "right" to do any of these things. There is, however, a *practical* case for democracy, and that is that other forms of government will inevitably be even more repressive.

In discussing democracy, people tend to confuse "the majority" with "the people." They say a law passed democratically reflects the will of the people. Though widely used, this phrase is correct only when there is unanimous agreement, which is rare. The correct term is "the will of the majority." And it's not clear why 49 percent or 10 percent or even 1 percent must become slaves of everybody else.

Liberal democracy does not solve this moral problem. Even with its checks on government power and guaranteed rights, it still provides for plunder (taxes, subsidies, regulation) and repression (conscription, censorship, state monopolies). Indeed, it gives this legalised theft and oppression a seal of approval that they don't deserve. In the end, the case for liberal democracy is a practical one. It is better than the alternatives. It reduces the likelihood that self-appointed elites will suppress the masses. It *minimises* authoritarianism, persecution, and the theft of people's wealth. It leaves space for individuals to own property, trade, and prosper.

A liberal democracy of decentralised power and referendums doesn't necessarily produce good government. But it does result in less bad government. Devolved, democratic governments can still abuse power. But they are far more likely than centralised states to allow people to live their lives in liberty and tranquillity — and that's the goal that democrats should always aim for.

8

THE ENVIRONMENT

The state
versus
the environment

It could be worse. You could be living in Czechoslovakia:

Belching smokestacks dot the landscape; open strip mines eat the flanks of mountains. At high noon, cars drive with headlights on, picking their way through stinking pea-soup smogs....
Two-thirds of Czechoslovakia's forests are being denuded by acid rain. Life expectancies have fallen five years over the last two decades; the incidence of cancer is up more than a third. An hour's stroll in Most amounts, roughly, to smoking a pack of cigarettes.
"Oh, look!" says Eva Janeckova, an ecologist at Most's Academy of Science, as she crosses a bridge over the oddly glimmering river Bila. "The water is red today."[1]

That's how *Newsweek* described the coal-mining and petrochemical-manufacturing town of Most, two months after the fall of the Berlin Wall. This was what it found in Poland:

Poland's southwest province of Silesia rivals Most as the armpit of Europe. Mines spew sulphuric dust into the air. Steel mills dump tons of salt and toxins into rivers. Tuberculosis is rampant; half of Poland's workers die before they reach retirement age. In Katowice, mothers of newborn infants receive coupons with which to buy uncontaminated milk; in Cracow, drinking water comes by delivery truck.[2]

In what was the Soviet Union, an ecologist lamented: "The territory of the entire country is essentially an ecological disaster zone." Air pollution in 70 Soviet cities is approaching life-threatening levels.[3] In the city of Astrakhan, children walk to kindergarten wearing gas masks to escape industrial pollution.[4] A Soviet television documentary reported that so much petrochemical waste was released into the Caspian Sea in 1988 that the sturgeon, the source of Russia's famous caviar, were being exterminated. But as economist Paul Craig Roberts and researcher Karen LaFollette wrote in *Meltdown*, their study of the Soviet economy published in 1990:

The concerns fall on deaf ears...as the factories bordering the basin still must produce to meet gross output targets. The environmental dangers are ignored in the rush to meet the plan.

The Black Sea, the Baltic Sea, the Barents Sea, and Lake Baikal face the same threat for the same reasons. Millions of dead fish wash ashore, and beaches are awash in sticky black gunk. The fabled Volga and Dnieper rivers are dying as well, unable to withstand the vast quantities of industrial waste and raw sewage dumped in them each year.[5]

The topsoil has been stripped on Soviet collective farms. Drinking water all over the country is contaminated. In Moscow, air and water pollution has cut life expectancies.[6] A TV documentary looked at the strife-torn city of Sumgait in the Azerbaijan region:

Footage shows hazardous working conditions in Sumgait's aluminium works, and the narrator reports that Sumgait's air supply is poisoned by 70 000 tons of toxic discharges each year, sickening many of the staff. The film then cuts away to show people living in a shantytown among industrial waste. A woman throws a bucketful of slops into a stagnant pond with a crowd of ragged children standing around. More than 20 000 live in the slums of Sumgait, and the area has the dubious distinction of having the highest infant mortality rate in the country.[7]

Environmental degradation on a vast scale was one of socialism's darkest secrets. The rulers of eastern Europe treated the land, water, and air as a nationalised rubbish dump. As South Africa drafts a green agenda, it can learn from the environmental destruction in eastern Europe and the pollution and havoc reported elsewhere in the world. Here are six guidelines.

1. Private property ownership is essential to protecting the environment. If you were a Pole or Czech or Russian and you didn't like what was happening, what could you do? You didn't own the property that was being destroyed. And nobody owned the polluting factories, either. When propertyless polluters meet propertyless pollutees, the result is an environmental disaster. Eastern Europe is the "tragedy of the commons" run amok.

But the problem isn't unique to eastern Europe. Wherever you find pockets of socialism, you find environmental damage. Consider South Africa's black townships — which have been owned and administered by the state like socialist-style work camps. It's not surprising that many of these patches of socialism are as dusty, smoky, treeless, and dreary as eastern Europe. The government owned the land that blacks lived on — it didn't restore the right of blacks to own urban land until 1986 — and the government controlled the transport, and hounded home businesses. The residents had no incentive to upgrade the areas. Why look after a plot of land that isn't yours and that might be taken away from you at any time? Now that the government has begun to privatise township properties — by restoring private property rights and selling or giving rented state housing to residents — they are being improved by their owners. The faster the privatisation of black townships proceeds, the faster the areas will break from their dirty socialist pasts. Likewise, rural and tribal lands in South Africa need clear private ownership to prevent collective abuse of them. The owners can then set sensible rules about who can use the land and under what conditions. This gives them the power to combat overgrazing and soil erosion.[8]

The capitalist West is also dotted with pockets of socialism, where private property rights are not defined or enforced, or resources such as forests and lakes are owned by the state. In these areas, the tragedy of the commons looms. As the American environmentalist Robert J Smith put it:

Ask yourself: Do we dump sewage in our swimming pools or in the nearby [state-owned] creek? Which is more polluted and suffers most from overuse, Disneyland or Yosemite Park? Will litter and garbage be greater in a private yard or in a town park? We cannot escape the fact that those resources which are unowned — air, rivers, lakes, and oceans — are treated as 'sinks' for the free disposal of our wastes and effluents. Since they belong to no one, and there is no way to sue for trespass or charge for their use, the cheapest way of disposing wastes is to dump them into the air and water.[9]

This lesson is lost on left-wing greens, who are blind to the pathetic track record of state control of resources. For example, the ANC's draft bill of rights, in its section on environmentalism, calls "the land, the waters, and the sky" the "common heritage" of all South Africans — an open invitation to everybody to treat the land, waters, and sky as a collective garbage dump.

2. Understand capitalism before you reject it. The strengthening of capitalism and private property rights should top the green agenda, but you'd never conclude this from mainstream discussions of the environment. The oft-repeated criticism of free enterprise is that it gives people the right to pollute as much as they want. Perpetrators of this myth fail to see what lies at the heart of capitalism: personal control over private property.

It is a clear violation of private rights to degrade somebody else's property — that is, to pollute. You don't have the right to set fire to somebody else's car or break into somebody's home. Similarly, you don't have the right to cover another person's land with soot, leak toxic waste into his water supply, or poison his air with smoke. There is no fundamental difference between arson, theft, and pollution.

Some people argue that pollution is the price of economic growth — that a company has the "right" to allow petrol to leak from its underground storage tanks into a neighbour's water supply as long as the company is contributing to the economy. This was the view in the Soviet Union and eastern Europe. But it's not a capitalist view. Under capitalism, a company cannot leak wastes onto neighbouring property unless the owner of that property agrees to it. The company might have to pay a hefty sum for that agreement. More likely, the neighbour will refuse to allow the company to pollute his or her land at all, forcing the company to install strict pollution-control devices. Either way, the company's cost of doing business is higher — but the neighbour is acting entirely within his rights in protecting his land.

If capitalism is so good at protecting property, why then is there so much pollution in capitalist countries, too? Mainly because capitalist rights have been thrown overboard by rampaging governments, which allow industries to pollute other people's land and water in the "public interest" or for the "common good." Individuals lose control over their land (and water and air). The resulting pollution is the result of creeping socialism, not rampant capitalism. Free-market capitalism doesn't give you a licence to pollute. If you want a licence to pollute, you have to ask a government.

3. Governments pose as defenders of the environment, but they are often the worst enemies. For decades, governments around the world have contributed to environmental havoc — something that emotional environmentalists tend to ignore.

In the western United States, the American government has subsidised multibillion-dollar dams and irrigation projects that have destroyed wildlife habitats and encouraged the waste of water by artificially lowering its price. Federal-government cash grants and subsidised crop insurance have encouraged farmers to drain wetlands and grow crops on ever-poorer land.[10] The US Forest Service has subsidised the destruction of public timberland in the Rocky Mountains by building logging roads and selling the harvested timber at huge losses. And a massive water project in North Dakota undertaken by the US Bureau of Reclamation destroyed tens of thousands of acres that were home to wildlife and waterfowl.[11]

In South Africa, the government has also carried out an assault on land, sea, and air. State road-building authorities have expropriated land to excavate gravel, and then abandoned the sites. The state has encouraged waste by keeping water costs artificially low through subsidised irrigation boards.[12] Agricultural subsidies have rewarded farmers for uneconomic and destructive land use. The government outlawed black land ownership and forcibly removed millions of people, undermining the development of stable communities that would have looked after the environment. The government owns large tracts of land — including vacant rural land and the army's vast holdings — that contribute to overcrowding and deterioration on the remaining land. And the government has hidden its controversial oil, gas, and nuclear energy projects behind official-secrets laws — projects that environmentalists claim produce pollution and hazardous wastes behind the veil of secrecy.

Other government actions affect the environment in less obvious ways and are often overlooked. Large bureaucracies and high taxes drive up costs for consumers, which leaves them less willing and less able to devote money to pollution control or conservation. Many countries could import the food they need, taking pressure off fragile farmland and eliminating the need to clear forests and drain swamps to grow more crops. But government-imposed trade barriers prevent this, forcing destructive farming and ranching.

Occasionally, of course, governments do something that environmentalists approve of, like creating a national park. But more often, governments curb trade, raise taxes, ravage state land, expropriate private land, subsidise uneconomic development, bless industrial pollution, and keep people poor, hungry, and homeless. This is the institution that's going to *save* the environment?

4. Be suspicious of claims that committees, experts, and an all-powerful minister of the environment will protect the environment. Socialist greens make the fatal mistake of assuming that strong government action always leads to a safer, cleaner environment. They forget that governments are made up of corruptible people, not angels.

Why will a strong government protect the environment rather than denude it? If a single minister is given sole power to issue permits to control pollution, what guarantee is there that the minister won't grant a permit to an influential overpolluting industrialist (especially if he is a generous supporter of the party in power)?

The governments of eastern Europe were strong. They could have squelched pollution with the same vigour with which they squelched dissent. But they didn't. They used their power for things like squeez-

ing out the production of one more shoe from an outdated, mismanaged, dirty factory.

Environmentalists put a lot of faith in the ability of a government to
strike a proper balance between production and pollution, an ability
that no government has ever demonstrated. And once a government is
given the power to ride roughshod over private property rights, what
hope is there for the environment?

Mainstream environmentalists, ignoring the rights of property owners, typically call for the government to run a cost-benefit analysis and
"objectively" rule how much pollution should be allowed — even if an
aggrieved property owner doesn't want to allow any. Take the case of
agricultural chemicals. Natal University plant pathologist Mark Laing
— writing in the book *Rotating the Cube: Environmental Strategies for the
1990s* — says there is a "conflict of interests" between farmers of sugar
cane, maize, wheat, and timber who use chemicals called "hormone
herbicides" and other farmers, like lettuce and tomato growers, whose
crops suffer when the chemicals spread to their land.[13] The chemicals
are generally sprayed from a plane or tractor, and the spray drifts into
other areas as far as a kilometre away, where it damages other people's
crops. For environmentalists who ignore property rights, the question
is simple: how much good is being derived from the use of the chemicals, and therefore how much suffering must other people tolerate for
the good of society? As Laing puts it: "For the short-to-medium term,
agrochemicals will remain essential to agriculture, and to our society's
well-being. It is the balance between use and abuse that needs our
careful monitoring."[14]

Some would agree. But that's not the liberal-capitalist position. If you
recognise private property rights, it's irrelevant how much good is
derived from the use of the chemicals. Farmers may use chemicals that
damage other people's land and crops *only* with the consent of those
people. If sugar-cane farmers want to continue using the chemicals,
they should either have to pay the lettuce and tomato growers for their
inconvenience and suffering, or spend money on a system that contains
the spray on their land. A system of private property rights does not
allow environmental degradation because it is "essential to agriculture" or contributes to "our society's well-being." The polluter has the
right to pollute only with the consent of those affected.

A nonenvironmental example helps clarify the principle. Suppose a
clever criminal takes your wallet and then does wonders with the
stolen money. He invests the cash, generates a lot of wealth, starts a
few businesses, employs several workers, and improves society's well-
being. Do these benefits to society justify his theft of your wallet? No. If

he believes he can put your money to good use, he must get it from you without force — perhaps by offering you interest or a cut of his profits. You could accept his offer, or you could refuse outright to part with your money. Neither the government nor "society" has the right to carry out a cost-benefit analysis to determine whether your money stays in your wallet or is taken by an entrepreneurial thug. Why, then, should a government have the right to do a cost-benefit analysis of your farmland? The lettuce grower's land is like his wallet. If another farmer wants to make lots of money by harming the lettuce grower's land with stray chemicals, he must get the consent of the lettuce grower. Otherwise, what he's doing is no different from street crime.

Unfortunately, this principled approach to pollution is widely ignored in favour of the dangerous notion that environmental protection requires a different set of rules — a kind of environmental fascism. Industrial policy, state ownership and control, lawmaking by experts and ministerial decree, and the violation of individual rights and private property: these are the new environmental policies. If they sound familiar, it's because they are the old socialist and fascist policies.

Consider this view of the environment:

Sufficient institutional arrangements and regulatory control are required to correctly apportion responsibility and usage of natural resources. The limits of finance and qualified manpower of developing organisations pose a serious threat to environmental conservation unless they are systematically improved.[15]

The message? The government can "correctly apportion" the use of resources. The writer? Bruce Corbett of the government's Development Bank of Southern Africa. Corbett also confidently calls for the government to require "balanced" regional development to promote "optimal" use of resources — a confidence shared by the former economic planners in eastern Europe.

Jeremy Ridl, an associate of the Institute of Environmental Law at Natal University, shows a similar faith in the authoritarian approach to environmental problems. Criticising the government's track record in policing mining developments, Ridl calls for the minister of environmental affairs to introduce a mandatory Integrated Environmental Management procedure whereby a committee of "unbiased experts" would impose environmental protection on new developments. He writes: "The proper implementation of the IEM procedure would more or less guarantee the wisest possible use of our natural resources."[16] Who are these wise experts? Whose property and whose resources will they lord over? And what recourse will there be if these unbiased experts turn out to be wrong, or take bribes from polluting industrialists or overzealous greens?

This cavalier attitude to people and their property, combined with a love of official committees, sounds a lot like the government's approach under apartheid. Are South Africans content to stick with authoritarian policies as long as they appear under a new, greener banner?

5. Don't keep people poor and expect them to rally around the ozone layer. Poor societies have more urgent things to worry about than environmental degradation. Even now, eastern European governments face a vexing problem: people can see that pollution is killing them, but they can also see that the store shelves are empty. Greens shouldn't be surprised if these people — ill-housed, poorly clothed, and hungry — democratically decide that a bit more pollution is a small price to pay for having consumer goods. If socialist economic policies continue in South Africa, the poor will probably exert similar pressure on the government not to divert a single cent to pollution control. Misguided green socialists say economic growth must be curbed to preserve the environment. In fact, high growth should be encouraged, to generate the billions of rands of new wealth that will make it easier to solve environmental problems — even from a socialist's perspective. As the poor get richer, the government would be able to spend more money on conservation, land rehabilitation, and pollution control, things that communist states and overregulated third-world countries simply cannot afford. Some citizens of socialism-torn Mozambique are so poor that they wear bark as clothing. Can you expect these people to applaud a government decision to prevent trees from being stripped of bark, or to shut down a trousers factory because it is polluting the air?

6. Inject some economics into environmentalism.

Outrage. They're cuddly and cute, and millions of them are slaughtered around the world to satisfy people's greed. But don't panic. They're in no danger of becoming extinct.

They're sheep.

Cattle, chickens, trout, and mink aren't endangered species, either.[17] The extinction of animals is popularly blamed on "man's greed." But this seems to be an incomplete explanation. People are "greedy" for beef, yet cows aren't an endangered species. Why? Because the equally greedy suppliers of cows are rewarded for meeting the huge demand.

Imagine a magazine article that warned: "In 1988 China passed Japan as the biggest importer of beef, which threatens cows with extinction by the year 2005." That's a fairly absurd warning about the future of cows.

How about this one? "In 1988 Hong Kong passed Japan as the biggest importer of ivory, which threatens African elephants with extinction by the year 2005." That's from a real article in *Newsweek*.[18]

But if demand increases, why must the supply automatically dry up? As demand for ivory soars, so does the price of ivory and the *value* of elephants. If elephant farming is profitable, then wildlife entrepreneurs will have an incentive to spend money on land for elephants, antipoaching measures, disease control, and research on breeding. Governments that remain involved in conservation could reduce the burden on taxpayers by earning revenue from sales of a valuable commodity: elephants.

Imagine a "Save the Cows" movement demanding a worldwide ban on trade in beef and leather. The number of cows would drop as farmers moved into more profitable commodities: what's the point of spending money on raising an animal that you can't do anything with? Yet halting trade in ivory is what some environmentalists believe will save the elephant. Not everybody agrees. In a hopeful sign that economic logic will prevail, many environmental bodies in South Africa, Botswana, and Zimbabwe are opposing a worldwide ivory ban. They have seen the economic benefits of culling elephants for their ivory.

The owners of private game farms in southern Africa are helping to popularise the connection between profits and conservation of wildlife. They make money by charging tourists admission fees, charging hunters a fee for each animal killed, and selling the meat and skins of harvested animals. Serious environmentalists — rather than sentimental environmentalists — should be trying to find ways to make wild animals even more useful to people if they want the animals to survive. This means calling on governments to decriminalise the farming of exotic animals and allow open trade in all animal products, including meat, tusks, furs, skins, and hair. It also means allowing people who have been displaced by government-owned game reserves to enjoy an *economic* benefit from the animals, rather than just haranguing people to support conservation.

In a pioneering project to conserve elephants in Namibia, the seminomadic people of Purros have begun charging tourists a levy to visit the communal land they share with wildlife. "It is as if we are farming wild animals," said one village elder after receiving his cut of the levy. "But instead of getting meat and skins for them, we get the money that the tourists pay to see them. That is why we must look after our wildlife."[19]

From ecology to economics

An injection of capitalist principles into environmentalism would also help people make rational decisions about things like alternative energy sources and recycling.

Consider solar power. Trendy environmentalists in South Africa want people to install solar panels in their homes to generate pollution-free electricity from the sun's rays. The reason this hasn't caught on is that it's cheaper just to flip a switch and use the electricity supplied by Eskom. Solar panels are expensive, so what's the incentive to use them? The environmentalists answer by saying consumers should consider the *real* costs of using Eskom's electricity, which includes the damage done to the air and rivers by Eskom's coal-fired electricity plants. They have a point. Solar energy might be cheaper if you considered *all* the costs of traditional energy supplies. But how can you count the costs accurately? The problem with industrial pollution today is that its costs are "externalised" — that is, the costs are borne by the local air breathers, land owners, and water users who are assaulted by the pollution, not by the offending company (and its distant consumers).

Enter property rights and prices. Suppose the victims could claim for compensation from Eskom for all water, land, and air pollution that it causes, as they would be able to do under a system of free-market environmentalism. Let's say the pollution from Eskom's power plants does damage to property owners of R5 billion a year. In other words, if Eskom were held responsible for its property-rights violations, it would have to pay R5 billion in compensation (or spend up to R5 billion on pollution-control equipment). That R5 billion would have to be recovered through higher electricity tariffs. *Then* consumers could see whether it pays to switch to solar energy. Pollution control (or compensation) should become another cost of doing business, so that prices finally reflect all the costs of a product. As long as pollution remains an externalised cost that taxpayers or private property owners have to cover, we can't make rational decisions about which energy supplies are really the most economic.

Now consider the great nappy war. Environmentalists in the US are waging war against disposable diapers because they take up huge amounts of space in landfills, are difficult to recycle, and create a toxic brew when mixed with human waste. Their solution: use cloth diapers. But economist Walter Block says the debate won't get very far until all the costs of polluting are internalised. He notes that there are environmental costs involved in using cloth diapers, as well: the electricity needed for washing, drying, and ironing, which requires gas, oil, coal, or nuclear power, and the resultant dirty, soapy water, which must be disposed of. So which nappy system is better? The only way to find out is to eliminate government subsidies at every step of production, distribution, and disposal and to make producers and consumers pay all costs. Block argues that once all resources are owned privately and the costs of pollution are reflected in prices, ecology will become a branch of economics — as it should be.[20]

The totalitarian temptation

None of this is to say that environmental problems are going to be easy to solve. Even a principled free-market approach raises many logistical problems. But they are problems that can be addressed through the normal institutions of liberal democracy: capitalism, property rights, and personal freedom on the one hand and accountable government, referendums, and innovative local lawmaking on the other. They won't be solved by grand socialist plans.

Unfortunately, grand socialist plans are being called for from all sides. The President's Council issued a report in 1991 that recommends central-government control over all aspects of the environment. It calls for a National Rural Development Strategy and centralised control of agricultural commodities. It calls for a centralised water-resource planning scheme, centralised noise regulations, and a national Waste Management Act. It recommends that legal control of hazardous waste be centralised in one statute. It says provincial laws governing conservation should be scrapped and replaced with a National Conservation Plan. It recommends that a single minister of environmental affairs be given power to do just about anything he wants, including overriding local policies and halting mining projects. And then, in case any lingering doubts remain, the report declares that "ultimate and final authority should lie with central government for all aspects of environmental management." It calls this a "National Environmental Management System."[21]

Maybe a little scepticism is appropriate here. Central planning in South Africa has been a costly failure again and again: in land, agriculture, housing, education, industrial development, communications, energy. Why should central planning suddenly succeed in "protecting the environment" — a task defined so broadly as to include everything from approving town-planning schemes to protecting flowers? There is little real-world evidence to suggest that a National Environmental Management System will be a success. National management systems of anything tend to lead to corruption, poverty, waste, and repression.

9

RIGHTS

Making sense
of a constitution
and bill of rights

Governments do things all the time that, if done privately, would be crimes. When thieves took over the streets in 1991, hijacking cars, burgling homes, and robbing banks, outraged South Africans demanded more police and tougher action against the thugs. Meanwhile, when finance minister Barend du Plessis announced late that year that he would extract R1 billion from motorists over the next 12 months by increasing the petrol tax 10 cents a litre, there was hardly a murmur of protest. People who fret about crime ought to ask themselves which is the bigger threat to their belongings — common criminals or the finance ministry?

When fellow citizens take your money at gunpoint, it's called theft. When the government takes your money at gunpoint, it's called taxation.

And that's not the only thing governments can do that ordinary people can't.

If you take somebody from his home and lock him up, it's kidnapping. When a government does it, it's preventive detention.

If you forcibly prevent a competitor from opening a store or staying open in the evenings, it's sabotage. When the government does it, it's business regulation.

If you force young men to work for you, it's slavery. When the government does it, it's national service.

If you print rands and spend them, it's counterfeiting. When the government does it, it's loose monetary policy.

Because governments can do these things, they wield enormous power over people. That's why they need to be controlled. But how? By instituting democracy, most people would answer. If everybody has the vote and majority approval is required for state action, a handful of people cannot call themselves the government and proceed to rob, assault, silence, and jail everybody else.

A handful can't, but what if a mob does? What if tyranny by a few people is replaced with tyranny by a lot of people? An action that has the approval of 90 percent of the people — or even 51 percent — is nominally democratic. But it is not necessarily sensible or just.

Suppose a band of criminals and their supporters form the "Plunder and Loot Party" and win 51 percent of the vote on a platform of counterfeiting, sabotage, kidnapping, and theft. They manage to persuade the majority that they'll flourish by abusing everybody else. Would this be democratic? Would it be moral? What should the PLP government be allowed to do to other people? Chop off their ears? Shut down their newspapers? Send them to work camps? Ban their books? Seize their land? Tax their incomes?

Now suppose a group of people form the "National Party" or "Democratic Party" or "Pan Africanist Congress" or "Inkatha Freedom Party" or "African National Congress" and muster 51 percent support on a platform of easy money, tough business regulation, reeducation camps, and wealth redistribution through taxation. Should there be any limits to what that party could do once in power — even if democratically elected?

Democracy — from the Greek *demos*, "the people," and *kratos*, "to govern" — describes a system in which the people rule. But what that means when applied to the real world is the subject of endless debate.

A liberal conception of democracy doesn't mean that a few people rule or even that many people rule. It means that all people rule — that everybody has a meaningful say in the collective laws they live under, while enjoying maximum control over themselves and their property. Democracy will never please everybody all the time. But a liberal-democratic constitution will try to ensure that every individual enjoys liberty — not that a bare majority of the people govern and live well while everybody else is suppressed. Only when everyone enjoys freedom, personal choice, and a say in government can it be meaningfully said that "the people" rule.

Roads and roadblocks

Together, a constitution and a bill of rights lay down the rules for

democratic government. But they pull in opposite directions. A constitution says what the government can do; a bill of rights says what it
can't. The constitution establishes the structures of the state: how the
government will operate, where powers will lie, and how voting will
take place. In doing so, it paves the way for government action. A bill
of rights, on the other hand, puts up roadblocks against government
action. It restricts state power.

Why put up roadblocks? Because without them, governments begin
to act like marauding gangs of thugs — gangs that include parliament,
city councils, politicians, the civil service, and bureaucratic boards.
Sure, they'll occasionally do things you'll applaud. They might build a
road or a school. But, more often, they'll take a big chunk of your
money to give to other people and then restrict what you can do with
what's left.

Of course, this is not what we learn about governments at school. In
textbooks, we're taught that government is a benign force, filled with
well-meaning individuals who represent the people. They debate and
agonise before passing laws. They promote the general interests of the
citizenry. (These textbooks are particularly popular in schools run by
governments.)

In real life, many people in government have a completely different
agenda. The general interest? They're far too busy looking after their
own self-interest. They dish out protection or subsidies to themselves
and their friends, harass their enemies, and please powerful lobbies in
exchange for support at the next election.

Some people are attracted to public life because they genuinely want
to help others. A few, untainted by the system, provide selfless service.
But many are corrupted. This isn't surprising. How would you behave
if you could collect lots of money from lots of people by passing a law?
If you could grant your friends their wishes? If you could make a
lifetime's earnings from a single bribe? The power that government
officials wield drives even the most well-meaning people into questionable dealings — around the world, all the time.

A constitution and a bill of rights should recognise how governments
behave in the real world, not in the textbooks. They should reflect a
healthy scepticism of the state.

A liberal vision

Authoritarians of the left and right — socialists and fascists — believe
in an active role for government. Liberals believe in a protective role
for government and an active role for people:

■ Suspicious of self-proclaimed leaders, liberal democrats call for universal franchise — one person, one vote — which prevents an unelected elite from governing in the name of the people.

■ Suspicious of thought control, liberal democrats call for free expression unhindered by any law. They tolerate diverse opinions and oppose censorship, even of speech they don't like.

■ Suspicious of the ability of a dominant or sole party to remain uncorrupted after a long stint in power, they oppose one-party systems and support multiparty democracy and political diversity.

■ Suspicious of the concentration of power, they call for government power to be diffused. Two-house parliaments, a cabinet, regional and local governments: with any luck, these government bodies will be so busy fighting with each other that they'll leave everybody else alone to get on with their lives.

■ Suspicious of creeping authoritarianism and personality cults, they support limitations on how long a person can hold any one government post.

■ Suspicious of backroom deals between government officials, they support open-meeting laws, or "sunshine laws," that require all government meetings to be advertised and open to the public.

■ Suspicious of the abuse of power, they support a court-enforced bill of rights that prevents the government — even if popularly elected — from violating basic rights, such as freedom of speech and the press, freedom of worship, freedom of association, and freedom to own property. This prohibits a government from dismantling the democratic structures that enabled it to come to power in the first place.

■ Suspicious of politicians and their powerful pals, they support referendums and the recall, which allow them to veto politicians' laws, propose their own laws, and throw misbehaving politicians out of office.

■ Suspicious of government control over people's lives, they support a civil society, private property, and a capitalist economy. Life should revolve around private institutions, not the state. As Gavril Popov, the mayor of Moscow, said in 1990: "State property is the basis of bureaucratic socialism. We cannot talk of freedom unless we have private property."[1]

Illiberalism, past and future

South Africa's white-minority governments have violated every one of these liberal tenets. They have historically rejected this liberal vision of open and accountable government, personal freedom, and private enterprise. A truly democratic revolution, therefore, would usher in a very different system of government. It wouldn't just change the rulers. It would change the rules.

And changing the rules is what the National Party is now proposing to do — often for the better. Faced with the prospect of losing power, it's exploring ways of devolving government power away from Pretoria. The government's Law Commission has proposed a bill of rights that — if its ominous state-of-emergency provisions are deleted — could, among other things, end political censorship and detention without trial and guarantee private property rights and freedom of association, movement, and enterprise. The Nationalists have a long way to go before they become liberal-democratic capitalists, but at least they occasionally make the right noises.

Perversely, many of the government's opponents aren't happy about this. Sammy Adelman, a former University of the Witwatersrand student-council president who was banned in 1981 and went into exile in 1982, complains that the government and big business have started promoting liberal values like federalism and the rule of law as "a way of protecting the minority's privileges rather than enlarging the freedoms of the majority."[2] And Rhodes University law lecturer Donald Leyshon similarly argues that the government's proposed bill of rights is designed to "preserve as much of the white South African way of life as is possible under a black-dominated government."[3]

The left is convinced that the problem in the past was the abuse of state power by an undemocratic white government, not the abuse of state power in and of itself. So they want to retain all the state power, but exercise it democratically and wisely. Unfortunately, if a new government inherits the powerful apartheid state, it is unlikely to act wisely. It is more likely to continue to run censorship boards, detain and silence opponents, take people's land, regulate business to death, and keep taxes high — by design, to fulfil its socialist plans, or by default, because it can't resist the temptations of power. Either way, the refusal to adopt liberal rights or roll back the state is hardly a formula for "enlarging the freedoms of the majority."

Restricting the power of the government will benefit blacks, who have suffered most under an intrusive government. The adoption of a liberal bill of rights and constitution that drastically reduce state power would not "preserve" the status quo. It would lead to radical changes away from centralised power and arbitrary government control of people and their property. Restricting state power would also benefit whites. All the talk about "white privilege" masks the fact that whites haven't fared all that well under the current regime. They've enjoyed far more freedom than blacks. But they have also suffered from an overregulating, overtaxing, unaccountable, dictatorial government.

Whites would also enjoy more freedom and prosperity under a new liberal order, even as they lose their privileges — so it shouldn't be surprising that some of them are pushing for liberal reforms.

Moreover, a liberal bill of rights wouldn't protect "white privileges," because a fundamental principle behind such a bill is that no people should be given privileges at the expense of others. Such a bill promotes equal citizenship, not favouritism. Dishing out privileges is what fascist, socialist, and apartheid systems do.

The assault on rights

What exactly do apartheid's left-wing critics want? It seems that they don't object to an all-powerful, overregulating, overtaxing, censoring, authoritarian government. What they object to is that they aren't the ones running it. After all, their grand plans will require the same degree of state power that apartheid did. Eager for its turn to run a strong government, the left is turning the notion of a bill of rights on its head. Albie Sachs is quite open about it:

> What needs to be done is to turn the Bill of Rights concept from that of a negative, blocking instrument, which would have the effect of perpetuating the divisions and inequalities of apartheid society, into that of a positive, creative mechanism, which would encourage orderly, progressive, and rapid change.[4]

In other words, Sachs rejects the concept of a bill of rights that protects people from the state and opts instead for a "bill of state action," which *requires* the government to boss people around. His bill of rights would instruct the state to meddle in people's lives, control their property, and undermine their freedoms — a perversion of rights. It would lead to a kind of warmed-over apartheid, with a strong central state free to interfere in every nook and cranny of people's lives under the ill-defined banner of affirmative action. As Sachs writes:

> Just as there is no area of South African life that apartheid has left untouched, so it will be necessary to extend affirmative action to every aspect of society — health, education, work, leisure, to mention but a few.[5]

Contrast this to Frederic Bastiat, the great liberal French economist and author, who wrote in 1850:

> It is not true that the function of law is to regulate our consciences, our ideas, our wills, our education, our opinions, our work, our trade, our talents, or our pleasures. The function of law is to protect the free exercise of these rights....[6]

In Sachs' illiberal view, shared by the socialist left and fascist right, the state exists to promote collectivism: to mould a society into some grand vision. No area of life can be outside the plan. People have no rights until the state creates them. And the state can force all "social institutions" — everything and everybody — to do as they're told.

In Bastiat's liberal view, rejected by socialists and fascists, the state exists only to protect people and their liberty and property. People have rights before they have a state. And those free people form a state for the sole purpose of defending their rights collectively. Bastiat writes:

If every person has the right to defend — even by force — his person, his liberty, and his property, then it follows that a group of men have the right to organise and support a common force to protect these rights constantly.[7]

It is illogical to argue that once that common force — government — has been created, it can then turn its power against individuals and restrict their rights to trade, invest, read, relax, think, learn, or associate. An institution designed to protect people and their property — that's what justifies the existence of government — should not become a tool to violate people and their property.

The generations of rights

Sachs' and Bastiat's views are fundamentally different. They disagree about the proper role of the state. But they also disagree about the very word *rights*, which both claim to support. Modern-day political scientists popularly divide human rights into three generations of rights: first, second, and third:

1. **First-generation rights** encompass civil liberties and legal rights, and they apply to everyone. These include the freedoms of private property ownership, trade, contract, association, speech, the press, thought, movement, travel, and worship, as well as equal citizenship and protection against torture, detention without trial, degrading treatment, and unwarranted searches by the police. First-generation rights are also called, rather unfortunately, negative rights, because they restrict what the state may do.[8]

2. **Second-generation rights** are the so-called social and welfare rights. These include the rights to health, education, food, employment, housing, holidays, child care, and recreation. They are called positive rights, because they give people a positive claim on the government. To fulfil these rights, the state is required to act.

3. **Third-generation rights** are also called peoples' rights, solidarity rights, collective rights, or group rights. Broad, sweeping, and vaguely defined, these include the rights to peace, development, social identity, and a clean environment. Like second-generation rights, they give people a collective claim on government.

Defining rights

There's just one problem with this popular classification of rights: second- and third-generation rights aren't rights at all. They are a mixed bag of privileges, promises, wishes, goals, claims, rewards, and benefits on the one hand and punishments, duties, and costs on the other. If you're on the receiving end, they are rewards. If you're on the giving end, they are duties. But whichever end you're on, they're not rights. As goals, many of them are excellent. Who doesn't want jobs, houses, and food for all? But that doesn't make them rights.

First-generation rights have unique characteristics that make them rights. They are universal — that is, they apply to everybody in a society at all times. To guarantee these rights, the government must simply refrain from initiating action against people (though, as the policing agency, the government may respond with action against people who are violating rights, such as thieves). They could be called "hands-off" rights because they restrict state power, leaving important spheres of life off limits to government. *First-generation rights*, in other words, is just a fancy phrase for people's classical right to life, liberty, and property. There are two aspects to this right: people *own* themselves and their belongings, and people have complete *control* over themselves and their belongings. You may agree that another person can use your property or your body, but no one has the right to do so without your freely given consent.

Consider robbery, rape, and murder. These are crimes because robbers, rapists, and murderers deprive people of their property, liberty, or lives without their permission. It's the principle of consent that is crucial.

After all, people take your money all the time. It's called shopping. So the act of taking money isn't necessarily robbery. It becomes robbery when somebody takes your money without your agreement.

Similarly, sexual intercourse is not a crime if you consent to it. But if it is forced upon you, it's rape.

And if you ask somebody to end your life because, for example, you are dying of cancer, it is mercy killing. You have consented, so it isn't murder (though many countries wrongly treat it as such).

Rights versus claims

These first-generation, or classical-liberal, rights are based on certain immutable principles:

■ people own themselves and their property and may protect themselves against aggression,

■ transactions require consent (or they are violations of rights), and, therefore,

■ people are prohibited from initiating violence or coercion against others (though they may defend themselves with violence).

Contrast this to second- and third-generation rights, which have no such underlying principles. They are cleverly called second- and third-generation rights, as if they flow naturally from first-generation rights. But they don't. They are of a different nature altogether.

Rather than complementing first-generation rights, they violate them. They give people a claim *against* other people's life, liberty, and property. Take the "right" to housing. It is actually a "claim" to housing. It says that if someone cannot afford a home, his "rights" are being violated, so the government must provide him with a home. To fulfil this claim, the government must force some people to pay for some other people's homes. This violates all aspects of rights. It's not a universal right, because some people are given homes while others have to pay for theirs. It's an attack on private property, because the state collects the money for the housing forcibly through taxation. There is no consent. You don't agree to pay for somebody else's house. Your money is simply taken from you. How is this anybody's right? The left never answers. It just says that "society" owes it to people — a rather flimsy definition of rights.

Guaranteed housing — like other so-called second- and third-generation rights — is actually a social or welfare claim. So is a guaranteed paid vacation or the right to strike without suffering the consequences. Employers and employees should be free to set their own rules governing employment. They may decide to include paid vacations in their agreement, and they may not. And their agreement should set the conditions under which the workers may go on strike and the conditions under which they cannot. Some employers might provide generous conditions to attract more workers. And, to make themselves more employable, some workers might demand fewer perks, such as paid vacations or paid work stoppages. But when the government forces companies to provide three weeks of paid holidays, or says employees may strike with impunity even if this violates a signed agreement with their employers, it is permitting employees to impose terms unilaterally on their employers.

And so it goes with these so-called rights. The debate is much easier to follow if we talk about "claims" to education, "claims" to food, and "claims" to electricity, water, health, housing, recreation, child care, communication facilities, or particular employment conditions.

A crucial difference between claims and rights is that a claim allows a party (the government or, through the government, the beneficiary of the claim) to institute violence or coercion to get what it wants. Where rights are involved, you can legitimately use force only against those who are violating you or your property.

Suppose you're not interested in being forced to look after other people, and you reject the claims — by refusing to pay the necessary tax or abide by the necessary regulation. If so, you are thrown into jail. So supporters of these claims, while pretending to support human rights, actually support human coercion. They support a Bill Of Tax Collection At Gunpoint, a Bill That Makes Everybody Subservient To The State, a Bill That Restricts Rights, or, more politely, a Bill of Claims.

The logic of rights

To see why claims are violent and unjust, consider the logic of rights. Say I own a home and invite somebody to dinner. I have that right, even though it means I don't invite the other 4 999 999 999 people on earth. I can discriminate against them because I am free to choose my dinner guest on whatever grounds I see fit. I can also decide whether I want the person to smoke in my home. If he wants to smoke and I don't want him to, he can turn down my invitation.

Now suppose I invite 10 people to dinner. I still have the right to invite whoever I want. I can invite only men or only women, blacks or whites, Jews or gentiles, the sick or the healthy. And, again, I can set the rules, including whether people may smoke.

Now suppose I invite 10 people and collect R30 from each to cover costs — and even make a few rands profit. Can I still set the rules? Of course. Introducing money into the equation doesn't affect my rights. If people don't want to pay — or don't like my other rules — they can refuse to attend. I cannot force anybody to come to dinner, but I can exclude people I don't want to be there.

Now suppose I invite 10 people and ask each to bring a friend. Can I still make the rules — about who may attend, about smoking, and about the cost of admission? Logically, yes. Even if I just open my door to strangers off the street, I have the right to decide who to admit and on what terms.

Now suppose I call this piece of property a "club" or a "restaurant"? Can I still set the rules?

If the area I live in upholds individual rights, I can. But if it is ruled by arbitrary claims of "society," I might not be allowed to. Under a bill of claims, the society around me is granted a social claim on my property, at some arbitrary and indefinable point between inviting one person to dinner and inviting a lot of people to dinner. Ownership remains private, but my private place has, by some mysterious alchemy, become a public place. Whether we call my property a "house" or a "restaurant," it's still my private property. Yet private restaurants (and shops and office buildings and cinemas) are routinely called public places today.

Now suppose the government bans smoking in "public places," including private restaurants. This is being done around the world to protect the "rights of nonsmokers." The problem is that nonsmokers have no such "right" on somebody else's property. Antismoking laws don't expand rights. They give nonsmokers a *claim against* the rights of restaurant owners. If a law prohibits smoking in my restaurant (or forces me to reserve some tables for nonsmokers), my rights are being violated. I have not agreed to the ban, so it is a unilateral invasion of my property. Antismoking lobbyists counter that smoking is a form of assault on nonsmokers — which is a violation of *their* right to life. But smoking, like any assault, is a violation of rights only if it is not agreed to. I could run a sadomasochistic restaurant at which diners are warned (or promised!) that a man will circulate among the tables and beat people up throughout the evening. If diners decide to come to the restaurant, they are agreeing to the abuse — that is an exercise of their rights. Similarly, if people agree to come to a restaurant that allows smoking, they are exercising their right to be harmed by smoke. The issue is consent. If diners don't want to be harmed by smoke, they can refuse to patronise the restaurant. They have no right to dictate the restaurant's rules. A smoking ban rides roughshod over private rights and grants nonsmokers a *claim*, not a *right*, to smoke-free restaurants. It enslaves restaurant owners, by forcing them to behave in a certain way against their will.

On the other hand, a restaurant (or a shopping mall or an office building) may decide it's a good idea to become smoke-free. It could choose to ban smoking. Some argue that such a ban violates "smokers' rights," but that's as wrong as the reverse case. Smokers do not have a "right" to smoke on somebody else's property. A person has no right to show up at my nonsmoking dinner party or nonsmoking restaurant and demand to be allowed to light up a cigarette. If smokers successfully lobby for a law that *prohibits* private smoking bans, they have not struck a blow for "smokers' rights." They have won a victory for "smokers' claims," which violates other people's rights.

Antidiscrimination laws, similarly, violate individual's rights — even if the goal is "good." A law that forces private restaurants or clubs to serve women does not expand women's rights. It creates a claim for women against the restaurant owner's rights. A law that forces private gay bars to admit straight people is not expanding heterosexual rights. It is granting heterosexuals a claim. And a law that forces a private company to hire white workers is not expanding white workers' rights. It's granting white workers a claim, or a privilege.

Rights, censorship, and shouting "fire"

When the National Party government censored people and newspapers, the left complained that the government was violating the right of free speech. But the left justifies its own censorship — of Nazis and racists — by arguing that free speech is not absolute. The proof: people don't have the right to shout "Fire!" in a crowded theatre and endanger fellow movie-goers. Similarly, left-wing censors say, people don't have the right to spout dangerous fascist propaganda. But their "proof" turns out to be a fiction. Under the liberal conception of rights, the government shouldn't be allowed to prevent people from shouting "fire" in a crowded theatre. It's a matter for the theatre owner to decide — just as I have the right to decide whether to permit shouting at my dinner party. You have to look at the property rights involved, and at the (written or unwritten) agreement entered into by the property owner and his guests. Why can't you shout fire in most theatres? Because you are violating that agreement. If you are the theatre owner and you shout fire, you are violating the property rights of the patrons, who have paid you so that they can enjoy a movie in peace and quiet. If you are a patron and you shout fire, you are violating the property rights of both the other patrons and the owner, who let you in on condition that you would not disturb the performance.

The government violates property rights when it gets involved in the theatre's decision, just as it violates property rights when it bans fascist speech. Some theatre owners, in fact, may expressly *allow* the shouting of fire — because they want to attract fun-loving clients who are excited by the prospect of a human stampede. Sensible people would avoid such theatres, just as sensible people avoid theatres that allow smoking. A private ban on shouting is no different from other rules that prohibit whispering, eating popcorn, shooting water pistols, or doing jumping jacks during the show. If you want to shout fire, whisper, eat, shoot, or exercise, don't go to the movie. You don't have a "right" to do those things on someone else's property without their consent.

The right of free speech means the *government* may pass no law that suppresses expression — it may not, for example, ban fascist language or communist language. It must leave decisions about communication to individuals or groups of individuals. Private suppression of speech happens all the time and is well within private rights: a Jewish newspaper refuses to run a pro-Hitler advertisement, an opera house demands silence during a performance, an ANC magazine refuses to run an article applauding the mass murder of blacks and communists, a company refuses to allow its employees to hold a political rally on its premises, a private radio station bans sexist language, a specialist newsletter covers only the topics it wants to. These are personal decisions to be made by the private owners involved. (Left-wing opponents of free speech often support this principle of private choice until they disagree with the choice. If a newspaper, for example, refuses to say nice things about the ANC, private choices suddenly become unacceptable and in need of being controlled, or "democratised.")

When the government imposes laws restricting expression, it violates the rights of individuals to make their own decisions on these matters. Government censorship can also come in the form of another so-called right, the "right of reply," which is advocated by the ANC. This, again, is a "claim of reply." It empowers the state to require a private newspaper, radio station, or newsletter to carry an opposing view. But forcing somebody to air *any* view is a claim, not a right. Like overt censorship, a claim of reply is an assault on rights — and a dangerous power to give to governments.

Individual rights and group claims
Now you can make sense of the dispute over individual rights and group rights.

Take the so-called group right to language or culture. In fact, this is just an individual right exercised by more than one individual at the same time. If the government may not outlaw an individual's language or culture — that is, if there is a *right* to language and culture — then it also may not outlaw a group's language or culture. But there's no reason to call this a group right. Similarly, if each individual is free to choose his friends and believe what he wants, then groups of individuals must logically be free to form groups under whatever rules they choose. If individual rights are secure, so are the rights of groups of individuals.

But other so-called group rights aren't rights at all. They are claims, or privileges. Past white governments used to say they were protecting "the rights of white workers" when they imposed job-reservation laws, which either excluded blacks from certain jobs outright or forced companies to hire a certain percentage of whites. In fact, they were creating a claim, or privilege, for white workers — a claim against the companies that were forced to hire them and against blacks who weren't allowed to compete with them.

The left, while opposing the government's "group rights," supports plenty of its own: rights (actually, privileges) for women, the handicapped, unionised workers, and blacks. Dismissive of individual rights but repelled by the tainted term "group rights," it prefers the trendier "collective rights."

The left's version of job reservation — called affirmative action — would force companies to hire a certain percentage of blacks. This creates a claim, or privilege, for black workers (against white workers and against company owners), not a right.

When labour law gives workers the power to force a company to recognise their union, the law is not expanding "workers' rights." There is no consent, which is required when rights are exercised. Rather, the law is creating "workers' claims" or "workers' privileges" — it is granting one group, workers, the power to violate the rights of other people, their employers.

Consider "women's rights." Women's rights are restored when laws are introduced that make them equal before the law — by eliminating restrictions that prevent them from holding certain jobs, abolishing discriminatory taxes, or ending second-class status for wives. But if the law dishes out favours to women — for example, by forcing employers to provide maternity leave even though the employment contract signed by the employer and employee doesn't require this — then the law is granting claims to women, not rights.

And take the "rights of the handicapped." If a law forces a private company to reserve parking near its entrance for the disabled, it is granting the disabled a claim against that company's property. It is not creating a right. The reason the debate becomes confusing is that people believe that things that sound good — that sound *right* — are "rights." It would be good if companies provided easy access for the disabled. And I'm not surprised when many governments require them to do so. But that doesn't make it a right. Nor is there a "conflict of rights," as some people argue. "Society" has simply decided in this instance that the claim of the disabled overrides the right of the company owner. This type of ruling — in which rights are made subservient to a "social good" — is dangerous, but common.

Most demands for group rights are, in fact, demands for group claims or privileges. They should be properly identified as such, so that when a government agrees to the demands, people can see that rights are being eroded, not expanded.

Rights, claims, and nonsense

While first-generation rights are principled and logical, supporters of second- and third-generation claims cannot offer a principled definition of their so-called rights — so they end up making all kinds of incomprehensible and contradictory comments about what will and won't be allowed in a democratic South Africa.

Take freedom of association. In its draft bill of rights released in 1989, the government's Law Commission explicitly proposed both the right to associate and the right to disassociate. Article 16 guaranteed the "right to associate freely with other groups and individuals," and Article 17 guaranteed the "right of every person to disassociate himself...from other individuals or groups." The commission was simply spelling out the logical flipside of the right to associate, which says you can work with, form clubs with, play with, or sleep with whoever you choose. But for every person you choose to associate with, there are 38 999 999 people in South Africa who you exclude, or disassociate, yourself from. *Every time* you associate, you also disassociate.

The left cannot stand this logic. They don't want to accept the implications of free choice, so they dismiss the right of disassociation as "bizarre" — that's the word Rhodes University's Donald Leyshon used to describe Article 17.[9]

Of course, the left supports a right of association when it suits them. So it's OK to form unions, women's organisations, black-advancement associations, and progressive youth pioneer groups. But they oppose a right of association when it doesn't suit them: it's not OK to form men's clubs and white-advancement groups or to refuse to join a union or hire unionised workers. Without any logical justification, they simply dismiss this second group of choices as unacceptable. But if these things aren't allowed, there is no freedom of association. What these left-wing critics should say is: "We oppose the right of association because some people will make choices that we don't like."

The left rejects private choice in education with the same distaste for logic. Albie Sachs says that "the power to ensure that your child goes to a whites-only school cannot be dignified with the word 'rights.'"[10] But why not? If people have the right to own property and educate their children, and if they enjoy freedom of association, then why *can't* they exercise these rights by electing to send their children to a whites-only school? Sachs supports freedom only when he approves of the *results* of exercising that freedom. If someone exercises his rights in a way that offends Sachs, he refuses to bless it with the label "rights." Notice that Sachs doesn't argue that "the power to ensure that your child goes to a blacks-only school cannot be dignified with the word 'rights.'" A blacks-only school would, of course, be acceptable. For many on the left, guaranteeing rights means nothing more than guaranteeing "things we think are OK."

The left also refuses to accept the logical implications of its own demand for a constitutional clause that would make all citizens equal in the eyes of the law. If a clause prohibits the state from making distinctions between people on the basis of race, it must logically prohibit both statutory apartheid and statutory affirmative action, since both require that the government classify people by race and treat them differently. But you'd never guess this from the way people on the left simultaneously call for a nonracial constitution and government-mandated racial quotas. For them, equality at law means: "All shall be equal before the law, except when we think they shouldn't be."

Principled rights versus feel-good rights
The exercise of true rights is a messy affair. The real world suggests that a rights-based society will be dynamic, entrepreneurial, tolerant, moderate, prosperous, and full of opportunities. Nonetheless, there will always be uncomfortable things happening on the fringes. Freedom includes the freedom to be eccentric and offensive. Some people are going to do things like run exclusive clubs and schools, print controversial views, read dirty magazines, make fun of women, smoke, drink, discriminate against people they don't like, and sleep with people of the wrong sex or colour. You won't like everything that happens around you in a liberal rights-based society.

Not so in the left's view of the world. For socialists, "society" has rights (actually, claims) and individuals do not. And since individuals cannot do whatever they want, nothing bad ever happens. "Bad" things are simply outlawed. You don't believe this? Just read Sachs' book *Protecting Human Rights in a New South Africa*. Nowhere in its 200 pages does Sachs' conception of rights lead to a single behaviour that he doesn't approve of. He defines out of existence any action he doesn't like as an obvious "violation of rights." For him, human rights is anything that makes him feel good.

Take the right to worship. Of course, there is the right to worship. Sachs writes:

> To believe or not to believe — that is one of the most important constitutional questions facing any country, and one of the most significant philosophical issues facing any individual. It is a question which each one of us answers in his or her own way. In some respects it touches on what might be the most fundamental human right of all, certainly the most intimate and personal, the right to conscience. No one should be compelled by the state or by anybody to believe, nor should anyone be forced not to believe....
>
> If there are Muslims who wish to attend mosque on Fridays, and Jews who refuse to ride on a bus on Saturdays, or Christians who believe it is sinful to catch fish on Sundays, that is their business and their right.

And:

Afrikaans-speakers who feel comfortable worshipping in the Dutch Reformed Church will be able to continue their prayers and hymns in the way to which they are accustomed, as well as to choose their spiritual leaders, and to develop their doctrine according to the internal teachings of the Church. In this sense there will be unfettered freedom of religious-cultural associations (one can think of many other groups — Jews, Muslims, Hindus, Greek Orthodox, as well as many African independent sects...).[12]

It is "their business and their right" to do these things, because it warms Sachs' heart. Such actions don't offend the new social architects.

However, Sachs adds:

What would not be permitted would be to deny membership on grounds of race etc. Nor would these socio-religious organisations be allowed to function as a cover for political mobilisation on a divisive, racist, or ethnic basis.[13]

Of course not — because those things make Sachs feel bad. Jews can refuse to patronise buses on Saturday, but conservative white Christians cannot decide who to admit to their churches on Sunday. If you're looking for a principle that holds these two positions together, you won't find one — except that the first action makes Sachs (and many of us) feel good and the second action doesn't.

To see the total lack of principle behind this conception of "rights," just reverse the ideology or colour of the participants in any example that comes from the left. Imagine a law that prevented churches from functioning as a cover for political mobilisation on a "uniting, integrationist, or multi-ethnic" basis. The left would oppose such a law as a violation of rights — because it's "bad." Or suppose a black church wanted to prohibit the admission of whites because it believes they are a heathen people stained with the blood of colonialism and apartheid. Here the left would allow the discrimination because it makes them feel good.

Sachs also goes on at length about "the right to be different and the right to be the same." Again, what this means is that Sachs will decide when people can be different and when they can be the same. He writes:

We cannot imagine a constitution which seeks to prescribe whom people should marry or not marry, or whom they should have as their friends or dinner guests or companions. Nor should it permit any state to dictate such matters.

Of course not, because privacy feels good. He continues:

At the same time, a democratic constitution could not acknowledge a right to bar people from hotels or restaurants or taxis or sports facilities because of the personal prejudices of the managers. In the former case the right to privacy would take precedence, in the latter the right to equal protection would prevail.[14]

Here, personal prejudice makes Sachs feel bad, so he deftly redefines rights to suit his purposes. In the liberal conception, the "right to equal protection" means that everybody is equal *at law* — in other words, that the state may not discriminate between people. How individuals choose to judge each other is left up to them. Sachs, however, twists "equal protection" to mean that people can be forced not to discriminate against others. This is, in fact, "unequal protection" because it empowers the law to grant one group (patrons) a claim against the rights of another group (property owners). It legalises coercion.

Before you accuse me of being racist, let me clarify this. As a rule, I don't approve of restaurants that refuse to serve blacks or Christians or Indians. I wouldn't patronise them and would avoid attending functions at them. But I cannot see what right I have to *force* them to conform to my standards, which is what an antidiscrimination law does. If I want my freedom, I have to allow them theirs. I don't intend to twist the definition of freedom to allow all the things I like and prohibit all the things I don't.

Anyway, I support discrimination in many instances. I think a private youth club should be able to refuse to admit drug users; a church should be able to refuse to ordain female ministers; a private bar for lesbians should be able to refuse men; a black lawyers' association should be able to exclude whites; a private black primary school should be able to choose the teachers and pupils that it wants; a private Jewish business person should be able to refuse to hire a self-proclaimed Nazi; and a private communist newspaper should be able to refuse to hire a liberal subeditor.

I also believe that many people on the left who say they oppose discrimination would agree with me in a lot of these cases — and would add many more of their own. I don't believe them when they say they oppose discrimination as a violation of "equal protection." What they oppose is *politically incorrect* discrimination — an incorrectness that they will judge. Sachs' "right to be the same and right to be different" means nothing more than the right of Sachs to draw the arbitrary line between acceptable and unacceptable behaviour.[15]

Sachs carries on with his flexible definition of rights, which includes only the right to do things he likes. Looking at the life of an Afrikaner business person under a new constitution, Sachs writes: "He will enjoy freedom of speech and information, but will not continue to have the right to propagate division and hatred on the grounds of race." So he will not enjoy freedom of speech and information once it begins to upset Sachs. Property rights? "His rights to personal property (a home, a motor car, a bank deposit, etc.) will be protected, while his rights to productive property will be recognised but subject to the principle of public interest and affirmative action." So he will not enjoy property rights. Association? "If he wishes as part of his private life to mix with and marry only Afrikaners, that will be his choice. Similarly, there will be no interference with the habits and customs of daily life, most of which will in fact be practised by many non-Afrikaners." But: "What he will have to learn to live with, however, is that in relation to anything outside the immediate private or family sphere, there will be constitutional norms of nondiscrimination" — flexible "constitutional norms" that will prevent "bad" discrimination by the Afrikaner business person but allow "positive" discrimination against the Afrikaner business person under affirmative action. Sachs' commitment to human rights would be more believable if he listed even a single private action — a thought, expression, association, or decision — that offends him but that would still be allowed within his conception of rights. As it stands, his feel-good conception of rights is an open invitation to a "society" (or, more likely, the society's intolerant rulers) to repress all who don't toe the line. That's not freedom. It's fascism.

Public policy versus rights

In modern democracies, governments obviously do more than just protect people and their property. Bastiat is right when he argues that the function of law should not be to regulate our ideas, wills, education, opinions, work, trade, talents, and pleasures. But, in modern times, that's exactly what the law does all the time. Governments finance housing, health, and education, impose laws on employers and employees, curb speech, and outlaw some forms of discrimination. My objection here is not that this happens (though I believe it shouldn't). My objection is that these actions are called an extension of rights when they are, in fact, a retreat from rights. Moreover, entrenching these so-called rights in a bill of rights is devious and makes a mockery of both a bill of rights and democracy. Why? Because it empowers the central government to meddle in housing, health, education, employment, and welfare without being subjected to public scrutiny and debate. A distant state would do as it wishes, and ordinary people would have virtually no control over vast areas of state spending and rule making.

Sachs clearly thinks this is a good idea. He calls for various committees filled with "highly qualified professional and technical" staff to oversee the implementation of the bill:

A carefully chosen Public Service Commission with a wide brief, highly technical competence, and general answerability to Parliament, could well be the body to supervise affirmative action in the public service itself. Similarly, a Social and Economic Rights Commission could supervise the application of affirmative action to areas of social and economic life, while a Land Commission could deal with the question of access to land. Finally, an Army and Security Commission could ensure that the army, police force, and prison service were rapidly transformed so as to make them democratic in composition and functioning....[16]

Having a bunch of distant committees implementing sweeping platitudes sounds more like dictatorship (and apartheid) than democracy. Voters in many democracies force fellow citizens to run their businesses in certain ways or to look after the poor and the homeless. Call these programmes privileges, gifts, a social safety net, or the fruits of plunder, depending on where your sympathies lie. But don't call them rights. Every such programme is a move away from a strictly rights-based society. Liberal critics warn against the waste and abuse inherent in these programmes, which, like all other aggressive state activities, should be hotly debated and tightly controlled.

My recommendation: let's call them claims, not rights. Then they can be kept as matters of public policy, which they are, and they can be openly debated in the public-policy arena, where they belong. Should South Africans enjoy a claim to housing? That should be debated and settled publicly, preferably at local level through referendums. It shouldn't be settled by a housing committee based in Pretoria — or by a constitutional court.

Towards a constitution and bill of rights

How best can the state be controlled and liberty protected? That's what the debate over a democratic constitution and bill of rights boils down to. Reacting to the Law Commission's proposed bill of rights, which endorses a nonracial franchise, Boerestaat Party leader Robert van Tonder, who supports the creation of a white homeland, said: "The commission neglected to make one final recommendation, namely that there should be a provision made to buy a dustbin into which the bill will be thrown after a black government takes over."[17]

Now, it's easy to dismiss such statements from right-wingers who have shown little respect for anybody's rights in the past. Still, stripped of its racial content, the statement raises a crucial issue: what *does* stop a new government from ignoring constitutional niceties and embarking on social engineering on a grand scale? Governments are inherently violent and coercive. So what structures are most likely to satisfy people's demands while preventing the abuse of state power? Do you support a court-enforced bill of rights — knowing that a court or commission that's given the final say might interpret the bill in strange ways? Do you support referendums, hoping that ordinary people are more sensible than vested interests — while knowing there's a risk that the mob of voters could be as vindictive, isolationist, jingoistic, and economically illiterate as the politicians? Do you support the decentralisation of power on the assumption that distant, centralised power is always abused — while accepting that some local governments could persecute people and impose unjust laws? How can ordinary people combat creeping bureaucracy, economic regulation, rising taxes, official intolerance, assaults on their rights, and power-hungry politicians? These are the questions that South African democrats have to tackle as they fight to have liberal tenets enshrined in a new constitution.

10

THE AFRICAN NATIONAL CONGRESS

The ANC's authoritarian roots

A week after Nelson Mandela was released from prison in February 1990, journalist Ken Owen had a go at him in his well-read weekly column. Owen criticised Mandela's socialist-style economics — for example, calling the looting of a liquor shop in Cape Town just before Mandela's Sunday-night address from city hall "an early example of appropriating other people's property to which Mandela immediately gave his support." Mandela, he complained, did nothing more than repeat "the drivel of the Freedom Charter."

David Dalling, a Democratic Party MP, immediately complained in a letter to Owen: "Insults, sarcasm, hostility, confrontation, and ridicule have no place in the challenges that lie ahead. They will serve only to destroy, not to build."

Replied Owen: "Sorry, I didn't know I was supposed to fawn. The writing style was honed on [former justice minister] Jimmy Kruger and [president] PW Botha — without protest from Dalling."[1]

That exchange reflects the confused logic surrounding debates on the ANC. Many historic opponents of apartheid —diplomats, journalists, business leaders, liberal politicians, activists, overseas politicians — have embraced the ANC with the reasoning that the enemy of their enemy is their friend. To justify this leap of faith, they project onto the ANC their own liberal-democratic credentials.

But this assumes that there are only two positions: you support the ANC or you support apartheid. In fact, both the NP and ANC have authoritarian pasts characterised by violence, socialist economics, political intolerance, and thuggish allies. Could you not logically oppose — or at least mistrust — both?

Liberals have shown a healthy scepticism of every reform move taken by the National Party government, from PW Botha's tentative steps to FW de Klerk's dramatic moves. Their misgivings about state power are welcome. But many of the same liberals have shown no corresponding scepticism of the ANC. Those who have fought decades of repression — the censorship, intolerance, unchecked government power, grand schemes, and economic controls of the Nationalists — might consider applying the same standards against those who could carry out decades more of it. At the very least, as the ANC puts forward constitutional proposals, they ought to consider reading the fine print.

What kind of democracy?

When the ANC talks about democracy, what kind is it referring to?

A report in *The New York Times* called the ANC's 25-clause draft constitutional guidelines — released in August 1988 — "astonishingly liberal." Journalists routinely refer to the ANC's support for western-style democracy, political pluralism, and civil liberties.[2]

Tom Lodge, a University of the Witwatersrand political scientist, said the guidelines are in line with "international understanding of what an acceptable democratic political settlement in South Africa should be."[3]

The ANC's Albie Sachs explained to the journal *Index on Censorship*:

The national executive committee of the ANC drafted a document called "Constitutional Guidelines," setting out the basic principles of a new constitutional law in South Africa. It comes down to an indivisible citizenship, equal citizenship, in a united South Africa, non-racial and democratic, with periodical parliamentary elections, a multiparty system, freedom of speech and assembly and basic due process, legal process, and a Bill of Rights, guarantee[ing] fundamental rights and freedoms.... [4]

Cassim Saloojee and Firoz Cachalia of the ANC-aligned Transvaal Indian Congress wrote shortly after the guidelines were released: "The guidelines directly challenge liberals because they commit the ANC to a liberal/democratic constitution — with multiparty democracy, a Bill of Rights, equality of law, etc."[5]

But a closer look suggests the carefully worded guidelines propose a democracy that's not liberal or multiparty at all.

Consider the spirit behind a liberal constitution. Liberal democracy has always been a reaction to abuse of state power — by kings, feudal landlords, imperialists, dictators, or self-appointed presidents-for-life. Liberal democracy seeks to protect individuals and their property from the whims of government power and to give people control of their lives.

The liberal-democratic view of society contrasts sharply with the authoritarian views of both left and right. Authoritarians — supporters of fascism, feudalism, socialism, Marxism, dictatorship, institutionalised racism, or other forms of government control — believe that the state is a force for good. More correctly, they believe that *their* state is a force for good; they generally don't like other people's states. So socialists in South Africa fight the abuses of the apartheid state but don't see that their own strong government would abuse power in much the same way.

The ANC's constitutional guidelines reflect the spirit of authoritarianism. They reject the liberal values of limited government, decentralised power, individual rights, a civil society, a capitalist economy, tolerance, and suspicion of state power.

Consider five differences between a liberal constitution and the ANC's recommendations:

1. Devolution of power. Diffusing power to regions, communities, and neighbourhoods reduces the potential for massive, nationwide abuses by a few people in a distant, centralised government. The ANC guidelines reject devolution, opting instead for something closer to what Lenin and Soviet-bloc governments called, rather misleadingly, "democratic centralism."[6]

The two relevant clauses:

(i) Sovereignty shall belong to the people as a whole and shall be exercised through one central legislature, executive, and administration.
(ii) Provision shall be made for the delegation of the powers of the central authority to subordinate administrative units for purposes of more efficient administration and democratic participation.

If lower tiers of government — state, provincial, regional, municipal — are simply "subordinate administrative units," there is no real devolution of power. Under a liberal order, lower levels of government wouldn't just *carry out* policies passed in Pretoria. They would have the power to legislate policies that conflict with Pretoria's wishes. That's the whole point of local government: to give people a say over laws that affect them and their communities, to allow a diversity of policies, and to avoid the concentration and abuse of power.

The ANC, because it wants the central government to shape society from the top down, rejects devolution. Zola Skweyiya, director of the

ANC's constitutional and legal-affairs department, explains the movement's proposal for popular participation within a centralised unitary state: "In terms of this conception, there can be no original, only derived, powers for regions and local authorities on major issues such as political power, land, economy, health, education, and housing policy."[7]

These should be fighting words for the civic associations, many of them ANC-aligned, which are pushing for grassroots democracy and nonracial municipalities. They have been remarkably silent on this narrow idea of popular participation, which, if implemented, would transform their grassroots democratic organisations into lackeys of the central state.

2. Checks and balances. Nothing in the guidelines suggests that any government could ever make a wrong decision or abuse power. There is no mention of any meaningful checks on government power. This turns the liberal notion of constitution building on its head. As University of the Witwatersrand law professor Johan van der Vyver wrote in the *South African Journal on Human Rights*:

A great misconception seems to prevail amongst politicians that...a good constitution makes for easy government. Nothing could be further from the truth: A good constitution is one that ties down those in authority, compels them to negotiate and compromise, and in general — within reason — forestalls the unbridled, unscrupulous, or rash exercise of state authority.[8]

The ANC guidelines express no such qualms about authority. Though the guidelines are relatively short, they require the state to do no less than eradicate race discrimination and sexism, outlaw hatred, promote binding loyalty, compel companies to promote social well-being, subsidise industry, subsidise language and culture, redistribute land and wealth, and guarantee education, social security, managerial skills, and employment for all. And they require much of this to be done "speedily."

3. Civil liberties and a bill of rights. At first glance, it seems the ANC supports the liberal planks of a classical bill of rights. It pretends to guarantee "the basic rights and freedoms, such as freedom of association, expression, thought, worship, and the press."

But the guidelines then subject these "guaranteed" rights to special clauses. This defeats the whole purpose of guaranteed rights. The clauses:

(i) The state and all social institutions shall be under a constitutional duty to eradicate race discrimination in all its forms....
(k) The advocacy of racism, fascism, nazism or the incitement of ethnic or regional exclusiveness or hatred shall be outlawed.

So the ANC would guarantee a free press — unless you advocate racism, fascism, Nazism, ethnicity, or regionalism. In other words, it would *not* guarantee a free press. The government would be given wide scope to define its enemies as racists or tribalists and then shut them up — under the banner of a bill of rights!

The National Party government also historically guaranteed freedom of the press and political expression — unless you threatened state security or advocated communism, or "the tenets of Karl Marx, Friedrich Engels, Vladimir Lenin, or Mao Tse-tung," or "any form of socialism or collective ownership."[9] And since these prohibitions were amorphous and could be interpreted in any way the government chose, it could silence and jail all sorts of people. When rights are subject to clauses, they are no longer rights.[10]

4. Multiparty democracy and political competition. Again, on the surface the ANC guidelines seem to welcome political diversity. "Every voter shall have the right to stand for election and be elected to all legislative bodies," the guidelines say. And they declare that "parties...have the legal right to exist and to take part in the political life of the country."

But not all parties. The right to form a political party is subject to clauses (i) and (k) above, plus clause (j):

(j) The state and all social institutions shall be under a constitutional duty to take active steps to eradicate, speedily, the economic and social inequalities produced by racial discrimination.

So armed, the ANC government could systematically ban all opposition parties, including those that now sit with it at the negotiating table:

■ The National Party and groups to its right — the CP, HNP, AWB — would be easy targets: they're racist, fascist, and, in the latter case, Nazi.

■ The liberal Democratic Party would be tougher to nail, but it could be called racist (for having participated in the tricameral parliament) and fascist (for being anticommunist and for supporting capitalist policies that, the ANC could declare, would not "eradicate, speedily," economic inequalities).

■ The black-consciousness Pan Africanist Congress and Azapo could be outlawed for being racist (since they supported black leadership in the struggle and opposed the "nonracial" ANC) and fascist (for objecting to the ANC's alliance with the SACP).

■ Parties rooted in the homelands, such as Zulu chief Mangosuthu Buthelezi's Inkatha Freedom Party, could be banned for being anticommunist and fascist , ethnic, and regional.

■ Coloured and Indian parties that participated in the tricameral parliament, such as the Labour Party and Solidarity, would be out for being racist, ethnic, and, perhaps, fascist.

■ Moderate and conservative black parties that participated in elections for segregated town councils, such as Sofasonke and the government-funded Federal Independent Democratic Alliance, would be banned for being racist and fascist.

So the ANC's constitutional guidelines seem to say that you're free to form a political party as long as you're the ANC. The authoritarian spirit of democratic centralism — of a participatory one-party state — comes through. The spirit of liberal democracy, of political competition, does not.[11]

This view is backed by Stellenbosch University political scientist Pierre du Toit, who says outright that the guidelines "contain the exact opposite of the liberal vision of a democratic constitution."[12]

The ANC's occasional calls for multiparty democracy? Du Toit says this is a "rhetorical device to enhance international legitimacy."[13] ANC representatives generally stick to the more ambiguous "nonracial democracy."

5. A civil society and a capitalist economy. The ANC rejects both. It sees social and market institutions as arms of the government. With the exception of the "family" and "parenthood," the guidelines make no reference to an independent anything. They take a strong collectivist approach, which lumps the public and private sectors together as if they're the same thing.

The guidelines call on "the state and all social institutions" to fight racism and inequality, failing to recognise that some private social institutions might prefer to be blacks-only or whites-only. They call for equal rights for women and men "in all spheres of public and private life," a plan that could shut down everything from exclusive men's clubs and housewives' leagues to executive women's associations and all-girl schools.

A robust, independent civil society would reflect South Africa's diversity. But the guidelines want the state to create "a single national identity and loyalty binding on all South Africans" — an identity and loyalty defined, of course, by the state. Meanwhile, the state would control the "entire economy" and oblige the private sector to "co-operate with the state" in promoting social well-being.

Most disturbing about the ANC's constitutional guidelines are the parallels to apartheid. The conventional wisdom is that South Africa's revolutionaries want to smash the apartheid state and usher in freedom. In fact, they seem quite content to seize control, retain the existing huge state, and use the old powers for *their* new purposes — embarking on "good" censorship, rallying people around their definition of "patriotic consciousness," and controlling the economy and civil life as they see fit.

Allaying white fears

The ANC's hatred of competing ideas is both morally wrong and practically disastrous, just as the National Party's was.

Morally, individuals in a free society should be free to advocate unpleasant things like fascism, racism, national socialism, and Marxism. Freedom of expression is meaningless if it's only freedom to agree.

Practically, governments delude themselves when they think that banning unpleasant ideas will make them go away. The ANC will be no more successful in banning swastikas and prohibiting people from calling for racism than was the NP in banning the hammer and sickle and persecuting people who opposed segregation. A ban on Nazism/racism/fascism would work for a while, especially if the government were sufficiently brutal. But it would eventually boost the stature of the banned ideas and turn their proponents into martyrs.

What the National Party — even the hardliners — finally realised is that it's easier to persuade people of the downside of communism and revolutionary socialism when you let the proponents have their say. The unbanning of the ANC and SACP stopped people from falling into the trap of thinking that if the government you hate silences communism, communism must be good for you.

The ANC's intolerance of ideas poses a further practical problem in the transition from white-minority rule. Calls to ban "fascists" and "racists" — and hints of punishing people for past actions deemed fascist in retrospect — reinforce the fears of nervous whites that all their rights and privileges will disappear on day one of liberation. The fear may be hypocritical from people who haven't worried much about other people's rights in the past, but it's not irrational. And the guidelines do little to allay it.

Practically, it is surely better to let people — *especially* crazy people — participate in a democratic debate. If they feel they've had their say, they're more likely to abide by the society's rules than to resort to guns and sabotage. Ban parties that advocate racial segregation and watch the bombs go off.

Whites who simply don't want blacks ruling over them will be difficult to convert to democracy. But many others would embrace a democratic future if they believed democracy isn't a code word for a new brand of tyranny.

Yet the ANC has reaffirmed its opposition to free speech and political pluralism again and again. In a speech to the Foreign Correspondents Association in November 1990, Mandela defended prohibitions on the advocacy of racism, Nazism, and fascism, saying: "Political doctrines and ideologies whose known consequences are harm to one's fellow citizens cannot be considered legitimate and on par with others."[14] Like the National Party before it, of course, the ANC believes it can decide which doctrines are "harmful." It will be the judge.

What the ANC doesn't say

More damning than what the ANC says about liberal-democratic values is what it doesn't say. Those who believe this critique is too harsh should ask: what single liberal value has the ANC ever endorsed, not subject to clauses?

If the ANC believed in a liberal-democratic future for South Africa, it could choose any number of role models: the United States, Switzerland, Germany, France, Sweden, Botswana, Japan. Instead, the ANC has historically extolled the virtues of patently undemocratic regimes: Cuba, Vietnam, Angola, Tanzania, Mozambique, Libya. In doing so, it has sided with unelected elites, rather than the masses who suffer under them. ANC leader Oliver Tambo called Zambian president Kenneth Kaunda "the world's greatest man" at a rally on December 16, 1990 — just 10 months before the masses who lived under the dictator threw him out of office when he finally got around to holding an election after 27 years.

Mandela, praising the unelected Angolan government for its support of the ANC, said, "We hope that one day we will be as free as you."[15] And on a trip to the United States, Mandela said in an interview with *The Washington Post* that the reason South Africa's black youth are so frustrated is that they are oppressed, whereas their "counterparts in the neighbouring states enjoy freedom in the fullest sense of the word," a patently absurd statement given the suffering and dictatorship in neighbouring states such as Angola and Mozambique.[16]

Mandela thanked Cuba — a country run by an unelected dictator for more than 30 years — because it provided arms to the ANC. He then added: "There's one thing where that country stands out head and shoulders above the rest. That is in its love for human rights and liberty."[17] On his first trip to Cuba in July 1991, Mandela said that "from its earliest days, the Cuban revolution has itself been a source of inspiration to all freedom-loving people." He denounced "a vicious imperialist-orchestrated campaign to destroy the [revolution's] impressive gains."[18] On a trip to the United States five months later, Mandela snapped back at critics of his support for Cuba. "Do not make the mistake of believing that your enemies are our enemies," he told a Washington press conference.[19]

The ANC has responded to the triumph of democracy in eastern Europe with a shrug. Said Mandela: "Regarding the changes taking place in Eastern Europe I must state that we can't be overworried over this matter, as the West is."[20] If the ANC were truly liberal, it would surely celebrate the collapse of dictatorships and the rise of democracy.

The SACP's pervasive influence

The ANC's alliance with the South African Communist Party is another sign that it's not a liberal-democratic movement.

In recent years, Communist Party members have dominated the ANC leadership. As recently as January 1990, just before Nelson Mandela's release from prison, the London newsletter *Africa Confidential* estimated that fully 27 of the 35 members of the ANC's national executive were SACP members.[21]

This number is generally accepted to have fallen, as prominent ANC leaders have quietly dropped out of the SACP. For example, international-affairs director Thabo Mbeki, today held up as a representative of the moderate wing of the ANC, was on the central committee of the SACP as recently as 1989, until the party's seventh congress, held in Cuba. Mbeki, like some others, is no longer believed to be an active member of the SACP, if even a member at all.

ANC executive Chris Hani confirmed the trend after he was elected SACP general secretary at the party's December 1991 congress. Referring to party membership by ANC members and executives who did not attend the congress, Hani said: "We allowed them to lapse quietly. They are no longer communists."[22]

The ANC expanded its national executive committee in 1991 to include 56 directly elected members. Estimates of how many of those 56 are SACP members ranged from 20 (by the *Sunday Star*) to 32 (by the International Freedom Foundation).[23] Joe Slovo applauded the ANC's move "to give well-known communists a most generous share" of top ANC posts.[24] But secrecy still surrounds the exact number — a secrecy reinforced when newly elected ANC secretary-general Cyril Ramaphosa instructed ANC executives to refuse to answer when asked whether they are SACP members.[25]

Still, many ANC members do not hide their membership, and many national and regional ANC posts are held by public SACP members. Among these are political-education officer Raymond Suttner, welfare head Cheryl Carolus, military leader Chris Hani, chief spokesperson

Gill Marcus, ANC-SACP-Cosatu liaison Sidney Mufamadi, public-relations chief Ahmed Kathrada, rural-mobilisation coordinator John Nkadimeng, Western Cape secretary Tony Yengeni, Natal Midlands leader Harry Gwala, Natal Women's League chairperson Nozizwe Madlala, and Joel Netshitenze, who edits the movement's mouthpiece, *Mayibuye*.[26]

Of the 30 people named to the SACP's central committee in December 1991, 10 also serve on the ANC's national executive.

But the debate over the exact numbers is not all that important. More significant, and largely ignored by South African liberals, is the party's inordinate influence over ANC policymaking.

Forget about who's a communist and who isn't. Just look at the illiberal policies the ANC supports. You see the hard left's influence in the ANC's choice of international friends (Gaddafi, Castro, Arafat, eastern Europe's old dictators, and Africa's current ones); its historic approval of "people's democracies"; its support for the Soviet invasions of Hungary and Afghanistan; its praise of places like East Germany as "anti-imperialist"; and its repeated calls for nationalisation. You see the influence in the language of the constitutional guidelines, with their references to "the people as a whole" and the calls to ban "fascism," outlaw political opponents, restrict speech, centralise state power, control thinking habits, and protect private property only if "for personal use and consumption." Much of the fascist-bashing language comes straight out of discredited socialist constitutions.

And the noncommunist members of the ANC hardly sound like liberals. Veteran leader Walter Sisulu has called himself a "scientific socialist." Albie Sachs, speaking after the collapse of communism in eastern Europe, said: "The basic socialist vision of a society based on principles of human solidarity, justice, equality, respect for everybody, a caring society, an unselfish society — that remains valid and it was socialism more than any other philosophy that put it firmly on the agenda. This essence in the socialist vision remains untouched by recent events."[27] When still head of the National Union of Mineworkers, Ramaphosa said: "Ultimately there has to be a system where there would not be any exploitation by anybody — a socialist system."[28] On a visit to Tanzania, Mandela applauded the neighbourhood "cells" set up by that country's brutal one-party government to monitor every citizen's actions.[29] And information chief Pallo Jordan said — in January 1992 — that "it would be foolish to abandon hope in the promise held out to humanity by the socialism of Marx and Engels."[30] With noncommunists like them in the ANC, who needs communists?

Even other left-wing opponents of the South African government have highlighted and condemned the communist influence in the ANC. Barney Desai, who sits on the Western Cape executive of the PAC, said in 1990 that "it has become clear that the ANC leadership is now in the absolute control of the Communist Party" and that "the SACP has given tacit support to every Soviet outrage." Desai added: "The world's number one Stalinist Communist Party outside of the Empire can never be the custodian of democracy in Azania."[31]

This general acknowledgement of communist influence in the ANC from conservatives, liberals, and radicals alike might come as a surprise to the ANC's fans outside South Africa. It has been fashionable for western supporters of the organisation to downplay the SACP link and mock those who even claim the existence of an alliance. US congressman Howard Wolpe, then chairperson of a House of Representatives subcommittee on Africa, for example, wrote in 1990 that communists are "certainly" not a majority on the ANC's national executive and that it is outrageous to characterise the ANC as a "dogmatic, ideological Marxist group" when "pragmatism and moderation...have been the organisation's hallmarks."[32] Meanwhile, at home, the ANC wallows in its formal alliance with the Communist Party and mocks liberal opponents who question it.

"The alliance between the ANC and SACP demonstrates the centrality of the working class in the national liberation struggle," says Jay Naidoo, the leader of the trade-union federation Cosatu, which is also allied to the ANC and SACP. "We reject attempts by imperialists and liberals to undermine this alliance."[33]

After his release from prison, Walter Sisulu told a rally: "Forward to peace and democracy! Long live the ANC! Long live our alliance with the South African Communist Party! Long live the working-class movement!"[34]

Nelson Mandela condemned "vicious attacks" on the alliance. "Those who imagine that they will cause a rift among us have understood neither the character of this alliance nor its historic role in our struggle for freedom," he told the ANC's National Consultative Congress in December 1990. "The ANC, like its allies, remains fully committed to the preservation and the strengthening of our alliance and no amount of pressure will shake our resolve."[35] On the eve of the July 1990 internal launch of the SACP, Mandela said: "The alliance between the ANC and SACP has been very strong — dating back to the '20s — and nobody is going to break that."[36]

Responding to a statement by President de Klerk that the SACP is a dying party clinging to the ANC and damaging its reputation, Joe Slovo, a leading figure in both organisations, said: "This is little more than a hopeful cry....As much as it may make their hearts bleed, our alliance with the ANC remains firmly in place."[37]

And Chris Hani, who visited the United States in April 1991 as a guest of the American Communist Party, said in an interview with Howard University TV in Washington:

For a long time now and after we are free, the party and the ANC will work together to consolidate democracy and independence. We shall tackle the huge socio-economic problems together and there's no question of the party and the ANC parting, at least in the near future.

Hani, an executive of both the ANC and SACP, added reassuringly:

We accept the mistakes and shortcomings of socialism in other countries. We are studying those shortcomings in order to ensure that when we rule that country as a communist country some day in the future — we ensure that we don't commit the same mistakes.[38]

An overstatement? A little verbal flourish?

Well, the ANC makes illiberal statements like this all the time, while continuing to pass itself off as democratic. Isn't it worth asking the ANC just what kind of "democracy" it's talking about?

11

AN ANC BILL OF RIGHTS

The new battleground

The 1955 Freedom Charter and 1988 constitutional guidelines were not the ANC's final words on its political vision. Under pressure to clarify its policies, and shaken by the democratic revolts against its old totalitarian allies in eastern Europe, the ANC responded with a fresh set of constitutional proposals and a draft bill of rights.

The constitutional proposals — released in April 1991 as a discussion document and called *Constitutional Principles and Structures for a Democratic South Africa* — seem a far cry from the 1988 constitutional guidelines.

The new document shows a suspicion of state power that was completely absent from the guidelines. Complaining that "South Africa has been a highly authoritarian society, characterised by arbitrary decision-making by officials and excessive secrecy," it calls for open government:

We must secure constitutional barriers to detention without trial, to spying on citizens, secret files, dirty tricks departments, disinformation, and the use of government money to promote party political objectives.

It rejects the forced unity implied in earlier ANC documents and welcomes diversity:

"[W]hen we speak of a united South Africa we do not envisage the elimination of cultural, linguistic, religious, and political differences. On the contrary, we regard the multiplicity of opinions, beliefs, faiths, tastes, cultures, and preferences as contributing towards the richness and texture of South African life."[1]

The ANC still supports strong central-government power. But it warns against "an over-centralised, impersonal, and over-bureaucratised country" and says "it is not the function of central government to involve itself in each and every decision that has to be taken at the regional or local levels."[2]

The new constitutional principles call for proportional representation[3], a maximum 10-year term of office for the state president, free access to government information, and an ombudsman to investigate complaints against civil servants and allegations of corruption. They say a second chamber of parliament based on regional representation should be considered. And they support a court-enforced bill of rights.

In short, it is a document that recognises that when you give a government power, it will find ways to abuse it.

So what's the catch?

The ANC has cleaned up its constitutional proposals and deposited all the debris in a draft bill of rights, released in November 1990. If you want to see the classical notion of a bill of rights turned upside down, look no further than this. Any liberal-democratic spirit in the new constitutional principles is snuffed out by this authoritarian bill of rights.

At first glance, the draft bill seems a huge step forward from the ANC's blatantly illiberal 1988 proposals. Gone are the heavy-handed references to outlawing parties that promote racism, fascism, Nazism, ethnicity, or regionalism — that is, everybody who isn't the ANC. Instead, there is an overt commitment to "multiparty democracy" (a phrase absent from the 1988 guidelines) and a call for basic procedures of law, including the ending of detention without trial.

But as the document progresses — it has 16 articles and 140 clauses — the initial guarantees of civil liberties turn out to be largely meaningless. At the same time, the draft bill requires the government to embark on an endless list of programmes that would control every aspect of South African life. So much for a bill of rights that's sceptical of state power.

But look at the good news first.

Justice for all
The legal proposals in the ANC's bill of rights are clearly stated and in line with the practices of western-style democracies. The ANC endorses, among other things, the right to a fair trial; an end to detention

without trial; trials within a reasonable time; the principle that one is innocent until proved guilty; independent courts; access to legal advice; the right to challenge evidence; the inadmissibility of evidence obtained through torture or degrading treatment; and the right to judicial review of administrative and executive acts.[4]

Other clauses that protect against a future police state are those that guarantee privacy; prohibit searches without reasonable cause; and ban interference with private communications, spying on people, and the keeping of secret files.

The document also declares: "All men and women shall have equal protection under the law."

The building blocks of democracy

The draft bill guarantees civil liberties and political pluralism. "South Africa shall be a multiparty democracy in which all men and women shall enjoy basic political rights on an equal basis," it proclaims. It calls for accountable government at all levels; regular, free, and fair elections on a common, nonracial voters' roll; and the right to form and join political parties "and to campaign for social, economic, and political change."

It guarantees other rights that are essential for democracy to thrive: the right to associate, assemble, and petition; the right to own property; and freedom of thought, speech, expression, opinion, and the press.

It guarantees freedom of conscience and, if there is conscription, offers the option of nonmilitary service for conscientious objectors.

The civil society

The ANC endorses the right to form independent organisations. In his introduction, Zola Skweyiya, the lawyer who chairs the ANC's constitutional committee, writes: "Extensive recognition is given to the right of people to organise their own associations in keeping with the principles of a vigorous civil society existing autonomously of the State." The bill calls for freedom of artistic activity and scientific inquiry, and the right to travel and emigrate.

It states:

There shall be freedom of association, including the right to form and join trade unions, religious, social and cultural bodies, and to form and participate in nongovernmental organisations.

And:

There shall be freedom of worship and tolerance of all religions, and no State or official religion shall be established.

Now back to the bad news.

Freedom, subject to clauses

The first round of bad news is that what the ANC's draft bill of rights gives with one hand it takes away with the other. Many of the freedoms listed above, even when initially proclaimed in the document, are immediately qualified. The document is littered with contradictions and exceptions.

The press, for example, is required to respect "the right to reply," which means the government must monitor the press to make sure it is being "fair." (The government could use this clause to halt publication of embarrassing information while it prepares a reply.) The press — along with schools, advertising, and "other social institutions" — would also be under "a duty to discourage sexual and other types of stereotyping." And it would be prohibited from inciting ethnic, racial, gender, or linguistic hatred.[5] So the bill guaranteeing press freedom rapidly degenerates into a bill outlining approved press behaviour.[6]

Civil society? The commitment to an autonomous, vigorous civil society isn't very deep. The bill is filled with rules, applicable to all "public and private bodies," that force conformity and unity. All institutions must observe the principles of nonracialism and nonsexism and must not incite racial, religious, or linguistic hostility. They must also do away with all structures and practices that divide the population by race, colour, language, or creed. Churches are free, but not free to prohibit entry on the grounds of race.

Autonomous organisations may be established in sport, recreation, and culture, but only if they are nonracial and draw on the talents and creative capacities of all South Africans — perhaps something to be monitored by the minister of sport, recreation, culture, and creativity.

Artistic activity and scientific inquiry shall be free of censorship, though subject to restrictions "generally accepted in open and democratic societies." Maybe this is just honest recognition that governments everywhere, for all their commitment to freedom, restrict individual rights as they carry out public policy. More likely, it is a vague clause that gives the government wide scope to censor.

Finally, the government is given power to compel all institutions to cooperate in the fight for social, economic, educational, and welfare progress, as the government defines it — meaning that, in fact, no institution is independent of the state.

Limits to justice

The ANC draft bill's protections against police abuse and invasions of privacy can be overridden by laws in circumstances "that would be acceptable in an open and democratic society." This phrase crops up several times in the bill. With little agreement on what democracy or an open society is, such an exception paves the way for massive state violations of individual rights to preserve some ill-defined "democracy." The government would simply declare all its laws, no matter how pernicious, to be "democratic."

The document also contains a clause stating that nobody should be subjected to slavery, servitude, or forced labour. However, it excludes services required in calamities and emergencies and work "which forms part of normal civil obligations" — disturbing exceptions that could justify labour brigades and reeducation camps in the name of "service to society."

The bill declares that no individual or group "shall receive privileges or be subjected to discrimination, domination or abuse on the grounds of race, colour, language, gender, creed, political or other opinion, birth or other status." It then proceeds to call for all sorts of privileges and group rights. It declares that women and blacks have group privileges to demand land and jobs. It grants unionised workers the privilege of negotiating collective contracts that will apply to nonunionised members.

The bill allows everybody to acquire, own, or dispose of property.[7] And it says no persons or legal entities will be deprived of their possessions — "except on grounds of public interest or public utility, including the achievement of the objectives of the Constitution." Compensation is not guaranteed.[8] The objectives of this draft bill are so broad and limitless that *any* seizure of property could easily be justified by the state.

So there's private property, unless the state can make better use of it. And there's press freedom, but not really. And an independent civil society, as long as it cooperates. And religious freedom, as long as you don't offend the sensibilities of the nonracial state. And no group rights and privileges, except for reasonable group rights and privileges.

With its explicit restrictions on personal freedom, the draft document should be called a Bill Against Rights. It carefully spells out how the state would assault classical rights and civil liberties.

Empowering the state, not the people
The second round of bad news is that, having restricted personal freedom, the draft bill goes on to require a huge, all-embracing state. The bill requires the state to: dismantle compounds and single-sex hostels; ensure that all homes have energy, clean water, and sewerage;

provide technical and vocational training; establish a national health service; guarantee unemployment benefits, workers' compensation, pensions, and paid holidays; prevent air pollution; develop nature reserves, parks, and recreational areas; protect historical and cultural sites; promote access to education, skills, jobs, and land for women and blacks; provide citizens with information; promote literature in all languages; and generally ensure that everybody has health care, nutrition, shelter, education, and income. Many of these are laudable goals. But they shouldn't be called "rights." In fact, when they are carried out by the state, they are privileges given to some groups (occasionally, the poor) at the expense of other people. The draft bill says the government must pursue these objectives "to the maximum of its available resources." And it must harness everybody in the fight. The bill is binding on the state and "on all social institutions and persons" — completely blurring any distinction between the state and private life. The thrust of the draft bill of rights is to force people and their private institutions to partake in the state's grand plan.

In the old days, the left wanted to abolish private institutions and individualism as part of the grand march toward socialism. Left-wing socialism having failed, it has now switched to right-wing socialism, or fascism. Under fascism, a government pretends that there are private institutions, a civil society, personal freedom, and private property. But it regulates those institutions to the point that they might as well have been nationalised. The ANC's bill of rights is a triumph of fascism — of state control and "cooperation" between capitalists, individuals, and the state. Ironically, for a movement aligned to a communist party, it espouses exactly what Marx warned against: a state/corporate partnership.

The first clause of its article on the economy — its guiding economic principle — is that business and the state must cooperate:

Legislation on economic matters shall be guided by the principle of encouraging collaboration between the State and the private, cooperative, and family sectors with a view to reducing inequality, promoting growth, and providing goods and services for the whole population.

The article guaranteeing a "progressively expanding floor of enforceable minimum rights" to nutrition, shelter, health care, education, and income, says:

The State may collaborate with nongovernmental organisations and the private sector in achieving these goals, and may impose appropriate responsibilities on all social and economic bodies with a view to their materialisation.

The state guarantees education "in collaboration with nongovernmental and private educational institutions where appropriate." The state guarantees shelter "in collaboration with private bodies where necessary."

On environmental rights:

Legislation shall provide for cooperation between the State, nongovernmental organisations, local communities, and individuals in seeking to improve the environment and encourage ecologically sensible habits in daily life.

So the bill aims to bolster state power, impose duties on people, and teach everyone "sensible habits." It's clearly not designed to protect personal rights.

Finally, in Article 15, ominously called "Limitations," the ANC's draft bill of rights says:

Nothing in this Constitution should be interpreted as impeding the right of the State to enact legislation regulating the manner in which fundamental rights and freedoms shall be exercised, or limiting such rights, provided that such regulation or limitation is such as might be deemed necessary in an open and democratic society.

The "right of the State"? The ANC's bill of rights turns out to be, quite shamelessly, a bill of *government* rights. It is not a shield for people to hold up to fend off the brute force of the state. It's the government's action plan. If the constitution cannot curb state power, there is nothing liberal about it. This bill of rights would give blanket approval to every step the government takes toward its definition of "genuine, nonracial democracy."

If that's what's meant by a bill of rights, the new South Africa would be better off without one. In fact, with that kind of bill, the new South Africa would be remarkably like the old.

The "right of the state" is exactly how the apartheid government justified its authoritarian laws. As interior minister Connie Mulder told a National Party congress in Natal in November 1976:

If it becomes necessary to choose between the freedom of the state and the freedom of the individual, we will choose the freedom of the state and abandon the freedom of the individual.[9]

The Star struck back with an exasperated editorial called: "How much power does he want?":

One wonders which particular freedoms [Mulder] now has in mind, what possible circumstances could justify the Government's taking more power than it already holds.

Already, the Minister of Justice may virtually at whim put anybody he chooses behind bars, entirely unanswerable to the courts. The Government already enjoys the power to withhold whatever information it chooses on matters of defence, security, nuclear power, prison conditions, foreign trade, and spending in several areas.

It has the power to restrict the movement of people; to withdraw citizenship and to expel anyone it chooses, even many who are South African born. It may move people at will, appropriate their land and their homes. It can change the race of some people at the stroke of a pen and refuse permission to travel abroad.

There appear to be very few facets of life in which the Government does not already hold absolute power in one way or another. We are not yet a police state, nor a total dictatorship. But individual freedom is severely curtailed. The State has more than enough powers to maintain law and order and enforce its distasteful racial policies.

We suggest that Dr Mulder, instead of talking loosely of "abandoning personal freedoms," should give more attention to restoring some of those the State has taken away.[10]

Those were the fighting words of South Africa's antiapartheid democrats in 1976. Let's hope that, two decades later, postapartheid democrats won't have to use them with equal force.

Conclusion

Ordinary people's power

How can the state be controlled by ordinary people, instead of ordinary people being controlled by the state? That's the question I've tried to answer in *No More Martyrs Now* — and the question that South Africans will have to answer if they want a constitution that ushers in democracy instead of new dictators.

The short answer? Don't let politicians of any stripe determine your future. Question their motives, doubt their promises, and keep them accountable.

Above all, fight to replace the stagnation of apartheid and socialism with the unlimited potential of capitalist democracy. It's the only system that will let individuals flourish — and that will allow South Africa to heal.

Documents

FREEDOM CHARTER 177

ANC CONSTITUTIONAL GUIDELINES 180

ANC CONSTITUTIONAL PRINCIPLES 182

ANC DRAFT BILL OF RIGHTS 192

SA LAW COMMISSION DRAFT BILL OF RIGHTS 204

SA LAW COMMISSION PROPOSED BILL OF RIGHTS 210

NP CONSTITUTIONAL PROPOSALS 222

■ African National Congress (1955)

The Freedom Charter

as adopted at the Congress of the People on 26 June 1955

THE PREAMBLE

We, the people of South Africa, declare for all our country and the world to know:

That South Africa belongs to all who live in it, black and white, and that no government can justly claim authority unless it is based on the will of the people;

That our people have been robbed of their birthright to land, liberty, and peace by a form of government founded on injustice and inequality;

That our country will never be prosperous or free until all our people live in brotherhood, enjoying equal rights and opportunities;

That only a democratic state, based on the will of the people, can secure to all their birthright without distinction of colour, race, sex, or belief;

And therefore, we the people of South Africa, black and white, together equals, countrymen and brothers adopt this FREEDOM CHARTER. And we pledge ourselves to strive together, sparing nothing of our strength and courage, until the democratic changes, here set out, have been won.

THE PEOPLE SHALL GOVERN!

Every man and woman shall have the right to vote for and to stand as a candidate for all bodies which make laws;

All people shall be entitled to take part in the administration of the country;

The rights of the people shall be the same, regardless of race, colour, or sex;

All bodies of minority rule, advisory boards, councils, and authorities, shall be replaced by democratic organs of self-government.

ALL NATIONAL GROUPS SHALL HAVE EQUAL RIGHTS!

There shall be equal status in the bodies of state, in the courts, and in the schools for all national groups and races;

All national groups shall be protected by law against insults to their race and national pride;

All people shall have equal rights to use their own language and to develop their own folk culture and customs;

The preaching and practice of national, race, or colour discrimination and contempt shall be a punishable crime;

All apartheid laws and practices shall be set aside.

THE PEOPLE SHALL SHARE IN THE COUNTRY'S WEALTH!

The national wealth of our country, the heritage of all South Africans, shall be restored to the people;

The mineral wealth beneath the soil, the banks, and monopoly industry shall be transferred to the ownership of the people as a whole;

All other industries and trade shall be controlled to assist the well-being of the people;

All people shall have equal rights to trade where they choose, to manufacture and to enter all trades, crafts, and professions.

THE LAND SHALL BE SHARED AMONG THOSE WHO WORK IT!

Restrictions of land ownership on a racial basis shall be ended, and all the land redivided amongst those who work it, to banish famine and land hunger;

The state shall help the peasants with implements, seed, tractors, and dams to save the soil and assist the tillers;

All shall have the right to occupy land wherever they choose;

People shall not be robbed of their cattle, and forced labour and farm prisons shall be abolished.

ALL SHALL BE EQUAL BEFORE THE LAW!

No one shall be imprisoned, deported, or restricted without fair trial;

No one shall be condemned by the order of any government official;

The courts shall be representative of all the people;

Imprisonment shall be only for serious crimes against the people, and shall aim at reeducation, not vengeance;

The police force and army shall be open to all on an equal basis and shall be the helpers and protectors of the people;

All laws which discriminate on the grounds of race, colour, or belief shall be repealed.

ALL SHALL ENJOY EQUAL HUMAN RIGHTS!

The law shall guarantee to all their right to speak, to organise, to meet together, to publish, to preach, to worship, and to educate their children;

The privacy of the house from police raids shall be protected by law;

All shall be free to travel without restriction from country to town, from province to province, and from South Africa abroad;

Pass laws, permits, and all other laws restricting these freedoms shall be abolished.

THERE SHALL BE WORK AND SECURITY!

All who work shall be free to form trade unions, to elect their officials, and to make wage agreements with their employers;

The state shall recognise the right and duty of all to work, and to draw full unemployment benefits;

Men and women of all races shall receive equal pay for equal work;

There shall be a forty-hour working week, a national minimum wage, paid annual leave, and sick leave for all workers, and maternity leave on full pay for all working mothers;

Miners, domestic workers, farm workers, and civil servants shall have the same rights as all others who work;

Child labour, compound labour, the tot system, and contract labour shall be abolished.

THE DOORS OF LEARNING AND CULTURE SHALL BE OPENED!

The government shall discover, develop, and encourage national talent for the enhancement of our cultural life;

All the cultural treasures of mankind shall be open to all, by free exchange of books, ideas, and contact with other lands;

The aim of education shall be to teach the youth to love their people and their culture, to honour human brotherhood, liberty, and peace;

Education shall be free, compulsory, universal, and equal for all children;

Higher education and technical training shall be opened to all by means of state allowances and scholarships awarded on the basis of merit;

Adult illiteracy shall be ended by a mass state education plan;

Teachers shall have all the rights of other citizens;

The colour bar in cultural life, in sport, and in education shall be abolished.

THERE SHALL BE HOUSES, SECURITY, AND COMFORT!

All people shall have the right to live where they choose, to be decently housed, and to bring up their families in comfort and security;

Unused housing space shall be made available to the people;

Rent and prices shall be lowered, food plentiful, and no one shall go hungry;

A preventative health scheme shall be run by the state;

Free medical care and hospitalisation shall be provided for all, with special care for mothers and young children;

Slums shall be demolished and new suburbs built where all shall have transport, roads, lighting, playing fields, creches, and social centres;

The aged, the orphans, the disabled and the sick shall be cared for by the state;

Rest, leisure, and recreation shall be the right of all.

Fenced locations and ghettoes shall be abolished and laws which break up families shall be repealed.

THERE SHALL BE PEACE AND FRIENDSHIP!

South Africa shall be a fully independent state, which respects the rights and sovereignty of all nations;

South Africa shall strive to maintain world peace and the settlement of all international disputes by negotiation, not war;

Peace and friendship amongst all our people shall be secured by upholding the equal rights, opportunities, and status of all;

The people of the protectorates Basutoland, Bechuanaland, and Swaziland shall be free to decide for themselves their own future;

The right of all the peoples of Africa to independence and self-government shall be recognised, and shall be the basis of close cooperation.

Let all who love their people and their country now say, as we say here:

"THESE FREEDOMS WE WILL FIGHT FOR, SIDE BY SIDE, THROUGHOUT OUR LIVES, UNTIL WE HAVE WON OUR LIBERTY."

■ African National Congress (1988)

The ANC's Constitutional Guidelines for a Democratic South Africa

THE STATE

(a) South Africa shall be an independent, unitary, democratic, and nonracial state.

(b) Sovereignty shall belong to the people as a whole and shall be exercised through one central legislature, executive, judiciary, and administration. Provision shall be made for the delegation of the powers of the central authority to subordinate administrative units for purposes of more efficient administration and democratic participation.

(c) The institution of hereditary rulers and chiefs shall be transformed to serve the interests of the people as a whole in conformity with the democratic principles embodied in the constitution.

(d) All organs of government, including justice, security, and armed forces, shall be representative of the people as a whole, democratic in their structure and functioning, and dedicated to defending the principles of the constitution.

FRANCHISE

(e) In the exercise of their sovereignty, the people shall have the right to vote under a system of universal suffrage based on the principle of one person/one vote.

(f) Every voter shall have the right to stand for election and be elected to all legislative bodies.

NATIONAL IDENTITY

(g) It shall be state policy to promote the growth of a single national identity and loyalty binding on all South Africans. At the same time, the state shall recognise the linguistic and cultural diversity of the people and provide facilities for free linguistic and cultural development.

BILL OF RIGHTS AND AFFIRMATIVE ACTION

(h) The Constitution shall include a Bill of Rights based on the Freedom Charter. Such a Bill of Rights shall guarantee the fundamental human rights of all citizens, irrespective of race, colour, sex, or creed, and shall provide appropriate mechanisms for their protection and enforcement.

(i) The state and all social institutions shall be under a constitutional duty to eradicate race discrimination in all its forms.

(j) The state and all social institutions shall be under a constitutional duty to take active steps to eradicate, speedily, the economic and social inequalities produced by racial discrimination.

(k) The advocacy or practice of racism, fascism, nazism or the incitement of ethnic or regional exclusiveness or hatred shall be outlawed.

(l) Subject to clauses (i) and (k) above, the democratic state shall guarantee the basic rights and freedoms, such as freedom of association, thought, worship, and the press. Furthermore, the state shall have the duty to protect the right to work and guarantee the right to education and social security.

(m) All parties which conform to the provision of (i) to (k) above shall have the legal right to exist and to take part in the political life of the country.

ECONOMY

(n) The state shall ensure that the entire economy serves the interests and well-being of the entire population.

(o) The state shall have the right to determine the general context in which economic life takes place and define and limit the rights and obligations attaching to the ownership and use of productive capacity.

(p) The private sector of the economy shall be obliged to cooperate with the state in realising the objectives of the Freedom Charter in promoting social well-being.

(q) The economy shall be a mixed one, with a public sector, a private sector, a cooperative sector, and a small-scale family sector.

(r) Cooperative forms of economic enterprise, village industries, and small-scale family activities shall be supported by the state.

(s) The state shall promote the acquisition of management, technical, and scientific skills among all sections of the population, especially the blacks.

(t) Property for personal use and consumption shall be constitutionally protected.

LAND

(u) The state shall devise and implement a land reform programme that will include and address the following issues:abolition of all racial restrictions on ownership and use of land; implementation of land reform in conformity with the principle of affirmative action, taking into account the status of victims of forced removals.

WORKERS

(v) A charter protecting workers' trade union rights, especially the right to strike and collective bargaining, shall be incorporated into the Constitution.

WOMEN

(w) Women shall have equal rights in all spheres of public and private life and the state shall take affirmative action to eliminate inequalities and discrimination between the sexes.

THE FAMILY

(x) The family, parenthood, and children's rights shall be protected.

INTERNATIONAL

(y) South Africa shall be a nonaligned state committed to the principles of the Charter of the OAU and the Charter of the UN and to the achievement of national liberation, world peace, and disarmament.

■ African National Congress (1991)

Constitutional Principles for a Democratic South Africa

PART 1

The African National Congress envisages a united, democratic, nonracial, and nonsexist South Africa, a unitary State where a Bill of Rights guarantees fundamental rights and freedoms for all on an equal basis, where our people live in an open and tolerant society, where the organs of government are representative, competent, and fair in their functioning, and where opportunities are progressively and rapidly expanded to ensure that all may live under conditions of dignity and equality.

When we speak of a united South Africa, we have in mind in the first place the territorial unity and constitutional integrity of our country. South Africa must be seen, as recognised by the international community, as a single, nonfragmented entity including Transkei, Bophuthatswana, Venda, and Ciskei.

Secondly, we envisage a single citizenship, nation, and a common loyalty. We speak many languages, have different origins and varied beliefs, but we are all South Africans.

Thirdly, all apartheid structures must be dismantled and replaced by institutions of government — central, regional, and local — which are truly nonracial and democratic. They must form an integrated and coherent whole, be drawn from all the people and be accountable to the whole community.

Fourthly, there must be a single system of fundamental rights guaranteed on an equal basis for all through the length and breadth of the country. Every South African, irrespective of race, colour, language, gender, status, sexual orientation, or creed should know that his or her basic rights and freedoms are guaranteed by the Constitution and enforceable by recourse to law.

Fifthly, the flag, names, public holidays, and symbols of our country should encourage a sense of shared South Africanness.

A unified South Africa requires a strong and effective Parliament capable of dealing with the great tasks of reconstruction, of overcoming the legacy of apartheid, and of nation-building.

We believe that there is a need for strong and effective central government to handle national tasks, strong and effective regional government to deal with the tasks of the region, and strong and effective local government to ensure active local involvement in handling local issues.

All such governmental structures and institutions shall be based on democratic principles, popular participation, accountability, and accessibility. A unified South Africa shall not be an overcentralised, impersonal, and overbureaucratised country. The precise relationship between central, regional, and local governments can be worked out on the basis of acknowledging the overall integrity of South Africa and the existence of fundamental rights for all citizens throughout the land.

The regions shall not be devised as a means of perpetuating privilege, ethnic or racial divisions along territorial zones, but should be based upon the distribution of population, availability of economic resources, communications, and urban/rural balance.

National tasks would include external links and representation, defence and ensuring the basic security of the country, general economic, fiscal, and tax policy, the creation of national policy framework, and the furnishing of resources for eradicating racism and racial practices and for the tackling of the vast problems of education, health, housing, nutrition, employment, and social welfare.

Regional tasks would include development and the carrying out of the basic tasks of the government at a regional level, bearing in mind regional particularities and resources.

Without detracting from basic constitutional rights and freedoms, provision could be made for special recognition of languages in the different regions.

Local tasks cover all the day-to-day aspects of living which most directly and intimately affect the citizen in an integrated and nonracial local authority area. The active local involvement of all sections of the population will be necessary in the fulfilment of these tasks.

The central government has the responsibility for ensuring that there is a common framework of principles and practices applicable to the whole country and for seeing to it that all areas of the country have equitable access to national resources. However, it is not the function of central government to involve itself in each and every decision that has to be taken at the regional or local levels. Such functions should clearly be delegated to these authorities and performed by them.

Similarly, when we speak of a united South Africa we do not envisage the elimination of cultural, linguistic, religious, and political differences. On the contrary, we regard the multiplicity of opinions, beliefs, faiths, tastes, cultures, and preferences as contributing towards the richness and texture of South African life. What the new Constitution should avoid at all costs is vesting political rights in different linguistic, cultural, ethnic, or religious groups.

A free South Africa must therefore ensure that these differences do not become the source of division or conflict or the means of perpetuating and promoting domination or privilege.

The new Constitution must consistently and clearly affirm the fundamental principle of equal and undifferentiated citizenship so that the differences of culture, interest, and personality can then express themselves in a constructive, free, and nonconflictual way.

The government must be democratic in the universally accepted meaning of the term. It must be the government of the people, by the people, for the people. It must be chosen by the people in free, fair, and regular elections. It must be removable if it loses the confidence of the voters. Elections must be based on the principle of universal suffrage on a common voters roll without distinction as to race, language, creed, class, social position, birth, or gender. Illiterate voters should not be disadvantaged. The precise method of voting and electoral system can be negotiated within the framework of these universal principles. The African National Congress favours the system of proportional representation, with regional and national lists.

Secondly, the legislature should be representative of the people as a whole, reflecting such differences of political views and interests as may be present in the community at any particular time.

Thirdly, the institutions of government should not be restricted to any language, religious, racial, ethnic, or cultural grouping. The central, regional, and local government structures including the law enforcement agencies and the administration of justice should reflect the composition of South Africa as a whole and draw on the talents and life experiences of all. Similarly, they should act in a fair and objective manner towards all, without fear, favour, or prejudice.

Fourthly, government must be open. Apartheid South Africa has been a highly authoritarian society, characterised by arbitrary decision-making by officials and by excessive secrecy. All South Africans have the right to be informed about the issues and to know what the basis of governmental decisions is.

There is far too much fear of the government. We must secure constitutional barriers to detention without trial, to spying on citizens, secret files, dirty tricks departments, disinformation, and the use of government money to promote party political objectives.

Fifthly, government should be based on the principle of active involvement of the people. The existence of civic associations, religious bodies, ratepayers organisations, trade unions, and other independent bodies should be encouraged. Similarly, government should collaborate with nongovernmental organisations, without interfering with their autonomy.

Finally, government should reflect the will of the majority, be effective but not all-powerful. It should operate within the framework of the Constitution, acknowledging a separation of powers and the existence of fundamental rights and freedoms as guaranteed in a Bill of Rights.

A nonracial South Africa means a South Africa in which all the artificial barriers and assumptions which kept people apart and maintained dominance are removed. In its negative sense, nonracial means the elimination of all colour bars. In positive terms it means the affirmation of equal rights for all.

It presupposes a South Africa in which every individual has an equal chance, irrespective of his or her birth or colour. It recognises the worth of each individual.

A nonracial Constitution can be adopted rapidly but a nonracial South Africa would take many years to evolve. Yet, although the massive discrepancies in education, health, and living conditions imposed by decades of racial discrimination cannot be eliminated by constitutional declaration, the Constitution must provide the positive means to reduce progressively the imbalance and inequalities and to ensure that everybody has an equal chance in life.

The new Constitution must reflect a commitment to full, free, and equal participation in the new South Africa. Law and practice keep South African women out of their rightful place in helping to build democracy and enable a new nation to evolve, and deprive them of their human rights as individuals.

The new Constitution must therefore:
■ guarantee equal rights for women and men in all spheres of public and private life;
■ create mechanisms whereby the discrimination, disabilities, and disadvantages to which women have been subjected are rapidly removed;
■ give appropriate recognition to reproductive and birth rights;
■ guarantee constitutional protection against sexual violence, abuse, harassment, or defamation;
■ ensure that women are heard in all issues and participate actively in all levels of society.

A Bill of Rights based on universally recognised principles of human rights should form an integral part of the new Constitution. In particular, it should guarantee all South Africans against the violations of human rights associated with apartheid and stress the principle of the equal dignity and worth of all South Africans.

The Bill of Rights should in clear and unambiguous language guarantee the rights of personal freedom and political expression. It should also protect and enhance rights of the individual to practise her or his religion and culture and speak her or his language. It should acknowledge the importance of securing minimum conditions of decent and dignified living for all South Africans.

It should create mechanisms for enforcing these rights. In particular, the courts should have a primary role in ensuring that the Bill of Rights is operative. A Constitutional Court that enjoys the respect of all South Africans, that draws on the experience and talents of the whole population, that is independent, and that functions in a manifestly fair and objective fashion, accountable only to the principles of the Constitution, should be created.

Similarly, a Human Rights Commission should be established to ensure that violations of human rights are investigated and appropriate remedies found, examine patterns of discrimination and make proposals for their elimination.

Finally the post of Ombud should be created to deal with questions of abusive, arbitrary, capricious, discourteous, and corrupt exercise of office by any official.

The Constitution should guarantee the free articulation of differences within the framework of equal rights and tolerance.

An open society requires guarantees for the free functioning of nongovernmental organisations, such as religious bodies, trade unions, sporting and cultural associations, subject only to respect for fundamental human rights as set out in the Constitution.

Nongovernmental organisations should be encouraged to collaborate with the Government in furthering the aims of the Constitution, without thereby compromising their identity or independence.

All men and women shall be entitled to all necessary information to enable them to make effective use of their rights as citizens, workers, and consumers and to impart such information.

There should be freedom of the press, and the media should be open, accessible, and respond to all the views, opinions, and interests of the community.

The three principal qualities of the civil service, the defence, police, and prison service shall be:

representativity, competence, and impartiality.

Representativity

All organs of government shall draw on the life experience and talents of all sectors of the community in such a manner as to instil a common South African perspective of public service. The present barriers based on race shall be eliminated and special steps shall be taken to redress patterns of discrimination attributable to apartheid.

Competency

It is in the interest of the population of a free South Africa that the standard and quality of service of the public service shall be as high as possible. To attain this goal and consistent with the principle of representativity, special programmes of training, retraining, and advancement shall be undertaken to enable the best South Africans to give the best possible service to all their fellow citizens.

Impartiality

The organs of government shall be accountable to Parliament and to the whole community. It is not their function to serve the interests of any party or sectional grouping. Impartiality presupposes a balanced composition of the bodies concerned and a sensitivity to the needs and aspirations of all sections of the community.

There should be adequate control and supervision over the civil service, defence, police, and prison service, an effective machinery to investigate complaints against these services, and the provision of redress.

Administration of justice

Without interfering with its independence, and with a view to ensuring that justice is manifestly seen to be done in a nonracial way and that the wisdom, experience, and judicial skills of all South Africans are represented on the bench, the judiciary shall be transformed in such a way as to consist of men and women drawn from all sectors of South African society.

In a free South Africa, the legal system shall be transformed to be consistent with the new Constitution.

The Courts shall be accessible to all and shall guarantee to all equal rights before the law.

A new South Africa can never evolve if the white part of the population lives in relative luxury while the great majority of black South Africans live in conditions of want, squalor, and deprivation.

Appropriate constitutional expression must therefore be found to guarantee basic human rights in relation to nutrition, shelter, education, health, employment, and welfare. Government should be under a constitutional duty to work towards the establishment of a guaranteed and expanding floor of social, economic, and educational rights for everybody.

It is particularly important that the Constitution facilitate access to education, employment, and land, so that people have real and effective opportunities for improving their situation and pursuing happiness.

THE STRUCTURE OF A CONSTITUTION FOR A DEMOCRATIC SOUTH AFRICA

PART 2

1. South Africa shall be reconstituted as a nonracial, nonsexist, democratic, and unitary republic.

2. South Africa shall consist of the whole territory recognised by the international community as South Africa and shall include the Transkei, Ciskei, Venda, and Bophuthatswana.

3.1. Provision will be made for the three branches of government: the Executive, Legislature, and the Judiciary.

3.2. The head of the Executive will be an elected President who will also be the Head of State. The question that arises is whether the President should be elected directly by the public and vested with greater executive powers, or whether s/he should be elected by and answerable to Parliament. This is a matter on which there must be greater public debate.

3.3. The President will act in consultation with a Cabinet of Ministers headed by a prime minister. The President will appoint a prime minister and other members of the Cabinet.

3.4. The President may only hold office for a maximum of two terms of five years each. He or she will be subject to removal only by a resolution passed for good cause by a two-thirds majority of the National Assembly.

3.5. The legislative branch of government will consist of two houses of Parliament. The first house of Parliament will be the National Assembly, which will be elected on the basis of proportional representation by universal suffrage in which all persons will have an equal vote without regard to race, gender, ethnic origin, language, or creed. The power of enacting legislation will primarily be vested in the National Assembly.

3.6. The second house of Parliament will be the Senate, which will also be elected according to universal suffrage without regard to race, gender, colour, ethnic origin, language, or creed. The Senate will neither be a corporatist chamber made up of interest groups (youth, labour, women, or business, or other groups) nor will it represent ethnic or so-called "community" interest. The electoral system will, however, be different to that adopted for the election of the National Assembly, and will make provision for representation on a regional but not on an ethnic basis.

3.7. The Senate will be the guardian of the Constitution, with power to refer any dispute concerning the interpretation or application of the constitution to the appropriate court for its decision and the power to review. Where appropriate the Senate may delay the passage of legislation passed by the National Assembly, but it will not have the power to veto legislation.

3.8. Elections for the Presidency, National Assembly, and the Senate will be held by secret ballot at periodic intervals of not more than five years and procedures will be enacted to ensure that the elections are genuine and are conducted in accordance with the principles and procedures consistent with those obtaining in a democracy.

3.9. All South Africans shall be entitled to stand for election as President, to Parliament, and to other elected offices. Elections will be supervised by an independent Electoral Commission, and conducted in accordance with the standard design to ensure that the elections are fair and free.

4.1. The National Assembly will be elected on the basis of proportional representation. The rationale behind proportional representation lies in the following factors:

(a) It encourages participation by groups which have significant followings. This is more satisfactory than forcing political or subversive activity outside parliament. Fringe parties would be excluded by imposing a threshold of 5 percent of the vote.

(b) Votes in excess of fifty percent would count and hence be an inducement to vote in areas where one party is dominant. Similarly "losing" parties' votes in those areas would also contribute to their overall performance.

(c) It leads to a more exact political reflection of the popularity of parties.

(d) It avoids the time, expense, and accusations of bias in the process of delimiting constituencies. This process can take months or years.

4.2. Proportional representation on the basis of a national party list system may present problems. Under such a system there is no way of ensuring adequate regional or local representation. Party bureaucracies benefit at the expense of local party structures or local sentiment. There is little direct accountability to constituencies.

4.3. Accordingly the ANC favours incorporating elements of a national list and regional accountability into the electoral system. This could be done most simply by combining a national list with a regional list. For example: regions could be allocated say half of the total seats, to be divided between the different regions in proportion to the registered voters in each region. The remaining half of the seats could be allocated on a national basis. Voters would vote for a party within their region and the regional seats will be allocated between the parties according to the percentages obtained by each party in each region. The second stage would be for regional votes to be aggregated so as to determine the national percentage of the total vote of each party. Each party would then be entitled to nominate from its national list the additional members needed to make up its total entitlement of seats.

4.4. The end result will be the representation of each party in the assembly in proportion to its total votes, but reflecting a regional choice of members as well. The system requires the electorate to cast one vote only. It will be easy to administer and easy for the voters to follow.

4.5. It is recommended that proportional representation, based on the list system, be the preferred system of voting for Senate, regional, and other elections.

5. It is important that there be a guarantee of free and fair elections and that procedures be enacted to see to this. It is therefore recommended that the conduct and supervision of all elections be vested in an independent electoral commission to oversee every aspect of elections from the printing of ballot papers to the adoption of regulations for access by parties to the public media and fairness to all political parties by the public media.

6. There will be an independent judiciary responsible for the interpretation of the Constitution and the application of the law of the land. The judicial power will include the power to review and set aside legislation and actions which are unconstitutional. A Constitutional Court, appointed by the President on the recommendation of a judicial service commission, or by other methods acceptable in a democracy, comprising of judges, practitioners, and academics would be set up.

7. Provision will be made for elected local and regional government on the basis of universal franchise without regard to race, gender, ethnic origin, language, or creed. Local and regional government will exercise delegated powers but will have wide discretions in regard to the priorities to be pursued at these levels, provided always that such policies do not conflict with national policies. Functions presently vested in the provincial administrations will be vested in the regional government. The boundaries of local and regional districts will be determined with due regard to economic and development considerations and without regard to race, colour, ethnic origin, language, or creed.

8. Provision shall be made for one common and equal citizenship

acquired by birth, descent, and naturalisation in accordance with conventional standards. Provision will also be made for the restoration of South African citizenship to persons who have lost their citizenship as a result of the denationalisation process through the homelands policy, or as a result of having gone into exile for political reasons, and provision will also be made for the acquisition of South African citizenship by the spouses and children of such persons.

9.1. All languages of South Africa will have equal status. They will be set out in a Schedule to the Constitution and will include in alphabetical order the following: Afrikaans, English, Sipedi, Sesotho, Siswati, Tsonga, Tswana, Venda, Xhosa, Zulu.

9.2. The State shall take all reasonable and necessary steps to protect, promote, and enhance the language rights of all the people of South Africa in relation to education and culture and in the functioning of the State at local, regional, and national levels.

9.3. The language policy of the state shall be directed towards promoting and encouraging multilingualism and preventing the use of any language or languages for the purposes of domination or division.

9.4. The State shall, however, be empowered to make reasonable provision by law for the use of one or more of the languages in different regions of the country, or for specific purposes.

9.5. The question may, of course, be asked whether there should be one official language for the country. But if this choice is made it would mean the demotion of some languages or the promotion of a single one. Also, it would mean that the official language would be one which most of the people either do not speak or do not speak fluently.

9.6. It would seem therefore that the most appropriate thing to do is to give equal status to all languages subject to the right of the Government to give primacy to one or more languages in any region or throughout the state as the language of administrative communication or judicial record, or for other purposes either throughout the State or in any area. But every one should be entitled to use her or his language for purposes of communicating with the public service.

10.1. There will be a justiciable bill of rights leaving the way open for legitimate state action but affirming and protecting internationally recognised rights and freedoms including equality before the law; freedom from detention without trial; protection against arbitrary arrest and detentions; protection against arbitrary search and seizure; the prohibition of forced labour; the right to fair trial; the prohibition of cruel and unusual punishment; protection of life including the abolition of the death sentence; protection of women's rights; protection of children; freedom from discrimination; the right to privacy; freedom of expression including a free press; the right to information; freedom of religion and conscience; freedom of assembly; freedom of association; freedom of movement including the rights of citizens to leave and return to South Africa; trade union rights including the right to work and the right to strike; the right to form political parties; the right to education, welfare, and health care consistent with the needs of the people and the resources of the state; environmental rights; family and cultural rights; and providing for just compensation to be paid for property taken by the state.

10.2. We do not propose to discuss here the formulation of each right and the enforcement of rights as this has already been done in a detailed fashion in a discussion paper The Draft Bill of Rights published in November 1990 by the African National Congress.

11. Provision will be made for discrimination to be eliminated in substance as well as in form. At all levels of government the state will be empowered to pursue policies of affirmative action for the advancement of persons who have been socially, economically, or educationally disadvantaged by past discriminatory laws and practices and in order to redress social, economic, and educational imbalances in South Africa resulting from such discrimination with special regard to the maldistribution of land and the need for housing. Special provision will also be made to redress the added discrimination which has been suffered by women and the victims of forced removals.

12. All discriminatory legislation and all other legislation inconsistent with the Bill of Rights will be invalidated by the Bill of Rights. All other legislation will remain in force unless repealed by parliament or set aside by a court under its power of judicial review.

13. There will be a public service commission charged with the responsibility of overseeing the recruitment, promotion, and dismissal to and from posts in the civil service. Such a commission will also be required to implement an affirmative action programme in regard to appointments to senior positions in order to redress existing race and gender disparities. Provision will be made for a representative structuring of the public service, the police service, and the defence services and to ensure that the public service will be accountable for its actions.

14. There will be an independent Ombud with powers to investigate complaints against members of the public service including the police and other holders of public and private power and to investigate allegations of corruption.

15. The Constitution will also make provision for a state of emergency to be declared when the life of the nation is threatened. Such a power will be subject to strict controls by Parliament and the judiciary. The Constitution will provide for the recognition and protection as far as possible of fundamental rights during the period of emergency.

16. The Constitution will be subject to amendment only if a majority of two thirds of the national assembly approve of the amendment or if approved by two-thirds of the votes cast at a national referendum.

■ African National Congress (1990)

A Bill of Rights
For A Democratic South Africa

Working Draft for Consultation

Article 1. GENERAL

1. All South Africans are born free and equal in dignity and rights.

2. No individual or group shall receive privileges or be subjected to discrimination, domination, or abuse on the grounds of race, colour, language, gender, creed, political or other opinion, birth or other status.

3. All men and women shall have equal protection under the law.

Article 2. PERSONAL RIGHTS

The Right to Life

1. Every person has the right to life.

2. No one shall be arbitrarily deprived of his or her life.

3. Capital punishment is abolished and no further executions shall take place.

The Right to Dignity

4. No one should be subjected to slavery, servitude, or forced labour, provided that forced labour shall not include work normally required of someone carrying out a sentence of a court, nor military service or national service by a conscientious objector, nor services required in the case of calamity or serious emergency, nor any work which forms part of normal civil obligations.

5. The dignity of all persons shall be respected.

6. No one shall be subjected to torture or cruel, inhuman, or degrading treatment or punishment.

7. Everyone shall have the right to appropriate protection by law against violence, harassment, or abuse, or the impairment of his or her dignity.

The Right to a Fair Trial

8. There shall be no detention without trial.

9. No persons shall be arrested or detained for any purpose other than that of bringing them to trial on a criminal charge.

10. Arrest shall take place according to procedures laid down by law, and persons taken into custody shall immediately be informed of the charges against them, shall have access to a legal representative of their choice, and shall be brought before court within 48 hours or, where that would be a Sunday or a public holiday, on the first working day thereafter.

11. Bail shall be granted to awaiting-trial persons unless a court rules that in the interests of justice they should be kept in custody.

12. No one shall be deprived of liberty or subjected to other punishment except after a fair trial in public by an independent court.

13. Trials shall take place within a reasonable time.

14. Everyone shall be presumed innocent until proven guilty.

15. No conduct shall be punished if it was not a criminal offence at the time of its occurrence, and no penalty shall be increased retrospectively.

16. No one shall be punished twice for the same offence.

17. Accused persons shall be informed in writing of the nature of the allegations against them, and shall be given adequate time to prepare and conduct their defence.

18. Everything that is reasonable shall be done to ensure that accused persons understand the nature and the import of the charges against them and of the proceedings, that they are not prejudiced through illiteracy or lack of understanding, and that they receive a fair trial.

19. Accused persons shall have the right to challenge all evidence presented against them, to be defended by a legal practitioner of their choice, and if in custody, to have access to a legal practitioner at all reasonable times.

20. If a person is unable to pay for legal representation, and the interests of justice so require, the State shall provide or pay for a competent defence.

21. No persons shall be required to give evidence against themselves, nor, except in cases of domestic violence or abuse, shall persons be required to give evidence against their spouses whether married by civil law or custom, their parents, or their children.

22. No evidence obtained through torture or cruel, inhuman, or degrading treatment shall be admissible in any proceedings.

23. Juveniles shall be separated from adult offenders.

The Right to Judicial Review

24. Any person adversely affected by an administrative or executive act shall have the right to have the matter reviewed by an independent court or tribunal on the grounds of abuse of authority, going beyond the powers granted by the law, bad faith, or such gross unreasonableness in relation to the procedure or the decision as to amount to manifest injustice.

The Right to Home Life

25. No one shall be deprived of or removed from his or her home on the grounds of race, colour, language, gender, or creed.

26. The privacy of the home shall be respected, save that reasonable steps shall be permitted to prevent domestic violence or abuse.

27. People shall have the right to establish families, live together with partners of their choice, and to marry.

28. Marriage shall be based upon the free consent of the partners, and spouses shall enjoy equal rights at and during marriage and after its dissolution.

The Right to Privacy

29. No search or entry shall be permitted except for reasonable cause, as

prescribed by law, and as would be acceptable in an open and democratic society.

30. Interference with private communications, spying on persons, and the compilation and keeping of secret files about them without their consent shall not be permissible save as authorised by law in circumstances that would be acceptable in an open and democratic society.

The Right of Movement

31. Everyone shall have the right to move freely and reside in any part of the country, to receive a passport, travel abroad, and to emigrate or return if he or she so wishes.

The Right to Conscience

32. The right to conscience shall be inviolate, and no-one shall be penalised for his or her beliefs.

Article 3. POLITICAL RIGHTS

1. South Africa shall be a multiparty democracy in which all men and women shall enjoy basic political rights on an equal basis.

2. Government at all levels shall be subject to the principles of accountability to the electorate.

3. Elections shall be conducted in accordance with an electoral law which shall make no distinction on the grounds of race, colour, language, gender, or creed.

4. Elections shall be regular, free and fair, and based on universal franchise and a common voters' roll.

5. All men and women entitled to vote shall be entitled to stand for and occupy any position or office in any organ of government or administration.

6. All citizens shall have the right to form and join political parties and to campaign for social, economic, and political change, either directly or through freely chosen representatives.

Article 4. FREEDOM OF SPEECH, ASSEMBLY, AND INFORMATION

1. There shall be freedom of thought, speech, expression, and opinion, including a free press which shall respect the right to reply.

2. All men and women shall have the right to assemble peacefully and without arms, and to submit petitions for the redress of grievances and injustices.

3. All men and women shall be entitled to all the information necessary to enable them to make effective use of their rights as citizens or consumers.

Article 5. RIGHTS OF ASSOCIATION, RELIGION, LANGUAGE, AND CULTURE

Freedom of Association

1. There shall be freedom of association, including the right to form and join trade unions, religious, social, and cultural bodies, and to form and participate in nongovernmental organisations.

Freedom of Religion

2. There shall be freedom of worship and tolerance of all religions, and no State or official religion shall be established.

3. The institutions of religion shall be separate from the State, but nothing in this Constitution shall prevent them from cooperating with the State with a view to furthering the objectives of this Constitution, nor from bearing witness and commenting on the actions of the State.

4. Places associated with religious observance shall be respected, and no one shall be barred from entering them on grounds of race.

Language Rights

5. The languages of South Africa are Sindebele, Sepedi, Sesotho, Siswati, Setswana, Afrikaans, English, Tsonga [Shangaan], Venda, Xhosa, and Zulu.

6. The State shall act positively to further the development of these languages, especially in education, literature, and the media, and to prevent the use of any language or languages for the purpose of domination or division.

7. When it is reasonable to do so, one or more of these languages may be designated as the language to be used for defined purposes at the national level or in any region or area where it is widely used.

8. Subject to the availability of public and private resources, and limitations of reasonableness, primary and secondary education should wherever possible be offered in the language or languages of preference of the students or their parents.

9. The State shall promote respect for all languages spoken in South Africa.

Creative Freedom

10. There shall be freedom of artistic activity and scientific enquiry, without censorship, subject only to such limitations as may be imposed by law in accordance with principles generally accepted in open and democratic societies.

The Right to Sporting, Recreational, and Cultural Activities

11. Sporting, recreational, and cultural activities shall be encouraged on a nonracial basis, drawing on the talents and creative capacities of all South Africans, and autonomous organisations may be established to achieve these objectives.

Article 6. WORKERS' RIGHTS

1. Workers shall have the right to form and join trade unions, and to regulate such unions without interference from the State.

2. Workers shall be free to join trade unions of their choice, subject only to the rules of such unions and to the principles of nondiscrimination set out in this Constitution, and no worker shall be victimised on account of membership of a union.

3. The right to organise and to bargain collectively on any social,

economic, or other matter affecting workers' interests shall be guaranteed.

4. In the furtherance of these rights, trade unions shall be entitled to reasonable access to the premises of enterprises, to receive such information as may be reasonably necessary, and to deduct union subscriptions where appropriate.

5. No law shall prevent representative trade unions from negotiating collective agreements binding on all workers covered by such agreements.

6. Workers shall have the right to strike under law in pursuance of their social and economic interests subject to reasonable limitations in respect of the interruption of services such as would endanger the life, health, or personal safety of the community or any section of the population.

7. Workers shall have the right to peaceful picketing, subject only to such reasonable conditions as would be acceptable in a democratic society.

8. Trade unions shall have the right to participate in lawful political activities.

9. Trade unions shall have the right to form national federations and to affiliate to international federations.

10. Employers shall be under a duty to provide a safe, clean, and dignified work environment, and to offer reasonable pay and holidays.

11. There shall be equal pay for equal work and equal access to employment.

12. The State shall make provision by way of legislation for compensation to be paid to workers injured in the course of their employment and for the benefits to be paid to unemployed or retired workers.

Article 7. GENDER RIGHTS

1. Men and women shall enjoy equal rights in all areas of public and private life, including employment, education, and within the family.

2. Discrimination on the grounds of gender, single parenthood, legitimacy of birth, or sexual orientation shall be unlawful.

3. Positive action should be undertaken to overcome the disabilities and disadvantages suffered on account of past gender discrimination.

4. The law shall provide remedies for sexual harassment, abuse, and violence.

5. Educational institutions, the media, advertising, and other social institutions shall be under a duty to discourage sexual and other types of stereotyping.

Article 8. DISABLED PERSONS

1. There shall be no discrimination against disabled persons.

2. Legislation shall provide for the progressive opening up of employment opportunities for disabled men and women, for the removal of obstacles to the enjoyment by them of public amenities, and for their integration into all areas of life.

Article 9. CHILDREN

1. All children shall have the right to a name, to health, to security, education, and equality of treatment.

2. The State shall, to the maximum of its available resources, seek to achieve progressively the full realisation of these rights.

3. No child shall suffer discrimination or enjoy privileges on the grounds of race, colour, gender, language, creed, legitimacy, or the status of his or her parents.

4. In all proceedings concerning children, the primary consideration shall be the best interests of the child.

5. Children are entitled to be protected from economic exploitation and shall not be permitted to perform work that is likely to be hazardous or harmful to their education, health, or moral well-being.

6. It shall be unlawful to oblige children to work or perform services for the employers of their parents or other family members.

Article 10. SOCIAL, EDUCATIONAL, ECONOMIC, AND WELFARE RIGHTS

General

1. All men and women have the right to enjoy basic social, educational, economic, and welfare rights.

2. The State shall, to the maximum of its available resources, undertake appropriate legislative and executive action in order to achieve the progressive realisation of basic social, educational, economic, and welfare rights for the whole population.

3. Such State action shall establish standards and procedures whereby all men, women, and children are guaranteed by law a progressively expanding floor of enforceable minimum rights, with special attention to nutrition, shelter, health care, education, and income.

4. In order to achieve a common floor of rights for the whole country, resources may be diverted from richer to poorer areas, and timetables may be established for the phased extension of legislation and minimum standards from area to area.

5. The State may collaborate with nongovernmental organisations and the private sector in achieving these goals, and may impose appropriate responsibilities on all social and economic bodies with a view to their materialisation.

6. In circumstances where persons are unable through lack of means to avail themselves of facilities provided by the State, the State shall, wherever it is reasonable to do so, give appropriate assistance.

Freedom from Hunger

7. In order to guarantee the right of freedom from hunger, the State shall ensure minimum standards of nutrition throughout the country, with special emphasis on preschool and school feeding.

The Right to Shelter

8. In order to guarantee the right to shelter, the State shall, in collabora-

tion with private bodies where appropriate, dismantle compounds, single-sex hostels, and other forms of accommodation associated with the migrant labour system, and embark upon and encourage an extensive programme of house-building.

9. The State shall take steps to ensure that energy, access to clean water, and appropriate sewage and waste disposal are available to every home.

10. No eviction from homes or from land shall take place without the order of a competent court, which shall have regard to the availability of alternative accommodation.

The Right to Education

10. In order to guarantee the right to education, the State shall, in collaboration with nongovernmental and private educational institutions where appropriate, ensure that:

there shall be free and compulsory primary education for all, with a school-leaving age of sixteen,

there shall be progressive expansion of access by all children as a right to secondary education,

there shall be progressive increase in access to preschool institutions and institutes of vocational training and of higher learning,

there shall be increasingly extensive facilities to enable adults to overcome illiteracy and further their education.

11. Education shall be directed towards the full development of the human personality and a sense of personal dignity, and shall aim at strengthening respect for human rights and fundamental freedoms, and promoting understanding, tolerance, and friendship among all South Africans and between nations.

The Right to Health

12. In order to guarantee the right to protection of health, the State shall establish a comprehensive national health service linking health workers, community organisations, State institutions, private medical schemes, and individual medical practitioners so as to provide hygiene education, preventative medicine, and health care delivery to all.

The Right to Work

13. In order to guarantee increasing enjoyment of the right to work, the State shall, in collaboration where appropriate with private bodies and nongovernmental institutions:

make technical and vocational training available to all,

remove the barriers which keep large sections of the population out of technical, professional, and managerial positions,

and promote public and other works with a view to reducing unemployment.

The Right to a Minimum Income and Welfare Rights

14. In order to guarantee the achievement of a minimum income for all, the State shall introduce a scheme of family benefits and old age pensions financed from general revenue.

15. In order to guarantee the enjoyment of basic social welfare rights, in particular unemployment benefits, compensation for injury, superannuation or retirement pensions, the State shall, in collaboration where appropriate with private bodies, establish a system of national insurance based upon contributions by employers, employees, and other interested persons.

Article 11. THE ECONOMY, LAND, AND PROPERTY

1. Legislation on economic matters shall be guided by the principle of encouraging collaboration between the State and the private, cooperative and family sectors with a view to reducing inequality, promoting growth, and providing goods and services for the whole population.

2. All men and women and lawfully constituted bodies are entitled to the peaceful enjoyment of their possessions, including the right to acquire, own, or dispose of property in any part of the country without distinction based on race, colour, language, gender, or creed.

3. All natural resources below and above the surface area of the land, including the air, and all forms of potential energy or minerals in the territorial waters, the continental shelf, and the exclusive economic zone of South Africa, which are not owned by any person at the time of coming into force of this Constitution, shall belong to the State.

4. The State shall have the right to regulate the exploitation of natural resources, grant franchises, and determine royalties, subject to payment of appropriate compensation in the event of interference with any lawfully vested interest.

5. The State may by legislation take steps to overcome the effects of past statutory discrimination in relation to enjoyment of property rights.

6. There shall be no forced removals of persons or communities from their homes or land on the basis of race, colour, language, gender, or creed.

7. No persons or legal entities shall be deprived of their possessions except on grounds of public interest or public utility, including the achievement of the objectives of the Constitution.

8. Any such deprivation may be effected only by or pursuant to a law which shall provide for the nature and the extent of compensation to be paid.

9. Compensation shall be just, taking into account the need to establish an equitable balance between the public interest and the interest of those affected.

10. In the case of a dispute regarding the amount of compensation or its mode of payment, provision shall be made for recourse to a special independent tribunal, with an appeal to the courts.

11. The preceding provisions shall not be interpreted as in any way impeding the right of the State to adopt such measures as might be deemed necessary in any democratic society for the control, use, or acquisition of property in accordance with the general interest, or to preserve the

environment, or to regulate or curtail monopolies, or to secure the payment of taxes or other contributions or penalties.

Article 12. ENVIRONMENTAL RIGHTS

1. The environment, including the land, the waters, and the sky, are the common heritage of the people of South Africa and of all humanity.

2. All men and women shall have the right to a healthy and ecologically balanced environment and the duty to defend it.

3. In order to secure this right, the State, acting through appropriate agencies and organs shall conserve, protect, and improve the environment, and in particular:

i. prevent and control pollution of the air and waters and degradation and erosion of the soil;

ii. have regard in local, regional, and national planning to the maintenance or creation of balanced ecological and biological areas and to the prevention or minimising of harmful effects on the environment;

iii. promote the rational use of natural resources, safeguarding their capacity for renewal and ecological stability;

iv. ensure that long-term damage is not done to the environment by industrial or other forms of waste;

v. maintain, create, and develop natural reserves, parks, and recreational areas and classify and protect other sites and landscapes so as to ensure the preservation and protection of areas of outstanding cultural, historic, and natural interest.

4. Legislation shall provide for cooperation between the State, nongovernmental organisations, local communities, and individuals in seeking to improve the environment and encourage ecologically sensible habits in daily life.

5. The law shall provide for appropriate penalties and reparation in the case of any direct and serious damage caused to the environment, and permit the interdiction by any interested person or by any agency established for the purpose of protecting the environment of any public or private activity or undertaking which manifestly and unreasonably causes or threatens to cause irreparable damage to the environment.

Article 13. AFFIRMATIVE ACTION

1. Nothing in the Constitution shall prevent the enactment of legislation, or the adoption by any public or private body of special measures of a positive kind designed to procure the advancement and the opening up of opportunities, including access to education, skills, employment, and land, and the general advancement in social, economic, and cultural spheres, of men and women who in the past have been disadvantaged by discrimination.

2. No provision of the Bill of Rights shall be construed as derogating from or limiting in any way the general provisions of this Article.

Article 14. POSITIVE ACTION

1. In its activities and functioning, the State shall observe the principles of nonracialism and nonsexism, and encourage the same in all public and private bodies.

2. All benefits conferred and entitlements granted by the State shall be distributed on a nonracist and a nonsexist basis.

3. The State and all public and private bodies shall be under a duty to prevent any form of incitement to racial, religious, or linguistic hostility and to dismantle all structures and do away with all practices that compulsorily divide the population on grounds of race, colour, language, or creed.

4. With a view to achieving the above, the State may enact legislation to prohibit the circulation or possession of materials which incite racial, ethnic, religious, gender, or linguistic hatred, which provoke violence, or which insult, degrade, defame, or encourage abuse of any racial, ethnic, religious, gender, or linguistic group.

5. All organs of the State at the national, regional, and local levels shall pursue policies and programmes aimed at redressing the consequences of past discriminatory laws and practices, and at the creation of a genuine nonracial democracy in South Africa.

6. Such policies shall include the implementation of programmes aimed at achieving speedily the balanced structuring in nonracial form of the public service, defence and police forces, and the prison service.

7. Without interfering with its independence, and with a view to ensuring that justice is manifestly seen to be done in a nonracial way and that the wisdom, experience, and judicial skills of all South Africans are represented on the bench, the judiciary shall be transformed in such a way as to consist of men and women drawn from all sectors of South African society.

8. In taking steps to correct patterns or practices of discrimination, special attention shall be paid to rectifying the inequalities to which women in South Africa have been subjected, and to ensure their full, equal, effective, and dignified participation in the political, social, economic, and cultural life of the nation.

9. Legislation may be enacted requiring nongovernmental organisations and private bodies to conduct themselves in accordance with the above principles.

Article 15. LIMITATIONS

1. Nothing in the Constitution shall be interpreted as implying for any group or person the right to engage in any activity or perform any act aimed at the destruction of any of the rights and freedoms set forth in the Constitution, or at their limitation or suppression to a degree other than is authorised by the Constitution itself.

2. Nothing in this Constitution should be interpreted as impeding the right of the State to enact legislation regulating the manner in which fundamental rights and freedoms shall be exercised, or limiting such rights, provided that such regulation or limitation is such as might be deemed necessary in an open and democratic society.

3. Any restrictions permitted under the Constitution to fundamental rights and freedoms shall not be applied to or used as a cover for any purpose other than that for which they have been expressly or by necessary implication authorised.

4. Any law providing for any regulation or limitation of any fundamental right or freedom shall:

i. be of general application;

ii. not negate the essential content of the right, but simply qualify the way that the right is to be exercised or the circumstances in which derogation from the right is permitted;

iii. as far as practicable, identify the specific clauses of the Constitution relied upon for the limitation of the right and the specific clauses of the Constitution affected by the legislation;

iv. specify as precisely as possible the exact reach of the limitation and the circumstances in which it shall apply.

Article 16. ENFORCEMENT

General

1. The fundamental rights and freedoms contained in this Bill of Rights shall be guaranteed by the courts.

2. Provision shall be made for the establishment of a constitutional court.

3. The terms of the Bill of Rights shall be binding upon the State and organs of government at all levels, and where appropriate, on all social institutions and persons.

4. All persons who claim that rights guaranteed them by the Bill of Rights have been infringed or threatened shall be entitled to apply to a competent court for an order for the declaration or enforcement of their rights, or for the restraining of any act which impedes or threatens such rights.

5. Any law or executive or administrative act which violates the terms of the Bill of Rights shall be invalid to the extent of such violation, save that the Court shall have the discretion in appropriate cases to put the relevant body or official to terms as to how and within what period to remedy the violation.

Human Rights Commission

6. Parliament shall have a special responsibility for ensuring that the basic social, educational, economic, and welfare rights set out in this Bill of Rights are respected.

7. Parliament shall establish by legislation a Human Rights Commission to promote observance of the Bill of Rights.

8. Such Commission shall have the right to establish agencies for

investigating patterns of violence of any of the terms of the Bill of Rights and for receiving complaints and bringing proceedings in court where appropriate.

9. The Commission shall monitor proposed legislation with a view to reporting to Parliament on its impact on the realisation of the rights set out in the Bill of Rights.

Ombudsman

10. With a view to ensuring that all functions and duties under the Constitution are carried out in a fair way with due respect for the rights and sentiments of those affected, the office of Ombudsman shall be created.

11. The Ombudsman shall be independent in the carrying out of his or her functions and may open offices in different parts of the country.

12. The Ombudsman shall receive and investigate complaints from members of the public concerning abuse of power or unfair, insensitive, capricious, harsh, discourteous, or unduly delayed treatment of any person by any official of government at national, regional, or local level, or any attempt by such official to extort benefits or corruptly to receive favours.

13. In accordance with his or her findings, the Ombudsman may initiate legal proceedings, refer the matter for prosecution, negotiate a compromise, or make a report to the department or organ concerned containing recommendations with a view to remedying the improper conduct, preventing repetition, and, where appropriate, making amends, including compensation.

14. Recourse to the Human Rights Commission or to the Ombudsman shall not oust the jurisdiction of the courts to hear any matter.

(Working draft prepared by the Constitutional Committee set up by the NEC).

■ South African Law Commission (1989)

The SA Law Commission Bill of Rights (1989) — Draft Copy

Bill of Rights

Part A: FUNDAMENTAL RIGHTS

The rights set forth in this part are fundamental rights to which every person in the Republic of South Africa shall be entitled and, save as provided in this bill, no legislation or executive or administrative act of any nature whatever shall infringe those rights.

Article 1

The right to life: Provided that legislation may provide for the discretionary imposition of the sentence of death in the case of the most serious crimes.

Article 2

The right to human dignity and equality before the law, which means that there shall be no discrimination on the ground of race, colour, language, sex, religion, ethnic origin, social class, birth, political or other views, or any disability or other natural characteristic; provided that such legislation or executive or administrative acts as may reasonably be necessary for the improvement, on a temporary basis, of a position in which, for historical reason, persons or groups find themselves to be disadvantaged, shall be permissible.

Article 3

The right to a good name and reputation.

Article 4

The right to spiritual and physical integrity.

Article 5

The right to be recognised legally, economically, and culturally as having rights and obligations and as having the capacity to participate in legal, commercial, and cultural affairs.

Article 6

The right to privacy, which shall also mean that a person's property or place of residence or employment shall not be arbitrarily entered, that he shall not be arbitrarily searched, that his property or possessions shall not be arbitrarily seized, and that there shall be no arbitrary interference with or interception of his correspondence or any other form of communication used by him.

Article 7

The right not to be held in slavery or subjected to forced labour, provided that legislation may provide for such labour as may be prescribed to be performed during detention resulting from a person's being sentenced to imprisonment by a court of law, or such compulsory military or civil service as may reasonably be acceptable in a democratic state.

Article 8
The right to freedom of speech and to obtain and disseminate information.

Article 9
The right to freely carry out scientific research and to practise art.

Article 10
The right to freedom of choice with regard to education and training.

Article 11
The right to the integrity of the family, freedom of marriage, and the upholding of the institution of marriage.

Article 12
The right to move freely within the Republic of South Africa and therein to reside, to work, or to carry on any lawful business, occupation, trade, or other activity.

Article 13
The right of every citizen not to be
A) arbitrarily refused a passport.
B) exiled or expelled from the Republic of South Africa.
C) prevented from emigrating.

Article 14
The right to freely, and on an equal footing, engage in economic intercourse, which shall include the capacity to establish and maintain commercial undertakings, to procure property and means of production, to offer services against remuneration, and to make a profit.

Article 15
The right to private property: Provided that legislation may, in the public interest, authorise expropriation against payment of reasonable compensation which shall, in the event of dispute, be determined by a court of law.

Article 16
The right to associate freely with other groups and individuals.

Article 17
The right of every person or group to disassociate himself or itself from other individuals or groups: Provided that, if such disassociation constitutes discrimination on the grounds of race, colour, religion, language, or culture, no public or state funds shall be granted directly, or indirectly, to promote the interests of the person who, or group, which so discriminates.

Article 18
The rights of citizens to freely form political parties, to be members of such parties, to practise their political convictions in a peaceful manner and to be nominated and elected to legislative, executive, and administrative

office, and to form and become members of trade unions: Provided that no person shall be compelled to be a member of a political party or a trade union.

Article 19
The right to assemble peacefully, to hold demonstrations peacefully and to obtain and present petitions.

Article 20
(a) The right of all citizens over the age of 18 years to exercise the vote on a basis of equality in respect of all legislative institutions at regular and periodical elections and at referendums.

(b) Subject to paragraph (a) hereof, the composition of the legislative institutions of the country shall be determined in the constitution.

Article 21
The right of every person, individually or together with others, to freely practise his culture and religion and use his language.

Article 22
The right of every person to be safeguarded from discrimination against his culture, religion, or language and to be safeguarded from preferential treatment of the culture, religion, or language of others: Provided that legislation may determine the official languages of a region: Provided further that when in proceedings instituted by an interested person or persons it is alleged that legislation or an executive or administrative act infringes the cultural, religious, or linguistic values of any individual or group of individuals, the court shall in adjudicating such allegation have regard to the interests of other individuals or groups of individuals.

Article 23
The right to personal freedom and safety, which also means that no person shall be deprived of his freedom, save in the following cases and in accordance with a generally applicable described procedure whereby his fundamental rights to spiritual and physical integrity are not denied:

(a) Lawful arrest or detention of a person effected in order to cause him to appear before a court of law on the ground of a reasonable suspicion that he has committed a crime or whenever it may be on reasonable grounds be deemed necessary to prevent the commission of a crime.

(b) Lawful detention upon conviction by a court of law or for noncompliance with a lawful order of the court.

(c) Lawful detention of a person in order to prevent the spread of infectious disease.

(d) Lawful detention of a person who is mentally ill or one who is addicted to narcotic or addictive substances, with a view to his admission, in accordance with prescribed procedure, to an institution or rehabilitation centre.

(e) Lawful detention of a person in order to prevent his unauthorised entry into or sojourn in the Republic of South Africa or with a view to the extradition or deportation of a person in accordance with prescribed procedure.

Article 24

It shall be the right of every person under arrest:

(a) to be detained and fed under conditions consonant with human dignity;

(b) to be informed as soon as possible, in a language which he understands, of the reason for his detention and of any charge against him;

(c) to be informed as soon as possible that he has the right to remain silent and that he need not make any statement and to be warned of the consequences of making a statement;

(d) within a reasonable period of time, but not less than 48 hours of the first court day thereafter, to be brought before a court of law and in writing to be charged or in writing to be informed of the reason for his detention, failing which he shall be entitled to be released from detention, unless a court of law, upon good cause shown, orders his further detention;

(e) within a reasonable period after his arrest, to be tried by a court of law and pending such trial to be released, which release may be subject to bail or guarantees to appear at the trial, unless a court of law, upon good cause shown orders his further detention;

(f) to communicate and to consult with legal representatives of his choice;

(g) to communicate with and to receive, in reasonable measure, visits from his spouse, family, next of kin, or friends, unless a court of law otherwise directs;

(h) not to be subjected to torture, assault, or cruel or inhuman or degrading treatment.

Article 25

The right of every accused person

(a) not to be convicted or sentenced unless a fair and public trial before a court of law has taken place in accordance with the generally applicable procedures and evidential rules;

(b) to be treated as innocent until the contrary is proved by the state;

(c) to remain silent and to refuse to testify during the trial;

(d) to be assisted by a legal representative of his choice and, if he cannot afford this, and if the case is a serious one, to be defended by a legal representative remunerated by the state;

(e) not to be sentenced to inhuman or degrading punishment;

(f) not to be convicted of an offence in respect of an act or omission which did not constitute an offence at the moment when it was done and not to receive a penalty heavier than that which was applicable at the time when the offence was committed;

(g) not to be convicted of a crime of which he was previously convicted or acquitted, save in the course of appeal or review proceedings connected with such conviction or acquittal;

(h) to have recourse by appeal or review to a court superior to the court which tried him in the first instance: Provided that if a Division of the Supreme Court of South Africa was the court of first instance it may be prescribed that leave to appeal shall first be obtained from that court or from the Appellate Division;

(i) to be informed as to the reasons for his conviction and sentence.

Article 26

The right of every person convicted of a crime and serving a term of imprisonment in accordance with a sentence of a court of law:

(a) not to be subjected to torture, assault, or cruel or inhuman or degrading treatment;

(b) to be detained and fed under conditions consonant with human dignity;

(c) to be given the opportunity of developing and rehabilitating;

(d) to be released upon expiry of the term of imprisonment imposed by the court of law.

Article 27

The right to cause civil disputes to be settled by a court of law and to appeal to a court of law by way of review against executive and administrative acts and against quasi-judicial decisions.

Article 28

The right to have the rules of natural justice applied in administrative and quasi-judicial proceedings and to have reasons furnished for any prejudicial decision.

Article 29

The right that the South African law, including the South African international private law, shall apply to all legal relations before a court of law: Provided that legislation may provide for the application of the law of indigenous groups or the religious law of religious groups in civil proceedings.

PART B

Article 30

The rights granted in this bill, may, by legislation, be limited to the extent that is reasonably necessary in the interests of the security of the State, the public order, the public interest, good morals, public health, the administration of justice, the rights of others, or for the prevention of disorder and crime, but only in such measure and in such a manner as is acceptable in a democratic society.

Article 31

The Supreme Court of the Republic of South Africa shall have jurisdiction upon application by any interested person acting on his own behalf or on behalf of a group of interested persons to determine whether any legislation or executive or administrative act violates any of the rights herein set forth or exceeds any of the limitations herein permitted and, if so, to the extent that the violation or excess takes place, to declare invalid the legislation in question or to set aside the executive or administrative act in question: Provided that finalised executive and administrative acts by which effect has been given the legislation declared invalid and which are not the subject of the proceedings concerned, shall not automatically become void.

■ South African Law Commission (1991)

The Bill Proposed By The South African Law Commission

Article 1: FUNDAMENTAL RIGHTS
The rights set forth in this Bill are fundamental rights to which every individual and, where applicable, also every juristic person in South Africa is entitled in relation to legislative and governmental bodies, and save as otherwise provided in this Bill those rights shall not be circumscribed, limited, suspended, or infringed by any legislation or executive or administrative act of any nature.

Article 2: THE RIGHT TO LIFE
Everyone has the right to protection of his or her life.

Article 3: EQUALITY BEFORE THE LAW
(a) Everyone has the right to equality before the law, which means, inter alia, that save as permitted in this Article, no legislation or executive or administrative act shall directly or indirectly favour or prejudice any person on the grounds of his or her race, colour, sex, religion, ethnic origin, social class, birth, political and other views, or disabilities or other natural characteristics.

(b) To this end the highest legislative body may by legislation of general force and effect introduce such programmes of affirmative action and vote such funds therefore as may reasonably be necessary to ensure that through education and training, financing programmes, and employment all citizens have equal opportunities of developing and realising their natural talent and potential to the full.

(c) The provisions of Sub-Article (a) hereof shall not be construed as making it compulsory for any female person to perform military service.

Article 4: THE RIGHT TO MENTAL AND PHYSICAL INTEGRITY
(a) Everyone has the right to the protection of his or her mental and physical integrity.

(b) No one shall be subjected to mental or physical torture, assault, or inhuman or degrading treatment.

(c) No exceptional circumstances whatever, whether a state of war or threat of war, internal political instability or any other public emergency or any order given by a superior officer or by any person holding office in government, shall serve as justification for acts mentioned in paragraph (b)

Article 5: PERSONAL LIBERTY AND SECURITY
Everyone has the right to his or her personal liberty and security, which means, inter alia, that no one shall be deprived of his or her liberty save in the following cases and in accordance with a prescribed procedure generally in force by which the fundamental right to his or her mental or physical

integrity is not denied:

(a) Lawful arrest or detention for the purpose of bringing a person before a court of law on the ground of a reasonable suspicion, which shall be justiciable by a court, that he or she has committed or is committing or is attempting to commit a crime;

(b) lawful detention pursuant upon conviction by a court of law or failure to comply with a lawful order of the court;

(c) lawful detention in order to prevent the spread of infectious disease;

(d) lawful detention of a person who is mentally ill or a person addicted to narcotic or addictive substances with a view to his or her admission, in accordance with prescribed procedure, to an institution or rehabilitation centre;

(e) lawful detention for the prevention of any person's unauthorised presence or sojourn in South Africa or with a view to his or her extradition or deportation in accordance with prescribed procedure.

Article 6: THE RIGHTS OF AN ARRESTED PERSON

Everyone who is arrested has the right —

(a) to be detained and to be fed under conditions consonant with human dignity and to receive the necessary medical treatment;

(b) to be informed as soon as possible in a language which he or she understands of the reason for his or her detention and of any charge against him or her;

(c) to be informed as soon as possible in a language which he or she understands that he or she has the right to remain silent and the right to refrain from making any statement and to be warned of the consequences of making a statement;

(d) within a reasonable period of time, but not later than 48 hours or the first court day thereafter, to be brought before a court of law and to be charged in writing or informed in writing of the reason for his or her detention, failing which he or she shall be entitled to be released from detention unless on good cause shown a court of law orders further detention;

(e) to be tried by a court of law within a reasonable time after arrest and pending such trial to be released, which release may be subject to bail or guarantees to appear at the trial, unless on good cause shown a court of law orders further detention;

(f) to communicate and to consult with a legal practitioner and a medical practitioner of his or her choice;

(g) to communicate with and to be visited by his or her spouse, family, next of kin, religious counsellor, or friends, unless a court of law otherwise orders;

Article 7: THE RIGHTS OF AN ACCUSED PERSON

Every accused person has the right —

(a) not to be sentenced or punished unless he or she had a fair and public trial before a court of law in accordance with the rules of procedure and evidence generally in force;

(b) to be presumed innocent until the contrary is proved by the state or other prosecutor;

(c) to remain silent and to refuse to testify at the trial;

(d) not to be convicted or sentenced on the ground of evidence so obtained or presented as to violate any of the rights under this Bill of the accused person or of the witness concerned or of any other person, unless the court, in the light of all the circumstances and in the public interest, otherwise orders;

(e) to be represented by a legal practitioner;

(f) to be informed by the presiding officer —

(i) of his or her right to be represented by a legal practitioner;

(ii) of the institutions which he or she may approach for legal assistance; and to be given a reasonable opportunity to endeavour to obtain legal assistance: Provided that failure or neglect so to inform an accused person or to give him or her such opportunity shall not result in the setting aside of the proceedings unless on appeal or review a court finds that justice was not done;

(g) not to be sentenced to an inhuman or degrading punishment;

(h) not to be convicted of a crime in respect of any act or omission which at the time when it was committed was not a crime and not to be given a sentence more severe than that which was by law applicable at the time when the crime was committed;

(i) not to be convicted of any crime of which he or she has previously been convicted or acquitted, save in the course of appeal or review proceedings relating to that conviction or acquittal;

(j) to have recourse, on appeal or review, to a higher court than the court of first instance: Provided that legislation may prescribe that leave to appeal shall first be obtained;

(k) to be informed in a language which he or she understands of the reasons for his or her conviction and sentence;

(l) to be tried in a language which he or she understands or, failing this, to have the proceedings interpreted to him or her;

(m) to be sentenced within a reasonable time after conviction.

Article 8: RIGHTS OF PERSONS CONVICTED OF A CRIME

Everyone who has been convicted of a crime and who in accordance with a sentence of a court of law is serving a term of imprisonment has the right —

(a) to be detained and to be fed under conditions consonant with human dignity and to receive the necessary medical treatment;

(b) to be given the opportunity to develop and to rehabilitate;

(c) to be released at the expiry of his or her term of imprisonment as imposed by the court of law;

Article 9: GOOD NAME AND REPUTATION AND DIGNITY

(a) Everyone has the right to the protection of his or her good name and reputation.

(b) Everyone has the right to the recognition and protection of his or her dignity.

Article 10: PRIVACY

Everyone has the right to the protection of his or her privacy, which means, inter alia, that his or her property or place of residence or employment shall not be entered, that he or she shall not be searched, that his or her property or possessions shall not be seized and that there shall be no interference with or interception of his or her correspondence or other forms of communication;

Article 11: FORCED LABOUR

Everyone has the right not to be subjected to forced labour: Provided that legislation may provide for —

(a) such labour as may reasonably be prescribed to be performed during detention pursuant to a sentence of imprisonment imposed by a court of law; and

(b) reasonable military or civilian national service so that, save during a state of war or the duration of a proclaimed state of emergency, each individual shall have a choice on grounds of religious or conscientious conviction between military and civilian national service of equal duration.

Article 12: FREEDOM OF SPEECH

Everyone has the right to freedom of speech and other forms of expression and to obtain and disseminate information.

Article 13: SCIENCE AND ART

Everyone has the right freely to engage in science and art.

Article 14: LEGAL COMPETENCE

Everyone has the right to perform juristic acts and thereby to acquire rights and to incur obligations.

Article 15: FREEDOM OF MOVEMENT

Everyone has the right to move freely within South Africa and to reside, to work or to engage in any lawful business, occupation, trade, or like activity at any place therein.

Article 16: PASSPORTS, CITIZENSHIP, EXILE OR EXPULSION, AND EMIGRATION

Every citizen has the right —

(a) not to be denied a passport or be deprived thereof;

(b) not to be deprived of his or her South African citizenship;

(c) not to be exiled or expelled from South Africa; and

(d) not to be prevented from emigrating.

Article 17: FREEDOM OF ASSOCIATION

Everyone has the right to freedom of association, which means, inter alia, that no legislation or executive or administrative act shall —

(a) debar or restrain individuals or groups from associating with other individuals or groups;

(b) compel individuals or groups to associate with other individuals and groups;

(c) directly or indirectly make available to an individual who or a group which on the ground of race or colour refuses to associate with any other individual or group, any public or state funds to foster the creation or maintenance of such discrimination or exclusion.

Article 18: RELIGIOUS, LINGUISTIC, AND CULTURAL RIGHTS

Everyone has the right, individually or in the community with others, freely to practise the religion of his or her choice, so that there shall be no prejudice to or favouring of anyone on account of his or her religion, culture, or language.

Article 19: FAMILY RIGHTS

Everyone has the right to protection of the integrity of his or her family and freedom to enter into marriage with any person of his or her choice, which includes the choice of entering a monogamous marriage and having entered into that marriage the maintenance of its monogamous character.

Article 20: RIGHTS OF CHILDREN

(a) Every child has the right to live with his or her parents and to be cared for and brought up by them, unless the interests of the child call for some other arrangement.

(b) Every child has the right to be cared for by the state if there are no relatives with a duty of support towards the child or other persons who are willing or able to care for the child.

(c) Every indigent child has the right to free state-aided medical care.

(d) Every child has the right not to be compelled to perform labour or render services harmful to his or her physical or mental health, upbringing or education or amounting to economic exploitation.

(e) Every child has the right not to be compelled to perform labour or render services for the benefit of the employer of either of his or her parents or any of his or her relatives.

(f) In all legislative, executive, and administrative proceedings the interests of the child shall in all circumstances be paramount.

Article 21: PUBLIC EDUCATION AND TRAINING

Everyone has the right to freedom of choice with regard to the available public educational and training institutions and fields of study: Provided that —

(a) free state education shall be provided up to the end of the primary school phase;

(b) no pupil or student shall on educationally irrelevant grounds be excluded from the available public education opportunities from which he or she may benefit with a view to the acquisition of knowledge, skills, and values;

(c) no state school or state-aided school or institution for education and training shall refuse to admit a pupil or student merely on the ground of his or her race, colour, religion, or ethnic origin;

(d) this Article shall not preclude the establishment and maintenance of private schools or institutions in which no state aid is involved, and such schools or institutions shall have autonomy of choice as to whom they admit;

(e) this Article shall not preclude the granting of state funds in aid of private schools or private institutions which do not discriminate against pupils or students on the grounds of their race, colour, or ethnic descent;

(f) every pupil is entitled, in so far as this is attainable, to be taught all school subjects through the medium of his or her mother tongue or some other language of choice from the first to the last school year.

Article 22: RIGHT TO PROPERTY

(a) Everyone has the right individually or jointly with others to be or to become the owner of private property or to have a real right in private property or to acquire such right or to be or to become entitled to any other right.

(b) Legislation may authorise the expropriation of any property or any other right in the public interest and against payment of just compensation, which in the event of a dispute shall be determined by a court of law.

Article 23: ECONOMIC ENTERPRISE

Everyone has the right freely and on an equal footing to engage in economic enterprise, which right includes the capacity to establish, manage, and maintain commercial undertakings, to acquire property and procure means of production, and to offer or accept employment against remuneration.

Article 24: POLITICAL RIGHTS

Every citizen has the right —

(a) freely to form and to be a member of political parties: Provided that no one shall be compelled to be a member of a political party or to take part in the activities thereof;

(b) to give expression to his or her political convictions in a peaceful manner; and

(c) to be appointed and elected to legislative, executive, and administrative office.

Article 25: ASSEMBLIES, DEMONSTRATIONS, AND PETITIONS

Everyone has the right to assemble and to demonstrate peacefully and unarmed and to canvass for and present petitions.

Article 26: FRANCHISE

Every citizen over the age of eighteen years has the right to exercise the vote on a basis of equality in accordance with the Constitution in respect of legislative and other institutions and other public offices at regular and periodical elections and at referendums.

Article 27: SOCIAL SECURITY

Everyone has the right —

(a) to form employees' or employers' organisations and, if he or she qualifies therefore, to become a member of any such organisation of his or her choice or not to become a member thereof;

(b) to obtain employment in accordance with the principles of supply and demand and accordingly to make use of the available opportunities of employment;

(c) lawfully to make provision for any costs that may arise from his or her mental or physical illness and that of his or her dependants, as well as the costs of pregnancy, loss as a result of unemployment, disability, accident, or age;

(d) lawfully to make provision for the maintenance of a reasonable standard of living for himself or herself and his or her dependants.

(e) lawfully to provide for his or her proper education and training and that of his or her dependants with a view to the development of each to his or her potential;

(f) to claim the available state assistance to provide for his or her own necessary subsistence and medical needs where he or she is unable to provide for such needs by reason of physical or mental illness or disability and where there is no person who may by virtue of a duty of support be compelled to provide for such needs.

Article 28: EMPLOYEES' RIGHTS

Every employee has the right —

(a) to work under safe, acceptable, and hygienic conditions;

(b) to work reasonable hours;

(c) to be given sufficient opportunity for rest, recreation, and leave;

(d) to receive equal payment with other employees for corresponding production of an acceptable quality, due regard being had to such aspects as qualifications, experience, the means of the employer, and the forces of supply and demand in the labour field;

(e) to the protection of his or her physical and mental well-being;

(f) to make provision against the risk of unemployment and accidents during the course of employment;

(g) to take part in collective bargaining;

(h) to take part in strikes and to withhold labour;

(i) not to be subject to unfair labour practices.

Article 29: EMPLOYER'S RIGHTS

Every employer has the right —

(a) to offer employment and to engage employees in accordance with his or her needs, due regard being had to the fitness, qualifications, and level of training and competence of the employee;

(b) to require of an employee adequate production of an acceptable quality and to lock out labour;

(c) to terminate the service of an employee in accordance with the common law or in accordance with his or her contract of employment with the employee, or in accordance with any relevant enactment, whichever of these or whichever combination thereof applies;

(d) of his or her free will to associate or to form a group with others, or not to do so;

(e) in accordance with the law to apply the principle of "no work, no pay";

(f) to run his or her business, particularly with a view to its economic viability and continued existence;

(g) where necessary, and in his or her own discretion, to make use of alternative labour to maintain production or service;

(h) to negotiate and to bargain collectively or individually;

(i) to be protected from unfair labour practices such as intimidation and victimisation.

Article 30: ENVIRONMENTAL RIGHTS

Everyone has the right not to be exposed to an environment which is dangerous to human health or well-being or which is seriously detrimental thereto and has the right to the conservation and protection of that environment.

Article 31: REVIEW OF ADMINISTRATIVE ACTS AND SUBORDINATE LEGISLATION

Everyone has the right to have civil disputes settled by a court of law and to have recourse to the Supreme Court to review, by virtue of its inherent jurisdiction, any subordinate legislation and any executive act and any administrative act.

Article 32: RULES OF NATURAL JUSTICE

Everyone has the right to have the rules of natural justice applied in administrative proceedings and actions in which, on the grounds of findings of fact and of law, the rights or legitimate expectations of an individual or a group are infringed or likely to be infringed, and in such cases every person having an interest in the matter has the right to be furnished on demand with the reasons for a decision.

Article 33: APPLICATION OF SOUTH AFRICAN LAW

Everyone has the right to have South African law, including the rules of South African Private International Law, applied in all proceedings before a court of law: Provided that legislation may provide for the application of the choice of legal rules relating to and judicial notice of the law of indigenous groups or the religious law of religious groups: Provided further that in civil proceedings such indigenous or religious law shall be applied only if all the parties agree thereto.

Article 34: CIRCUMSCRIPTION AND SUSPENSION

(1) Circumscription

With the exception of the rights, procedures, and institutions referred to in Articles 1; 3; 4(b) and (c) ; 5; 6(a) to (e) inclusive; 7; 8; 9(b) ; 11; 16(c) and (d) ; 17; 18; 19; 20; 21; 22(b) ; 24(a) and (b) ; 31; 32; 34; 35; 36; 37; 39; 40, and 41, the rights, procedures and institutions set forth in this Bill may be circumscribed by legislation of general force and effect:. Provided that such circumscription —

(a) shall be permissible only in so far as it is reasonably necessary for considerations of state security, the public order and interest, good morals, public health, the administration of justice, public administration, or the rights of others or for the prevention or combating of disorder and crime; and

(b) shall not derogate from the general substance of the right in question.

(2) Suspension

(a) The rights set forth in this Bill may be suspended only in accordance with enabling legislation relating to a state of emergency, such legislation to be passed by the highest legislative body and to be of temporary operation.

(b) Where such suspension is so effected the following requirements shall be complied with:

(i) A state of emergency shall be proclaimed only where the security or continued existence of the state is threatened by war, invasion, or general insurrection and the proclaiming of a state of emergency is reasonably necessary to bring about peace or order;

(ii) A state of emergency shall not be proclaimed for a period exceeding six months from a given time.

(iii) The said legislation relating to the proclamation of a state of emergency shall provide that, within three weeks after the proclamation of the state of emergency, not less than two-thirds of the directly elected members of the highest legislative body shall ratify the proclamation of the state of emergency and the rules and regulations that will apply during the state of emergency.

(iv) Legislation relating to the state of emergency or regulations made thereunder shall not permit, authorise, or sanction the cruel or inhuman treatment of persons, the retroactive creation of crimes, detention without trial, indemnity of the state or any officer of the state for acts done during the state of emergency, or the subjective discretionary use of force by any officer of the state or government: Provided that —

(aa) the foregoing notwithstanding, Articles 1; 2; 3; 4; 5; 6(a) , (b), (c), (e), (f) and (g); 7; 8; 9; 11; 14; 16(b) and (c); 17(b) and (c); 18; 19; 20; 21; 22; 24; 26; 31; 32; 33; 34; 35; 36; 37; 39(b) ; 40; and 41 shall remain of force and effect and shall not be suspended;

(bb) any person detained under the emergency measures shall within seven days or on the first succeeding court day thereafter be brought under a court of law and be charged in writing or informed in writing of the reason for his or her detention, failing which he or she shall be entitled to be released from detention unless on good cause shown a court of law orders further detention.

Article 35: TESTING RIGHT OF THE COURTS

(a) Any law, enactment, or regulation of whatever nature of any legislative body in South Africa or any executive or administrative act which violates any of the rights set forth in this Bill or which exceeds any of the circumscriptions or suspensions herein permitted shall to the extent of such violation or excess be invalid.

(b) Any court in which an alleged violation or excess as referred to in paragraph (a) hereof is raised shall be competent to pronounce judgement thereon.

(c) The Constitutional Chamber of the Appellate Division shall hear all appeals before the Appellate Division, in which, in the opinion of the Chief Justice, the only or main issue or issues arise from the provisions of the bill of rights, the other provisions of the Constitution Act, the Constitution in general, and executive or administrative acts. The Chief Justice shall therefore place all appeals to the Appellate Division on the roll of either the General Chamber or the Constitutional Chamber.

(d) Any individual, juristic person, or association has the capacity on behalf of himself or herself or itself or any other individual or any group or class of persons to test by virtue of the provisions of this Bill, the validity of any legislative, executive, or administrative act by applying to the appropriate Division of the Supreme Court for a declaratory order not-withstanding the fact that the applicant is able to prove only an indirect interest or indirect prejudice.

Article 36: HUMAN RIGHTS COMMISSION

(a) There shall be a permanent, full-time Human Rights Commission under the chairmanship of a Judge of Appeal or retired Judge of Appeal which shall —

(i) assume responsibility for and coordinate education and informa-tion in respect of democratic values and human rights in South Africa and initiate educational programmes and information projects;

(ii) fulfil an advisory function in respect of —

(aa) any question as to the consistency with this Bill of proposed legislation at any level of government;

(bb) any question as to the consistency with this Bill of any existing legislation;

(cc) any question as to any need that may exist for the extension of the protection of human rights and shall make recommendations to the legislature and the executive and administrative authorities regarding additional measures of any nature whatever;

(iii) inquire, on its own initiative or on the grounds of complaints lodged, into alleged violations of human rights and publicly and in writing report thereon to the highest legislative body.

(b) Further provision shall be made in the Constitution for the compo-sition and additional functions of the said Commission.

Article 37: OMBUDSMAN

(a) There shall be a permanent full-time Ombudsman who shall on his or her own initiative or in response to representations made —

(i) investigate complaints of maladministration by executive or ad-ministrative bodies or persons, including the violation of human rights as contained in this Bill;

(ii) investigate complaints against state institutions or administrative bodies or officers or employees thereof regarding unfair, unjust, and discourteous conduct which infringes or has infringed human rights as contained in this Bill;

(iii) act on behalf of groups of individuals, including patients in hospitals, taxpayers, pensioners, prisoners, children, and other groups, whose individual rights have been prejudiced or are likely to be prejudiced by a specific act or acts by the executive authority or the administration;

(iv) generally watch over the upholding and respecting of human rights by the executive and administrative bodies and officers, and himself or herself take the initiative in protecting the human rights set forth in this Bill;

(v) institute enquiry as to whether or not acts done by the executive or administrative authorities under powers conferred by subordinate or delegated legislation and which appear to infringe the human rights set forth in this Bill are unconstitutional;

(vi) through investigation, mediation, conciliation, and negotiation endeavour to reach a settlement between the complainant and the body or person complained of, which may include obtaining an apology, revoking a decision or ruling, reconsidering the complainant's application or request, or effecting a change in policy or practice;

(vii) cooperate with the Human Rights Commission with a view to attaining the aims and objects of the Commission;

(viii) in respect of every investigation carried out by him or her report in writing, at least once each year, to the highest legislative body concerning his or her findings relating to the infringement of human rights and the steps and actions taken or recommended by him or her, such report to be published for general information simultaneously with submission thereof to that legislative body.

(b) Further provision shall be made in the Constitution for the functions of the Ombudsman.

Article 38: POSITIVE PROMOTION OF ALL HUMAN RIGHTS

Apart from the duty of all legislative and executive and administrative institutions of the state not to infringe the fundamental rights set forth in this Bill, all the said institutions shall use those fundamental rights as guidelines in instituting and carrying out legislative programmes and executive and administrative planning and action for the promotion of those rights.

Article 39: OPERATION IN RESPECT OF THIRD PARTIES

(a) The rights set forth in this Bill shall be exercised by every individual in such a manner as will not infringe the rights granted under this Bill to any other individual.

(b) In the interpretation of all legislation, including legislation regulating only the relations between persons, the court shall have regard to the provisions of this Bill and shall as far as may be appropriate construe the said legislation in a manner consonant with the values enshrined in this

Bill.

Article 40: APPLICATION OF BILL

The provisions of this Bill shall apply to all existing and future legislation and to all executive and administrative acts done after the date of the coming into operation of this Bill.

Article 41: AMENDMENT OR REPEAL

This Bill, including this Article, shall not be amended or repealed save by a two-thirds majority of the votes of all the directly elected members entitled to vote in the highest legislative body, ratified by the same majority of votes cast in a referendum in which everyone entitled to vote in an election for the said body may cast his or her vote.

■ National Party (1991)

Constitutional Rule in a Participatory Democracy

National Party proposals for a future democratic South African constitution

BASIC POINTS OF DEPARTURE

The National Party has repeatedly committed itself to the creation of a new constitutional dispensation through negotiation. Such a new dispensation must be based on certain fixed points of departure. A system must be sought which, inter alia

■ ensures that universally accepted values and norms in South Africa are maintained
■ is based on universal franchise in a democratic structure of government
■ is free from apartheid and discrimination in any form
■ is free from domination
■ establishes an ordered and orderly society
■ makes good government possible
■ ensures justice for all
■ promotes a market-oriented economy coupled with private initiative and social responsibility
■ accommodates the cultural differences in South Africa
■ enables all South Africans to share in peace, progress and prosperity.

There are considerable differences of opinion as to the specific constitutional model in which these basic points of departure may best be realised. In order to achieve the best possible result the National Party is striving for

■ negotiation at national level in order to reach agreement on the broad structure of government and to establish the position of central, regional, and local authorities within that structure
■ negotiation at regional level so that the needs, aspirations, and problems of the residents of such a region may be properly accommodated and
■ negotiation at local level in order to accomplish cooperation and harmony at grassroots level.

STRUCTURAL PRINCIPLES

A Three-Tier Government

The National Party proposes a three-tier government in which full legislative and executive functions and authority are conferred on central government and regional and local authorities. Regional and local authorities are therefore not merely administrative extensions of the central government; they are not merely the consequence of decentralised administration. On the contrary, every tier is "government" in its own right, with

its own
■ elected authority that is responsible to the voters
■ legislative and executive power
■ tax base.

A three-tier system of government takes account of
■ the rich diversity of the population of South Africa, the needs of communities in regional and local context, and the consequent need for self-determination in regional and local context
■ the need to bring government as close to the people as possible, so that decisions can be taken at a level where the citizen's position is best understood
■ the need for a rationalised and effective state administration.

The question is how the boundaries of regions are to be determined for regional government purposes. It is essential in any event for the present multiplicity of second-tier governments, consisting of four provinces, six self-governing territories, and three own affairs administrations, to be simplified and included in a single system of regional government. It is suggested that the present nine development regions may present a good starting point for negotiation about new regional boundaries. Naturally adjustments to these will have to be considered. The present development regions which may be used as a starting point currently comprise

Region A (Western Cape), Region B (Northern Cape), Region C (Orange Free State and Qwaqwa), Region D (Eastern Cape), Region E (Natal and Kwazulu), Region F (Eastern Transvaal and KaNgwane), Region G (Northern Transvaal, Lebowa, and Gazankulu), Region H (the PWV area and KwaNdebele) and Region J (Western Transvaal).

Although the present development regions include the four independent national states (the TBVC states) in terms of agreements for purposes of cooperation regarding regional development, their relationship with a new South Africa will have to be negotiated with each state individually.

As far as local authorities are concerned, municipal boundaries will have to be delimitated on an appropriate geographical basis so as to replace current boundaries based on race. A delimitation authority could handle this task. A question which requires attention is whether the concepts "municipality" or "city council" should possibly be extended to include the whole of a district (that is, a town together with its rural district).

The Separation of Powers

A clear separation of the legislative, executive, and judicial powers is a characteristic of modern democracies. Such separation is accepted as an essential feature of a new dispensation in South Africa.

The separation of powers prevents an overconcentration of power being vested in a specific part of government and contributes to achieving checks and balances. Consequently the constitution must contain arrangements that
■ prevent the executive authority from dominating the legislative author-

ity, and vice versa
- confer on Parliament the authority to call the executive to account
- confer on the judicial authority jurisdiction, based on the Constitution and the Charter of Fundamental Rights, to test and set aside Acts of Parliament and actions of the executive.

PARTICIPATORY DEMOCRACY: TWO PILLARS

For the framework sketched above to really satisfy the unique needs of the South African situation, and to conform to our basic points of departure, it is necessary to frame the constitution in such a way that
- a constitutional state is established
- a system is designed which will ensure the realisation of a participatory democracy.

The First Pillar: A Constitutional State

The term rule of law is used in constitutional debates to express the pursuit of justice and a limit on the power of the state.

The National Party accepts the rule of law as the foundation on which such endeavours must be based. However, this term was developed within the distinctive milieu of the Westminster system and an unwritten constitution. The term constitutional state is therefore used to indicate that we are striving for a system that may rightfully be described as "constitutional government": a system in which the constitution and the law are the source of justice, and at the same time serve to curtail the powers of government.

The concept "constitutional state" expresses the view that the constitution of a country should regulate the power of government in such a way that freedom, justice, and legal certainty are guaranteed for all.

Thus we are concerned with a constitutionally entrenched legal dispensation involving seven principles:
- The constitution must be the all-embracing criterion and guideline for the state and the citizen. Consequently it will enjoy a higher status than all other law; it may only be amended if special procedures are followed and compliance with its prescriptions will be enforceable by the courts.
- A Charter of Fundamental Rights must be constitutionally protected and legally enforceable. This will equip the citizen to protect himself against unlawful action by government. Effective protection of the fundamental rights of the individual will at the same time offer important protection of the interests of groups and communities.
- An independent judiciary is a cornerstone of the constitutional state. An independent court structure must have the jurisdiction to declare Acts of Parliament and actions of the government null and void if they do not comply in all respects with the criteria of the Constitution and the Charter of Fundamental Rights. The individual must have free access to the courts.
- Organisations and institutions that function in nonpolitical spheres must enjoy the highest possible measure of self-determination in respect of their own fields of interest in the community. Full recognition must be given to their autonomy in this regard.

■ Mechanisms must be built in to prevent the abuse of government power and state structures. The office of an independent and objective Ombudsman must be instituted. The Auditor-General, the Public Service Commission, and the Reserve Bank must be vested with greater autonomy, and a procedure for the appointment of judges must ensure the objectivity, professionalism, and independence of the Bench.

■ The integrity of the constitution must be ensured. The constitution must be protected against infringements. A system must be developed that ensures effective and balanced control over the security forces as the instrument for maintaining the constitution at all times.

■ An impartial and professional civil service with career security for employees must be ensured and the Commission for Administration must be vested with sufficient authority.

Building these seven principles into the constitution effectively, will ensure that

■ the interests of the citizens, as entrenched in the constitution, are respected by government

■ the fundamental rights of the individual, including rights exercised in group and community context, are protected against infringement

■ the government remains subject to the law, and cannot take arbitrary decisions

■ the government will not interfere in fields where there is no legal authorisation for doing so

■ the abuse of power and maladministration are prevented

■ the constitution is maintained.

The Second Pillar: Participatory Democracy

By "participatory democracy" is meant that a system of government is developed in which a number of political parties effectively participate and in which power-sharing therefore takes place. This is in contrast to the Westminster system in which one party exclusively enjoys power.

Participatory democracy takes into account the diversity of South African society and the reality of the existence of a multiplicity of socioeconomic and cultural interest groups. Such groups do not exist in the community because they have been created or recognised in terms of legislation, but by virtue of the fact that people naturally and voluntarily associate with one another because they have some kind of interest in common. In its Five Year Action Plan of 1989 the National Party undertook to seek, through negotiation between leaders, a more just and meaningful basis than race and colour on which groups may be defined for purposes of political participation. In the constitutional sphere the political party is the most effective means of furthering the interests of such groups. In other spheres interest groups define themselves in terms of other criteria. The National Party's conviction is that a new constitution should offer the opportunity for every viable political party to play an effective role at local, regional, and central government levels.

This concept may be put into effect in two ways:

■ First, political power may be divided among various authorities. Most important here is the distribution of power among the different tiers of government. This is normally referred to as the principle of devolution of power.

Functions must be distributed among the different tiers of government in such a way that the constitution confers autonomous authority on every tier (that is, original and entrenched authority with which the other tiers of government may not interfere). The constitution must therefore stipulate which powers and duties are to be vested in the central government, regional government, and municipal or local government. In each case it must be determined which tier of government can perform a particular function in the most appropriate and effective manner. While some functions may as a whole be allocated to one of the three tiers, it will be appropriate to spread other functions among all three tiers so as to allocate to each tier that aspect of a function which can be handled there most effectively in the interest of the community.

■ Secondly, an effective say and participation in state power for a number of parties may be brought about.

These principles are elucidated below by outlining the framework of a model.

PARTICIPATORY DEMOCRACY: A POLITICAL MODEL

Introduction

This exposition presents the framework of a model embodying the above principles. The National Party has already received a mandate from the voters to negotiate a new constitution based on these principles. This particular model is not necessarily a final proposal which cannot be amended. It may be revised as a result of further reflection in the NP and by negotiations and also in the light of the expected reports of the South African Law Commission on fundamental rights and on constitutional models that may be appropriate for the South African situation.

CENTRAL GOVERNMENT

Parliament

It is proposed that Parliament should consist of two Houses. Both houses must adopt legislation.

The First House

The First House is elected proportionally, so that each political party receives a number of seats in accordance with the share of the political support which that party enjoys nationally on the strength of a general election. The electoral system may further be so organised that voters are also given the opportunity to express their preference for specific candidates in particular electoral districts, without the requirement of proportionality being sacrificed.

Legislation will be passed by a simple majority, but will be subject to a weighted majority (e.g., two-thirds) in respect of those issues entrenched in the Constitution.

The Second House

A Second House, which is smaller than the First House, is proposed. An equal number of seats in the Second House will be allocated to each region. Each political party which has gained a specified amount of support in the election in the region's legislative body will be allocated an equal number of seats for that region in the Second House. Thus every democratic party which enjoys a significant amount of support in the region, will be represented in the Second House. This will result in equal representation of both the regions and those political parties with significant support.

The functions of the Second House are to

■ deliberate on the bills which are approved by the First House and for which increased majorities are not required and to pass them by a simple majority

■ deliberate on and pass by a weighted majority legislation which
   ❑ amends the constitution
   ❑ relates to the interests of minorities
   ❑ relates to the interests of regions
   ❑ is entrenched in the constitution

■ initiate legislation relating to circumscribed matters and which affects the specific interests of minorities and regions.

Executive Authority

The core of the National Party's proposals is that the executive should not be constituted from one party alone, but from members of a number of the major parties.

Thus a multiparty government (of which Western European coalition-style government is an example) is preferred to a system where the majority party alone forms the executive of government. (The Westminster system usually results in this situation.)

The present constitution excessively concentrates functions and authority in a single person, the State President. Instead, it is proposed that the office of head of state and of government should be vested in a collective body known as the Presidency. The Presidency will consist of the leaders of the three largest parties in the First House. In the event that the three largest parties do not together represent the majority of the voters, the Presidency will be supplemented by as many additional leaders, in order of the size of their party, as may be required to represent a joint majority. A party that qualifies in these terms may however, if it so wishes, abstain from participating.

The chairmanship may rotate among the members on an annual basis. Decisions are taken by consensus. Likewise, a State President may be elected on a rotating basis from the ranks of the Presidency.

The Presidency, by consensus, appoints ministers who form a multiparty Cabinet and who are obliged to carry out the policy of the Presidency.

The two Houses of Parliament may pass a motion of no confidence in the Presidency collectively (but not in individual members), in the Cabinet, and in individual Ministers.

REGIONAL GOVERNMENT

Introduction

It has already been mentioned in the preceding section that provision is made for the representation of the different regions in the Second House of the central Parliament; also, that the present nine development regions may be used as a point of departure for the planning of a regional government dispensation. The composition of such a regional government is suggested as follows:

To ensure participatory democracy and power-sharing for a number of political parties, measures for effective minority protection must also be built in at the second and third levels of government in accordance with the principles already embodied at the first level.

The Legislative Authority

An elected Legislative Council for every region is proposed, in which

■ the numerical strength is determined by the size of the voting population

■ the representatives are elected from electoral districts within the region on a proportional basis

■ indirect nomination of part of the Legislative Authority by third-tier authorities, or possibly by subregions, may also be considered

■ decision-making procedures provide for the protection of minority interests and certain circumscribed matters.

The Executive Authority

The Executive Committee of a region may be made up of three to five leaders of those political parties which have a predetermined minimum representation in the Legislative Council, according to the same system as already set out in regard to the Presidency at the first level. The Executive Committee must function collectively as a unit, and each of its members must be responsible for a specific portfolio.

Sub-regions

Within regions, the possibility of sub-regions or district authorities for districts with particular interests and cohesion may be provided for as an option.

LOCAL GOVERNMENT

Constitutional Framework

The National Party proceeds from the following points of departure:

■ the basis of the local government system — namely that local government is a democratically elected, autonomous tier of government, which within its own area of jurisdiction is in each case vested with legislative, executive, and fiscal authority — must be laid down in the constitution and entrenched.

■ A national Local Government Act, which must be a product of the (national) constitutional negotiation process, must establish the broad principles and structural framework of local government.

■ Following negotiation at local level, a formal agreement or charter must be drawn up for every local authority and promulgated under the Local Government Act, to serve accordingly as the "local constitution" of the local authority concerned.

Participatory Democracy at Local Level

At local government level the term participatory democracy gains a particular meaning. At this level, where people live, work, and take their recreation from day to day, it is essential that a framework be created to promote good order and cooperation. It is unfortunately true, however, that this is precisely where the large gap between developed and underdeveloped areas becomes evident. In the interest of the development of stable communities (and therefore in the interests of South Africa's future), a dispensation must be established that is politically fair to all components of society. This balance must be given practical expression in the composition of the political authority at local level, the city council. Within the boundaries of every town or city only one nonracial local authority will be established with one administration and one tax base.

The City Council

Participatory democracy may be put into effect at local level in various ways, inter alia by

■ electing the City Council on the basis of the representation of wards, and accepting property valuations and voter numbers in a fair proportion to one another as the basis for the delimitation of wards

■ determining the franchise in accordance with both the interests of all lawful residents and the particular interests of owners, lessees, and ratepayers

■ considering a combination model in which, for example, half of the city councillors are elected by a voters' roll on which the names of all residents appear, and the other half by a voters' roll containing only the names of owners, lessees, and ratepayers.

■ providing for special decision-making procedures, such as increased majority votes in the city council, in respect of certain circumscribed sensitive matters.

Neighbourhood Councils

The National Party acknowledges the need to provide, within the broad boundaries of a municipal area, for the exercise by a geographical neighbourhood of an option of self-determination over community interests. This concept involves that

■ a geographical area within a municipal area may decide on a voluntary basis to institute a Neighbourhood Council

■ a Neighbourhood Council may be elected by the residents of the neighbourhood

■ autonomous power may be entrusted to the Neighbourhood Council over neighbourhood matters, such as

❏ the regulation of norms and standards for the residential environment
❏ the granting of licenses/permits in regard to the use of property
❏ the provision of communal facilities
❏ security matters and civil protection
❏ matters that may be allocated to a Neighbourhood Council in terms of other legislation, for example education and welfare
■ the Neighbourhood Council may impose an additional levy on the residents for specific projects within its area of jurisdiction.

Ratepayers' associations and civic organisations can play an important role in the establishment of Neighbourhood Councils.

FREEDOM AND JUSTICE FOR ALL IN THE NEW SOUTH AFRICA

The main points of the National Party's thinking on constitutional affairs are outlined in this document. The principles which the National Party would like to see built into a constitution must form a framework within which a variety of arrangements together form a network in order to guarantee true freedom and justice for all. Thus reliance is not placed on single prescriptions or arrangements to protect the rights of individuals or minority groups. The proposed guidelines in fact all combine to protect the interests of all South Africans in three fields in particular:

Political Say and Effective Participation in Government Structures

The proposed guidelines are aimed at ensuring a say in political matters and effective participation in the entire spectrum of government structures. In this regard attention is drawn in particular to the important role played by the Second House: It has the important function of protecting the constitution and minority as well as regional interests. The fact that the executive power is vested in a Presidency in which the most important leaders are included guarantees participation across the widest possible political spectrum. Finally, the arrangement proposed for the local level aims to achieve a sound balance, while the concept of neighbourhood councils can ensure an orderly and peaceful residential environment. Domination is eliminated by these proposals.

Protection Against the Abuse of Power

The point of departure that South Africa should be a constitutional state is regarded by the National Party as being of cardinal importance. In the guidelines sketched in this document the emphasis consequently falls on matters such as checks and balances, the distribution of power, a Charter of Fundamental Rights, the integrity of the constitution, and above all the supremacy of the law, which by means of an independent judiciary protects the freedom of each citizen. The arbitrary exercise of power is eliminated by these proposals.

The Recognition of Free and Autonomous Fields of Interest of Communities

The guideline that government intervention in the autonomy of institutions in the nonpolitical sphere should be limited has important implications for the citizen. This guideline, which fits into the whole network of constitutional arrangements, takes account of the fact that numerous activities in a society are performed by a variety of groups, often in nongovernmental organisations and institutions, and that it is precisely here that freedom to proceed without interference by the state must be protected. Cultural, religious, and sporting activities are specific examples of these, as well as various occupational, professional, and other spheres of interest, which contribute to the orderly structure of society through autonomous institutions. The reality of groups, legitimate group interests, and the fact that there are always minority groups in society, are acknowledged in the National Party's guidelines. Therefore it is suggested that the government's ability to interfere unneccesarily should be limited. By building this principle into the constitution effectively (as well as by giving it further expression in the Charter of Fundamental Rights) communities are guaranteed self-determination in regard to business and professional life, trade union affairs, education and culture, sport, religion, language, tradition, and nonpolitical community life.

Notes and readings

1. Civil society: The triumph of private life

1. "Ciao, Ceausescu," *The New Republic*, January 22, 1990, p 7.
2. Andrei Codrescu, "Big Chills: My high school reunion, in Romania," *Harper's Magazine*, November 1990, p 72.
3. Michael Meyer, "In Romania's Rubble," *Newsweek*, May 28, 1990, p 14.
4. "Ciao, Ceausescu," *The New Republic*, p 7.
5. Patrick Brogan, *Eastern Europe 1939 - 1989, The Fifty Years War* (London: Bloomsbury Publishing, 1990), p 225.
6. *Ibid*.
7. "Ciao, Ceausescu," *The New Republic*, p 7.
8. Brogan, p 230.
9. "Will the Romanian tragedy continue?," *Freedom Bulletin*, International Freedom Foundation, May 1990, p 5. Also, Brogan, p 226.
10. *Newsweek*, May 28, 1990.
11. *The Star*, February 9, 1990.
12. Some definitions of civil society exclude the productive base of the economy, saying civil society is life away from state power *and* capitalist power. But that's not convincing. It seems more like a last-ditch, futile effort by socialists to pretend that the power a company has (having to lure money from you) is the same power a state has (taking your money at gunpoint). It's also problematic because such definitions tend to include trade unions. This means organised workers can be part of civil society but organised employers cannot be, a fairly hairsplitting position. I think civil society works better as a broad term for the private sector, serving as a reminder of the pluralising and democratising effects of competitive capitalism — and the stultifying and dehumanising effects of socialism and fascism.

    Other definitions and uses of the term civil society in South Africa include this one by political analyst and former liberal opposition leader Frederik van Zyl Slabbert, writing in the *Sunday Times* of December 29, 1991:

    > Civil society is that arena in the individual's social life in which he or she can participate free from direct party-political or government control, eg communal life, voluntary associations in churches, charities, sports clubs, ratepayers' associations, etc.
    >
    > In authoritarian society this part of societal life was politically managed: where we slept, made love, went to school, bought property, went to church, played sport, etc....
    >
    > Will the old political management of civil society be replaced by new political management, or will civil society be allowed to develop autonomy?

13. Mark Swilling, a researcher at the University of the Witwatersrand's Centre for Policy Studies, distinguishes three arenas of life: civil society, political society, and the state.

Civil society, he writes in the book *Policy Options for a New South Africa* (Pretoria: HSRC Publishers, 1991, pp 88-89), "comprises the institutions and in[n]umerable base organisations that facilitate and co-ordinate everyday social existence outside the state and beyond the private [personal] sphere. The church, the schools, cultural formations, the workplace, and the communities where people reside are the five most important arenas in civil society within which people organise themselves for daily life."

He continues: "Within them, a wide range of value systems, practices and social relationships coexist that are shaped by more than the state or relations to the means of production. Civil society is where the broad mass of people exist, interact, work, communicate, and develop common-sense perceptions of one another on a daily basis."

Political society, he says, contains organisations that explicitly compete for political power: "parties, fronts, political elites, leaders, alliances, elections, legislatures, and certain types of media." In South Africa, when black political society was harassed and outlawed, some organs of black civil society stepped in to perform the mobilising, political function.

And, finally, *the state* is made up of all the components of government from the parliament and the president to state agencies.

Swilling writes:

> It is possible to determine the relative democratic nature of a given state by specifying (a) the degree to which it is controlled by or dominates political and civil society, and (b) the relative balance of each state institution within the overall organisation of state power. It is possible to claim that, ideally, a democratic state should be controlled by an elected party that should, in turn, be accountable in terms of rules determined in political society. Political society, in turn, should facilitate the expression of the full range of interests and groups in civil society. If these conditions pertain, then it is theoretically possible for the state to govern with minimal levels of direct coercion. In reality, however, politics is about the competitive manipulation of power to secure degrees of control of the state which is, in turn, the most powerful institution in society.

14. *Sapa Reuter*, July 20, 1990.
15. *Ibid.*
16. Alan Berlow, "Ballots and Bullets," *The New Republic*, June 4, 1990, p 22.
17 *The Star*, April 27, 1990.
18 Koigi wa Wamwere, "Kenya — independence without freedom," *Index on Censorship*, 7/1990, p 17.
19. "Kampuchea, National reconciliation or civil war?," *New Era*, June 1989, p 23.
20. *Amnesty International Report, 1988* (London: Amnesty International Publications, 1988), p 193.
21. *Ibid*, p 107.

22. *Ibid*, p 235.
23. *Ibid*, p 70.
24. *Human Rights Around the World - ISHR Report 1987* (West Germany: International Society for Human Rights, 1987), p 276.
25. *The Star* , April 27, 1990.
26. *Weekend Mail*, July 27-29, 1990
27. "Castro's Economic Woes Cast Doubt on Survival," *Developing World Monitor*, Vol 1, No 3, July 1990.
29. *Weekly Mail*, April 5-11, 1990.
30. "For the love of the game: A short history of soccer in South Africa," *Learn and Teach*, No 5, 1990, p 10.
31. "The case for urgent economic intervention," *Work in Progress*, Nov/Dec 1989, p 38.
32. "Onto the Offensive," *New Nation*, July 14-20, 1989, p 12.
33. Saul Molobi, "A Roarrr from the Bush," *Learn and Teach*, No 4, 1990, p 38.
34. *Saspu National*, Vol 1 No 2, 1990, p 10.
35. *South*, May 17-22, 1990.
36. *Sunday Times*, September 16, 1990.
37. Albie Sachs, "The gentle revenge at the end of apartheid," *Index on Censorship*, No 4, 1990, p 3.
38. "An Interview with Comrade Joe Slovo," *Learn and Teach*, No 4, 1990, p 12.
39. Karl von Holdt, "Insurrection, negotiations, and 'war of position,'" *South African Labour Bulletin*, September 1990, p 14.
40. *Ibid*, p 17.
41. Timothy Garton Ash, *We The People* (Cambridge: Granta Books, 1990), p 147.
42. Edward H Crane, "The Revolution in Eastern Europe Is Coming West," *Cato Policy Report*, May/June 1990, p 2.

2. Apartheid economics: Apartheid was socialism

1. WOSA. "Statement on behalf of the Central Committee to the First National Conference of the Workers' Organisation for Socialist Action, Johannesburg, May 31, 1991." Pamphlet.
2. *Sunday Star*, June 9, 1990. See also "Political Report. Presented by Joe Slovo, General Secretary of the SACP, 5 December 1991." Mimeo.
3. *Sunday Times*, March 24, 1990.
4. *Business Day*, June 28, 1990.
5. Jay Naidoo spoke on March 1, 1987, at Soweto's Funda Centre to a Health Workers Association Conference. Quoted in Don Caldwell, *South Africa: The New Revolution* (Johannesburg: Free Market Founda-

tion Books, 1989), pp 53, 229.

6. See Merle Lipton, *Capitalism and Apartheid* (Cape Town: David Philip, 1986) and Walter Williams, *South Africa's War Against Capitalism* (Cape Town: Juta, 1990).

7. Lawrence Mavundla and Mehlaleng Mosotho, *Freedom to be Enterprising* (Johannesburg: Pavement Books, 1991), p 40.

8. *Saturday Star*, April 27, 1991.

9. *Sunday Times*, November 24, 1991.

10. *Business Day*, November 29, 1991.

11. Blacks, especially, enjoyed virtually no capitalist rights. Until recent deregulation, the government owned all the land in black townships, owned the houses, owned the schools, ran or controlled transportation, and shut down home businesses. Blacks lived without rights in these pockets of state socialism.

    Whites, though heavily controlled (and, in some instances, heavily protected and subsidised), at least enjoyed some capitalist rights. In white-designated areas, people could own property, invest, trade, and build. So these areas developed. Whites would have enjoyed higher living standards without the apartheid-inspired controls, but they suffered far less than their black countrymen.

12 William Hutt, *The Economics of the Colour Bar* (London: Andre Deutsch, 1964) p 130.

13. Rian Malan, *My Traitor's Heart* (London: The Bodley Head, 1990), p 19.

14. Lipton, p 293.

15. *Ibid*, pp 35, 269.

16. Hutt, p 159.

17. *Ossewa Brandwag: Vanwaar en Waarheen?* (Johannesburg: Afrikaanse Pers, 1942), p 20.

18. Lipton, p 327.

19. *Ibid*.

20. Capitalism is not a free-for-all, as less-informed critics maintain. It is a system of contracts enforced by courts, in which fraud and the initiation of force are not allowed. Think of a game with referees and players. Government administration of the courts — as a "referee" — is technically a violation of advanced libertarian capitalism (libertarians make the case for private courts and defence). But for this discussion, only laws that make the government a "player" are considered anti-capitalist and illiberal. In South Africa's case, the government has been both an aggressive player and a biased referee, imposing illiberal laws and then frequently overriding judicial attempts to temper such laws.

21. Apartheid and industrial racism flourished only with the help of state-socialist laws — and, then, only for a while. The state's love of racism could not withstand the market's drive for efficiency and equal rights. This liberal view of history questions the views and prejudices of both right and left.

The right must be asked: if blacks are lazy workers and incompetent business people, if they can't manage private property, if they are terrible farmers, if they are wholly unprepared to live in a modern society, why did the government have to seize their land, shut down their businesses, condemn their houses, and reserve jobs for whites? Why did whites need so many laws to protect them from black competition if that competition was no threat?

The left must be asked: if whites are naturally racist, especially white capitalists, why has the government been fighting a century-long battle to force whites to be racist? Why not just let racism blossom under capitalism? Why do you need laws preventing whites from trading with, selling land to, and employing blacks, if whites naturally refuse to do these things in the market?

It's also important to note that, contrary to socialist mythology, "capitalists" did *not* support all apartheid laws. They furiously opposed and circumvented those that raised their costs and ran against their economic interests. As a general rule (individual business people reacted differently, depending on their morals), profit-seeking business owners in the cities supported laws, like the hut tax and Land Acts, that artificially increased the size of their labour pool, thus pushing wage costs down. But they opposed job reservation, influx control, and white/black hiring quotas that prevented them from taking advantage of lower-priced black labour. Left-wing historians would have us believe that business owners gave blanket support to apartheid laws. That would mean that they supported laws creating a pool of "cheap black labour" and then supported job-reservation laws that prevented them from taking advantage of that labour pool, an absurd and contradictory position.

Meanwhile, "capitalist" farmers generally supported laws that forced blacks off the land and supported laws, like job reservation, that made it difficult for blacks to get jobs in the cities. White workers supported laws that kept blacks out of the cities and curbed job opportunities for black competitors who made it to the cities — the opposite position of white industrialists and a similar position to white farmers. (This is why the National Party was historically supported by an alliance of white farmers and white workers.)

Shopkeepers, hotel owners, restaurateurs, and theatre owners — again, as a general rule — opposed social apartheid laws that effectively cut down their pool of customers by 85 percent. This is evidenced by their intensive lobbying efforts to get social apartheid removed and the speed with which private facilities were integrated when race laws were removed. (An example of a hotel owner who *would* support a whites-only segregation law: a racist who doesn't want blacks at his hotel but who doesn't want competing hotels to profit from serving blacks. In other words, he supports the law because it allows him to enjoy his prejudice without being undermined by nonracist competition.)

It is illogical to say that whites supported apartheid in unison, when any particular race law had costs and benefits to different parts of the white community. But the point here is that where whites — "capitalists," farmers, workers — supported an apartheid law, they were supporting a *law*. They couldn't achieve their anticompetitive racist goals without resorting to the power of the state. A free market was not sufficiently racist for them.

22. Hutt, pp 135, 136.
23. *Handhaaf*, August 1980, p 15.
24. Lipton, p 85.
25. "Address by Comrade Jay Naidoo, general secretary of Cosatu, to the 84th National Congress of the South African Communist Party." December 1991. Mimeo.
26. *Weekly Mail*, November 16-22, 1990.
27. *Business Day*, February 21, 1990.
28. *Learn and Teach*, No 4, 1990, p 12.
29. *The Daily Mail*, August 15, 1990. *The Star*, October 22, 1990.
30. Albie Sachs, *Protecting Human Rights in a New South Africa* (Cape Town: Oxford University Press, 1990), p 114.
31. *The Star*, February 26, 1990.
32. *Sunday Times*, April 29, 1990.
33. *Business Day*, July 4, 1990.
34. *Business Day*, February 23, 1990.
35. *Sunday Times*, October 16, 1990.
36. *Financial Times*, August 1, 1990. Reprinted in *The Star*, August 3, 1990.

3. Taxes: Bringing taxes under control

1. For the most part, Sachs seems unaware that his proposed benefits even *have* costs. He simply trots out more and more programmes that the state must undertake. Occasionally, he realises that *somebody* has to pay. For his plan to uplift children, he recommends "appropriate budget backing." He says legal-services centres should be paid for by workers, employers, local governments, central government, and lawyers ("either in terms of a direct levy or of some kind of turnover tax, for example on large conveyances or on the liquidation of huge estates after death"). And he says "parents, employers, and the state" should pay for education, until "free, compulsory, and universal education becomes the order of the day" — in which case, presumably just the "state" would pay. This adds up to vague recommendations to soak companies, lawyers, and the dead. There's no mention of how high

corporate tax rates would have to go or how many rich people would have to die to finance all of his sweeping promises.

2. *Business Day*, January 30, 1989.

3. Don Caldwell, "The poverty of economics," *Financial Mail*, February 3, 1989.

4. Francis Wilson, "Poverty, the state, and redistribution: Some reflections," in N Natrass and E Ardington, eds, *The Political Economy of South Africa* (Cape Town: Oxford University Press, 1990), p 239.

5. *Ibid*, p 236.

6. *Business Day*, October 3, 1991.

7. The tax was increased five cents in March 1991, and another 10 cents in September 1991, bringing it to 50,9 cents. So at the beginning of 1992, when the price of petrol was R1,43 a litre in Johannesburg, more than a third of the price was tax. This does not include other state-mandated charges in every litre of petrol sold: 4 cents for a mandatory insurance programme, 9,2 cents to the state's pipeline network, and 7 cents to an equalisation fund, which is used to steady the petrol price.

8. *Business Day*, November 20, 1990.

9. In my mock "headlines," I am conforming to the standard newspaper headline style of using "2%" to refer to "2 percentage points." The two are, of course, entirely different. A rise in VAT from 10% to 12% is a 20% rise in VAT, or a 2 percentage point rise, but not a 2% rise.

10. *Business Day*, July 10, 1991.

11. *The Star*, October 23, 1991.

12. Albie Sachs, *Protecting Human Rights in a New South Africa* (Cape Town: Oxford University Press), p 165.

13. A major difference between the multiplier effect and the divider effect is that it is possible to see what the government builds — water pipes, homes, schools — while it is impossible to see the wealth it destroys from taxing to pay for it. This is why people believe that the government stimulates growth: they don't see that it destroys at least as much wealth as it creates.

14. In several other passages, it recommends a variation of corporate tax: forcing companies to provide some services ("private corporations would be required to direct resources to training schemes," for example). And it says the state would require that company pension funds invest in government-backed "national development objectives." These fascistic state directives are popular among politicians because they finance pet projects without having to call for a "tax." But they are subject to the same analysis as overt corporate taxation.

15. *Saturday Star*, September 21, 1991. See also *Business Day*, September 23, 1991.

16. *Business Day*, December 19, 1991.

17. These are plans to control government meddling in the economy and people's lives, not abolish it, which I would prefer. None of these tax-

and-spending proposals is guaranteed to eliminate a large, corrupt, antigrowth, plundering government. The proposals simply aim to make it clear to people that when they ask for more government, they are collectively agreeing to take each other's wealth. Each programme embarked on by the government beyond its basic roles of providing police, courts, and defence is a move away from the classical-liberal vision. It is difficult to find a moral justification for this. Also, economic history suggests that each programme, even if approved by voters, will inevitably be corrupt and wasteful.

18. In *South Africa: The New Revolution*, I recommend scrapping anticapitalist laws, dismantling much of the central government, and funding what's left — law and order, courts, defence — with an above-board tax, such as a 5 percent sales tax with no exceptions or a flat 10 percent income tax on each individual's earnings over R10 000 a year. One of these low, broad taxes — or a modest combination of the two — would easily raise the, say, R8 billion needed for the central government to run a lean justice and defence system.

This would be approximately a 90 percent tax cut from the nearly R80 billion the central government planned to collect in 1991. There could still be other taxes at regional and local levels if voters there demanded more services. And police functions could be devolved to communities and regions, and paid for through local taxes.

Also, in the transition to a free economy, I recommended other state spending, specifically school vouchers and golden handshakes to civil servants to get them into the private sector. How to pay for this? The best bet would be to sell off the government's huge portfolio of assets. For example, a R15 billion annual education-voucher programme could be funded for six years by selling off the assets of Eskom (R39 billion), Transnet (R25 billion), the post office (R13 billion), and the Land Bank (R11 billion). At the end of six years of virtually nonexistent taxes, the economy across the country would be much stronger and education funding could then be privatised or funded by local taxes. Another option to pay for these programmes would be to increase sales and income taxes — but still keep them simple and visible.

There are other things that people think the government should do: maintain roads, subsidise health care, give handouts to inefficient businesses that would otherwise die in the marketplace (called "industrial development"). These are best done at the local level, far from Pretoria. There, voters could decide what other government services they want and what taxes they are willing to suffer to pay for them.

Finally, I recommend that the intensive democracy I call for in this book — including regular referendums — also be paid for with privatisation revenues, privatising the state's more than R250 billion of assets as fast as necessary to cover the administrative costs. Before long, referendums would pay for themselves, however. Voters would need to veto only a few wasteful multibillion-rand projects to more than make up for the cost of referendums.

19. Voting on every single spending proposal would be fairly easy at neighbourhood and local levels of government but would arguably be cumbersome at regional or national levels (though as technology advances, direct electronic voting will become much easier and more widely demanded). Even so, voters should at least have to approve overall budgets — health, education, administration — even if they don't vote on every item. And there should be a standard procedure whereby they can petition to force a vote on specific items within a department's budget. This would give voters final veto power over ridiculous projects sneaked into big budgets.

20. *The Star*, March 13, 1991.

21. *Business Day*, May 7, 1991.

22. *The Star*, April 30, 1991.

23. *Weekly Mail*, October 18-24, 1991.

24. Dave Barry, *Dave Barry Talks Back* (New York: Crown Publishers, 1991), pp 281-282.

25. The petrol tax isn't the only hidden tax that needs to be brought into the open. The government imposes hidden, discriminatory sales taxes on a wide range of goods — but it calls these excise duties, import duties, and import surcharges. They are then absorbed into the price of the good, invisible to consumers. In effect, these duties are like having a higher rate of VAT (or GST) on cigarettes, booze, tires, soft drinks, perfume, and innumerable imported goods from computers to textiles. If voters approve of this tax discrimination, it should be made visible.

How? Simply have a two-tier sales tax or VAT, one for normal goods and one for "luxury," "sinful," or imported goods. There could be a 5 percent tax on standard items and a 10 percent tax on the other items. The cashier at a shop could simply press the 10 percent tax button for cigarettes, tires, imported cameras, computer software, or whatever else voters have ruled to be subject to higher taxes. This would remind consumers every day that the government raises the price of some goods more than others. Then we'll see a real debate on the fairness of this discriminatory treatment — which happens secretly today.

Note that I'm not recommending a higher VAT *in addition to* today's excise and import duties — which is what some in government and on the left are calling for. I'm recommending a two-tier rate of VAT *only* if it is implemented to replace today's invisible discriminatory taxes.

4. Affirmative action: Look who's racist now

1. *The Star*, June 20, 1991. Figures quoted in parliament by Gene Louw,

minister of home affairs.

2. *Sunday Star*, February 17, 1991. The act was officially repealed in June 1991.

3. Dinesh D'Souza, *Illiberal Education: The Politics of Race and Sex on Campus* (New York: The Free Press, 1991), p 57.

4. *Ibid*, p 58.

5. Albie Sachs, *Protecting Human Rights in a New South Africa* (Cape Town: Oxford University Press, 1990) pp 22, 150, 19, 186, 60.

6. Herman Belz, *Equality Transformed* (New Brunswick and London: Transaction Publishers, 1991), p 152.

7. "Discussion Document on Economic Policy by the ANC Department of Economic Policy. DEP Workshop, Harare, 20-23 September 1990." Mimeo, p 10.

8. See Thomas Sowell, *Preferential Policies: An International Perspective* (New York: William Morrow and Company, 1990).

9. Affirmative-action laws inevitably lead to government-imposed or court-imposed racial quotas — even if they begin as innocuous-sounding "equal opportunity" or "antidiscrimination" laws. Once the government gets involved in determining whether a hiring practice is racist, it must become race-conscious. Roger Pilon, writing in *Regulation* magazine ("Uncivil Rights," Summer 1991, pp 9-13) explains why laws that are supposed to promote nonracialism degenerate into discriminatory laws requiring apartheid-style racial headcounts:

> [T]he idea behind the Civil War amendments to the [US] Constitution, and the civil rights acts that implemented them, was straightforward and simple: blacks, just as other Americans, were to enjoy equal rights to buy and sell property, to make and enforce contracts, to sue and be sued, to be parties, to give evidence, and generally to enjoy the full and equal benefit of all laws and proceedings for the security of persons and property. In practice, this meant that employment had to be voluntary, either by contract or at will. When at will, as most employment was, both employer and employee would be free to enter into a relationship or to end one at will — that is, for any reason, fair or unfair, or for no reason at all. No one imagined that there was anything such as a right not to be discriminated against in the Fourteenth Amendment's privileges and immunities, much less in its due process or equal protection clauses, or that it was the business of the law to inquire about an employer's motives, which were almost always complex in any event. Freedom of association, grounded in individual liberty, meant essentially the right not to associate, whatever the reason.
>
> Did this arrangement permit discrimination? Of course it did. And discrimination there was, on all manner of grounds. Much of it was "legitimate" (Chinese waiters in a Chinese restaurant tend to make life easier in the kitchen), much of it was not. But we thought that those subjective calls were best left to the parties themselves to make, especially since the criteria the government might use in regulating hiring practices would likely be no better, and might be worse, than the criteria individuals themselves were using. Human prejudice being what it was, we thought it was not the business of government to try to stamp out discrimination through forced associations.

In the South, of course, discrimination took on a particularly noxious character in the form of Jim Crow laws aimed at enforcing both public and private segregation by race. A principle target of the civil rights movement of the 1950s and 1960s, therefore, was the discrimination that had been brought into being through the force of law. It was one thing to allow people not to associate if that was their preference and quite another to force them not to associate. Until such laws were stricken, freedom of association could hardly be realised.

The Civil Rights Act of 1964 at long last abolished what remained of Jim Crow. But the act did not stop there. Instead, it went on to bar all manner of private discrimination, as in Title VII, which prohibited discrimination in the private workplace on the basis of race, colour, religion, sex, or national origin. That is where our current problems began, as a brief discussion will show.

To summarise, the 1964 act created, in effect, a right not to be discriminated against on the stated grounds, which amounted, by implication, to rolling back the right of association by saying that employers (but not employees) could no longer refuse to associate on any of the stated grounds. This meant, of course, that the employer's reasons for refusing to associate, however simple or complex, would now come to the fore. No longer could the employer refuse to associate for any reason or for no reason at all. Now, as a defence against the charge of discrimination, he had the burden of coming forward to show that he was refusing to associate only for a "good" reason. This meant in turn that the courts would increasingly get into the messy and, in principle, infinitely complex business of second-guessing the reasons why an employer may have hired, promoted, or fired as he did. And that led inevitably to quotas. To avoid the costly and often fruitless litigation that was aimed at defending their reasons for doing what they did, employers simply started getting their numbers right.

To understand more fully how Title VII works, we must first come to grips with the idea of *discrimination*, and with the question whether that term should be limited, as one might think, to intentional discrimination or whether it should include something more....

The Equal Employment Opportunity Commission, one of four agencies charged with enforcing Title VII, decided early on, in effect, to [both infer discriminatory intent and to broaden the meaning of *discrimination*]. Recognising the difficulty of proving intentional discrimination, especially when employers might hide behind such seemingly neutral employment practices as job tests, degree requirements, or height-and-weight standards, the EEOC wrote guidelines that prohibited not only "disparate treatment" — the intent test — but those practices that had a "disparate impact" — the effects test — on members of a relevant class. More precisely, once a practice was shown to have a disparate impact — to select against blacks or women, for example — a prima facie case of discrimination was established. The burden then shifted to the employer to validate, modify, or eliminate the practice. Thus, in the end, whether the employer was intentionally discriminating was irrelevant. Because of the difficulties of enforcement, an inference of discrimination was made from the effects of the practice. If the employer could not justify that practice, he had discriminated.

Not surprisingly, the outcry over those enforcement procedures was intense and is by now familiar. Employers with no history of discrimination were incensed that the EEOC was presuming them guilty simply because their workforce composition did not reflect some seemingly arbitrary workforce pool. Disputes about the relevant pool were exceeded only by complaints about the demise of the presumption of innocence. When the Supreme Court sanctioned the EEOC's procedures in 1971 in *Griggs v Duke Power Co* and went on to say that the test by which employers might justify their practices was one of "business necessity," which lower courts later expanded, employers soon realised that they were at a disadvantage. While not impossible, the burden of demonstrating the validity of most selection procedures proved so costly and uncertain that the prudent course was simply to get the numbers right.

Thus, while quotas are no explicit part of the 1964 act — in fact, the act states that nothing in Title VII "shall be interpreted to require any employer...to grant preferential treatment to any individual or group" — quotas are in the act as a practical reality, as any employer who undertakes the costly and often fruitless litigation needed to defend his practices soon discovers....

We are still faced in the end with the question whether the government should be trying to so regulate the millions of personnel decisions that are made every day in the American employment market. Most Americans oppose racism and sexism. But the effort to encode and enforce that opposition has proven a nightmare for employers and many employees alike, however much it may have been a boon for lawyers, politicians, and civil rights professionals. Yet we seem bent on proceeding apace, despite every sign of failure—[unless] the real goal *is* employment by the numbers. Thus, after citing a *Fortune* poll in which CEOs admit that their companies have "specific quotas for hiring and promoting," the administration sanctimoniously adds that the use of quotas "represents a perversion of Title VII and of disparate impact law" and cites Justice Sandra Day O'Connor to the same effect.

If anything should be clear after careful, candid analysis, it is that quotas are *not* a perversion of Title VII: they are a necessary, inescapable product of this entire effort, through law, to stamp out discrimination in the workplace. Employment decisions have about them an inherent element of subjectivity. Yet it is precisely that element—not the underlying unobjectionable acts of hiring, promoting, or firing—that we are trying to regulate when we inquire about an employer's reasons or motives. Not surprisingly, as the business necessity language makes clear, that subjective element is difficult, if not impossible, to regulate—not least because the objective underlying act is *not* itself objectionable. When the law attempts to deal with the subjective alone, it is at its worst. We have here, in fact, a variation on the common law maxim that if an act is not actionable per se, it is not actionable simply because done from a bad motive. Thus, if we have a right not to associate per se, we have a right not to associate for a bad reason. To put the point the other way, proving motive, absent an underlying wrongful act, is so difficult and uncertain that when the law fastens on motive to make wrong what is otherwise unobjectionable, people are forced, as a defence, to try to objectify their behaviour. That is precisely what getting the numbers right is all about.

None of this, of course, is to defend unjustified discrimination, which should be condemned at every turn. Rather, it is to defend the *right* to discriminate, which is a very different thing. It is fortunate that most Americans *do* condemn racism and sexism. But like so much else we condemn, from flag burning to certain forms of "politically incorrect" behaviour, there are better ways to do so than by resorting to the force of law. Imagine that Title VII was abolished tomorrow and that employers were told that they could discriminate at will. Would they do so? Some would, of course. But who would imagine that the executives from the Business Roundtable who sat down recently with the civil rights establishment to try to hammer out a new civil rights bill would start closing their doors to qualified minorities and women? And if they did, who would imagine that they could long afford to do so, either in the marketplace of financial survival or in the marketplace of public opinion—arguably the more powerful market in matters of this kind? Would the behaviour of and responses to any other employer differ? Are those not the two markets in which all employers have to survive?

Forcing the regulation of employment decisions, however, gives rise to some fairly predictable consequences: employers' behaviour changes from cooperative and constructive to defensive and even adversarial. Moreover, the misuse of force, which is inevitable when motives are second-guessed, breeds suspicion and resentment. Who can doubt what poll after poll is showing—that after more than a quarter of a century of efforts to impose fairness in the workplace, ethnic consciousness and hostility in America are at unprecedented levels? In the name of civil rights, attitudes and behaviour are becoming increasingly uncivil. The time may be near to rethink fundamentally our approach to civil rights. If we are serious about equality, perhaps we should give serious thought to returning to the idea that civil rights are the rights we all—employer and employee alike—have equally in civil society. These rights include the right to full freedom of association. If it is respect that civil rights are ultimately all about, only free association can ensure that end.

10. Sowell, p 108.
11. D'Souza, p 163.
12. *Ibid*, p 200.
13. Thomas Sowell, *The Economics and Politics of Race* (New York: William Morrow and Company, 1983), p 29.
14. Sowell, *Preferential Policies*, p 28.
15. *Ibid*, p 50.
16. *Ibid*, pp 82-83.
17. Sowell, *Economics*, p 47.
18. This analysis is concerned with government-mandated (or court-mandated) racism and affirmative action. Private racism is a different matter. A liberal, nonracial constitution would make the government colourblind and prevent it from passing any law that makes reference to race. However, private individuals (and private companies, associations, schools, and clubs) should be able to choose to be racist or not. Some would opt for racist policies (like affirmative action) and others would ignore race.

To see why private discrimination is acceptable, consider the case of the HerdBuoys, a black-run advertising company formed in 1991 that trades off its blackness with the slogan: "Now adding a touch of colour to adland." Racist? Who cares? If you don't like their approach, don't hire them. But there should be one set of rules for everybody: all people and all businesses — black, white, Jewish, Christian, male , female — should have the same freedom as the HerdBuoys to determine who they will associate with, who they will hire, and how they will market themselves. They will reap the benefit or suffer the consequences, depending on how wise their personal choices are.

Nonetheless, private companies that choose to embark on affirmative action (and blacks who support such voluntary policies) should still consider the ill effects outlined in this chapter. Many of my concerns with state-mandated affirmative action apply equally to private discrimination.

19. Interview with author, 1991.
20. Wayne Allen, "Affirmative Action and the Rise of Neotribalism," *The World and I*, May 1991, p 555.
21. In Britain, researchers for the Inner London Education Authority have reported that some minorities do better than whites and some do worse. Black Afro-Caribbean and Bangladeshi pupils were, on average, underachieving educationally, while other Asian groups performed better than both the general and white averages. If discrimination by whites explains everything, why is it that some nonwhites do better than whites? This is too confusing for Britain's racial-equality activists. (*Encounter*, July/August 1990, p 65.)

Their solution? Make successful nonwhites disappear to keep the issue black and white. So affirmative-action supporters group all nonwhites, including Asians, in the "black" category. That way, the success of overperforming nonwhites (in education, income, job advancement, or whatever) is swamped in the new "black" category by underperforming nonwhites — preserving the "proof" that whites discriminate against blacks. (Sowell, *Preferential Policies*, p 176.) But imagine how black-blacks would react if British institutions used Asian-blacks to meet black targets.
22. D'Souza, p 170.
23. *Ibid.*
24. *The World and I*, May 1991, p 557.
25. "Political Report, presented by Joe Slovo, general secretary of the SACP, December 5, 1991." Mimeo, p 8.
26. Sowell, *Economics*. The figures are drawn from Chapter 2, "The Overseas Chinese"; Chapter 3, "Emigrants from Europe"; and Chapter 5, "An International Perspective."
27. *Ibid*, p 139.
28. *Ibid*, p 136.
29. Sowell, *Preferential Policies*, p 132.
30. Figures provided in January 1992 by the Public Auditors and Accounting Board and the Association of Black Accountants of South Africa.
31. D'Souza, p 4.
32. Shelby Steele, *The Content of Our Character* (New York: St. Martin's Press, 1990), p 90.
33. D'Souza, pp 37, 38.
34. *Ibid*, p 39.

35. *Ibid*, p 49.
36. *Ibid*, p 138.
37. *Sunday Star*, September 29, 1990.
38. D'Souza, p 49.
39. *Ibid*, p 4-5.
40. Jim Sleeper, "In The Mix," *The New Republic*, February 18, 1991, p 28.
41. Richard Blow, "Mea Culpa," *The New Republic*, February 18, 1991, p 32.
42. *Mau-Mauing the Media: New Censorship for the New South Africa* (Johannesburg: South African Institute of Race Relations, 1991), p 35.
43. D'Souza, p 167.
44. *Ibid*, p 169.
45. *Tribute*, January 1992, p 1.
46. D'Souza, pp 33-34.
47. *Ibid*, p 45.
48. *Financial Mail*, December 13, 1991.
49. *Sunday Times*, December 9, 1990.
50. Desiree Hansson and Dirk van Zyl Smit, eds, *Towards Justice?* (Cape Town: Oxford University Press, 1991), preface.
51. Merle Lipton, *Capitalism and Apartheid* (Cape Town: David Philip, 1986), p vii.
52. "Dr SM Motsuenyane: Keynote speech delivered at the Euromoney Conference on November 26, 1991 in Cape Town." Mimeo. See also *Sunday Times*, December 2, 1991.

5. Free speech: No more censors now

1. "Towards a Bill of Rights in a Democratic South Africa," *South African Journal on Human Rights*, Vol 6 Part 1, 1990, p 13.
2. *South African Journal on Human Rights*, Vol 7 Part 1, 1991, p 108. This is from an article in which Haysom refers strangely to the draft bill's "unambiguous commitment to a democratic society" and "clear affirmation" of classical civil and political rights.
3. Denis Beckett, "Press freedom and democracy are indivisible," *Sunday Star*, October 28, 1990 — a highly recommended attack on threats to political expression.
4. *Weekly Mail*, May 3-9, 1991.
5. Don Caldwell, "The Non-Racial Thought Police," *Frontline*, February 1991.
6. *South African Journal on Human Rights*, Vol 1 Part 1, 1985, p 34.
7. Gilbert Marcus, "Reasonable Censorship," Hugh Corder, ed, *Essays on Law and Social Practice in South Africa* (Cape Town: Juta, 1988), p 355.
8. *South African Journal on Human Rights*, Vol 1 Part 2, 1985, p 106.
9. *Images of Defiance — South African Resistance Posters of the 1980s* (Johan-

nesburg: Ravan Press, 1991), p 174.
10. "Protect Minority Rights — ANC," *Five Freedoms Forum Newsletter*, May 1990. Suttner amplifies this in a lengthy essay in the *South African Journal on Human Rights*, Vol 6 Part 3, 1990, pp 372-393, in which he calls for "the suppression of doctrines such as apartheid and fascism, which threaten democracy," along with "certain utterances" of fascism, warmongering, and incitement to racism.
11. Suttner, *South African Journal on Human Rights*, Vol 6 Part 3, 1990, pp 379-380.
12. The case for censorship — from whatever direction it comes — is typically riddled with logical errors.

■ **Logical error one.** If expression offends a segment of the population, it must be banned in the interests of those people.

But why don't those people simply refuse to read the offending tract? Freedom of speech does not prevent people from ignoring individually — or even boycotting collectively — the offensive speech.

If huge numbers of Christians will be offended by a film, they shouldn't go to see it — rather than calling in the police to prevent others from going. Likewise, if blacks or communists don't like the way they are characterised in a right-wing newspaper, they shouldn't buy the newspaper — rather than passing a law to shut the paper down.

■ **Logical error two.** The only way to fight a bad idea is to outlaw it.

A better way is to organise a boycott of the disliked newspaper or movie. An even better way is to fight the offensive expression with reason and counterargument — swamping bad ideas with good.

■ **Logical error three.** Once an idea has been shown to be bad, the government must ban it.

Even if it were possible to come up with an objective and unambiguous definition of hate speech or hate literature, there is still no logical justification for banning it. Many ideas are repulsive to many people. But what right does that give them to prevent others from hearing it or expressing it?

■ **Logical error four.** If you don't ban a bad idea, you endorse it, or if you oppose a ban, you endorse the banned view.

The government used to claim that anybody calling for the ANC to be unbanned was an ANC-supporting stooge. Today, the government and its right-wing opposition are still far from embracing a liberal order of free expression. But at least some members have realised, even if grudgingly, that one way to undermine their enemies is to let them spout their slogans. Justifying the unbanning of communism, Adriaan Vlok, then the law-and-order minister, said: "We believe that by openly allowing it, people will be exposed to its real colour." (*Business Day*, July 2, 1990.) And at the Idasa press-freedom conference in November 1990, Koos van der Merwe, a Conservative Party MP, said, only partly in jest: "I think they should get Chris Hani on TV more" — suggesting that the

ANC-SACP leader's bellicose statements bolster the Conservatives' case against the ANC-SACP. Meanwhile, with their calls to ban racist and fascist speech and political movements, the left are fast becoming the new reactionaries.

■ **Logical error five.** If an offensive idea is banned, it will go away.

Shooting the messenger doesn't make the message disappear. Totalitarian governments in eastern Europe finally learned in 1989 that shutting up dissidents doesn't make opposition go away. American universities have been trying to purge student bodies of racism, sexism, and otherisms by silencing their expression. The bizarre belief is that we will all love each other if we can't express our hatred. But gagging people doesn't change the way they feel. In fact, gagging usually backfires. On some American campuses, the racial thought police — through compulsory race-consciousness courses, anti-free-speech codes, and special rules for black students — have accentuated racial differences and arguably heightened racial tension. If a black-led government in South Africa silences racists, the last thing that it will bring about is a decrease in racism.

But ignore the philosophical case and consider the practical consequences of censorship, which suggest that it's inevitably a disaster.

Go back to President de Klerk's watershed speech at the opening of parliament on February 2, 1990, when he announced the unbanning of the PAC, ANC, and SACP. Suppose that, in the same speech, he banned the Conservative Party, the Herstigte Nasionale Party, and the AWB — declaring that there is no room in the new South Africa for parties and ideologies that organise around race and apartheid.

Imagine the outcry. Such a ban would be a recipe for civil war. Conservatives and neofascists would be turned into instant martyrs. Deprived of their parties, symbols, pamphlets, and newspapers, they would turn to mass protests or violence. This would be countered by a massive deployment of police, some of whom would defect to the warring right-wing side. It takes a huge leap of the imagination to see how this would have made South Africa safe for democracy.

But silencing the racist right is exactly what ANC representatives regularly propose to do. At a Lawyers for Human Rights debate in 1991 in Johannesburg, Joe Slovo, an ANC-SACP leader, said that if his recommended constitutional clause prohibiting the promotion of racism caused the Conservative Party to be banned, "so be it."

13. "No Platform for Racists: What should the view of the Left be?," *South African Journal on Human Rights*, Vol 6 Part 3, 1990, pp 397-398.

Similarly, Wits law professor Johan van der Vyver, commenting on the ANC's proposals to outlaw racist speech, argues that a new government should allow "the rhetoric of racial prejudice" to contaminate the air rather than trying to police it out of existence: "Non-racialism has so much to be said in its favour from literally every angle of human existence and behaviour, that the viability of persuasion rather than coercion as a means of promoting its cause ought at least to be put to the test." ("Comments on the Constitutional Guidelines of the African National Congress," *South African Journal on Human Rights*, Vol 5 Part 2, 1989, p 143.)

14. Denis Beckett, *Sunday Star Review*, April 7, 1991.
15. Albie Sachs, *Protecting Human Rights in a New South Africa* (Cape Town: Oxford University Press, 1990), p 105.
16. *Pretoria News*, September 3, 1987. Quoted in *South African Journal on Human Rights*, Vol 4 Part 1, March 1988, p 83.
17. *The Star*, May 1, 1991.
18. *Weekly Mail*, August 31 to September 7, 1990.
19. *Rhodes University Journalism Review*, November 1990, p 9.
20. *Film: What the Censors Think*, Anti-Censorship Action Group (Johannesburg, 1989), p 6
21. Likewise, the government, in its Publications Act of 1974, called for the maintenance of standards that "uphold a Christian view of life" — these to be maintained by a government that was involved in torture, forced removals, spying on mixed-race couples, and the shutting down of mission schools. The government could have outlawed its own un-Christian statute books.
22. "The American Clear and Present Danger Doctrine and SA Publications Control," *South African Journal on Human Rights*, Vol 2 Part 1, March 1986, p 34. Cheh's essay is well worth reading.
23. *Index on Censorship*, No 5, 1990, pp 22-28.
24. *The Star*, January 17, 1991.
25. *Africa Report*, November/December 1990, p 8.
26. *Amnesty International Report, 1988* (London: Amnesty International Publications, 1988) p 78.
27. *Foreign Policy*, Winter 1989-1990, p 148.
28. Anita Coulson, "Press freedoms beckon...but the door is only half open," *Index on Censorship*, 5/90, p 27.
29. In 1987, Stoffel Botha told an international conference on press freedom hosted by *The Star* that freedom of expression will not be allowed to such an extent that it fosters violence, revolt, or "confusion." He added: "But even in trying circumstances we will endeavour to maintain civilised standards." Harvey Tyson, ed, *Conflict and the Press* (Johannesburg: Argus Printing & Publishing Company, 1987), p 137.
30. *Financial Mail*, July 18, 1986.
31. *Mau-Mauing the Media* (Johannesburg: South African Institute of Race Relations, 1991), pp 11, 13.
32. *Ibid*, p 15.
33. *Ibid*, p 58.
34. *Ibid*, p 28.

6. The recall: Keeping government accountable

1. Six of the 15 states exempt judges. Thomas E Cronin, *Direct Democracy:The Politics of Initiative, Referendum, and Recall* (Cambridge, Massachusetts: Harvard University Press, 1989), p 125.
2. *Ibid*, pp 144-148.
3. Jacques Pauw, *In the Heart of the Whore* (Halfway House: Southern Book Publishers, 1991), p 29.
4. *Sunday Times*, February 25, 1990.
5. *Ibid*.
6. *The Star*, March 6, 1990.
7. *The CCB: Origin, actions, and the future of the Civil Cooperation Bureau.* Special Report SR-9. Issued by the Human Rights Commission in association with the David Webster Trust, September 1990.
8. *The Star*, November 14, 1990. *Weekly Mail*, November 16-22, 1990.
9. *Sunday Times*, November 18, 1990.
10. *Sunday Star*, November 18, 1990.
11. *Weekly Mail*, November 16-22, 1990.
12. *The Star*, November 23, 1990.
13. *Business Day*, February 7, 1991.
14. *The Star*, February 20, 1991.
15. *Pretoria News*, February 20, 1991.
16. *The Star*, February 22, 1991.
17. *The Star*, February 21, 1991.
18. *Ibid*.
19. *Business Day*, February 25, 1991.
20. *Weekly Mail*, February 22-28, 1991.
21. *Business Day*, March 8, 1991.
22. *Business Day*, April 10, 1991. *Sunday Star*, April 7, 1991. See also "Open letter to State President De Klerk and his Cabinet from the NEC of the ANC," *History in the Making*, May 1991.
23. *Business Day*, April 10, 1991.
24. *The Star*, April 12, 1991.
25. *The Star*, April 11, 1991. *Business Day*, April 12, 1991.
26. *The Star*, April 12, 1991.
27. *Business Day*, July 22, 1991.
28. *Sunday Star*, July 28, 1991.
29. *The Star*, July 30, 1991.
30. *Business Day*, July 30, 1991.
31. *Ibid*.
32. *Weekly Mail*, December 13-18, 1991.
33. *The Star*, December 15, 1991.
34. *Sunday Times*, December 22, 1991.
35. *Weekly Mail*, January 3-9, 1992.

36. *Citizen*, January 6, 1992.
37. "Address by the State President Mr FW de Klerk at the opening of the fourth session of the ninth parliament of the Republic of South Africa." Cape Town, January 24, 1992. Mimeo.
38. *Sunday Star*, August 8, 1990.
39. *Sunday Star*, August 12, 1990.
40. The number of signatures required for a recall election in the US varies from place to place. Some states base the calculation on the number of registered voters. For example, before a statewide recall vote can be held in Montana, petitioners must collect signatures equalling 10 percent of registered voters in the most recent election. To stage a local recall in Montana, 15 percent of registered voters in the last election in the official's jurisdiction must call for the recall. Other states base the calculation on the number of votes cast in a previous election. In Kansas, for example, the signature requirement is fully 40 percent of votes cast in the last general election for the targeted office. For more details, see Cronin, *Direct Democracy*.
41. If voters recall an *appointed* civil servant, the government would appoint a replacement. It would probably do this with care, since the newly appointed official could be recalled, too.
42. It's unlikely that activists will be able to run successful petition drives against one rude postal clerk or one abusive traffic cop (though that option should remain open). More likely, they will be able to rally support for a petition drive against the employee's bosses: mid-level or high-level postal or police officials. They are responsible for the abusive and incompetent behaviour of their subordinates, and the threat of losing their jobs would be a powerful incentive for them to respond to citizen complaints.
43. *Saturday Star*, September 8, 1990.
44. *The Star*, November 21, 1990.
45. *Sunday Times*, December 22, 1991.
46. *Sunday Times*, February 17, 1991.
47. *Ibid.*
48. *The Star*, December 4, 1990.
49. *Sunday Times*, January 20, 1991.
50. *Sunday Star*, February 25, 1990.
51. *Sunday Times Metro*, February 17, 1991.
52. "Voting for Change," *Leadership*, Vol 6 No 2, 1987, p 48.
53. *Sunday Times Metro*, December 8, 1990.
54. *Sunday Times Metro*, December 2, 1990.
55. *Sunday Star Review*, July 14, 1991.
56. *Weekly Mail*, October 5-11, 1990.
57. *Report of the Committee for Constitutional Affairs on Decision-making and Conflict Resolution Mechanisms and Techniques in Constitutional Systems.* (Pretoria: Government Printer, President's Council 1/90).

58. *Ibid*, pp 77, 102.

7. Maximum democracy: Referendums, local choice, and majority rule

1. I'm using the figure of 5 billion to simplify the mathematics, although that includes children. Parents are assumed to vote in their children's interest.
2. Again, to simplify the mathematics, I'm using the term "51 percent" for the majority instead of the correct "50 percent plus one." But, to illustrate, I'm using 2 500 000 001, which is 50 percent plus one.
3. Legislative — lawmaking — power, as well as administrative functions, must be assumed by these new units of government for devolution to increase democracy. If higher levels of government can simply overrule lower-level policies, devolution fails.
4. As with the world example above, only adults would vote, not the entire population. But the point remains.
5. *Business Day*, May 21, 1990.
6. A thorough case for decentralising government power is made by Frances Kendall and Leon Louw in *South Africa: The Solution* (Johannesburg: Amagi, 1986) and *Let the People Govern* (Johannesburg: Amagi, 1989) and by Kendall in *The Heart of the Nation*. (Johannesburg: Amagi, 1991). See also: Denis Beckett's *The Fallacy of Heroes* (Johannesburg: Saga Press, 1988) and Don Caldwell's *South Africa: The New Revolution* (Johannesburg: Free Market Foundation Books, 1989).
7. *The New Rand McNally College World Atlas* (Chicago/New York/San Francisco: Rand McNally & Company, 1985) and *The Heart of the Nation*.
8. And this does not include degrees of yes and no, as with a partial tax increase. The figure 1 024 is 2 to the 10th power. The formula is x to the nth power, where x is the number of choices — yes or no, in this case — and n is the number of issues. If there are three choices — increase, keep the same, decrease — and 10 issues, the number of combinations is 59 049, or 3^{10}.
9. Frances Kendall and Leon Louw, co-authors of *South Africa: The Solution* and *Let the People Govern*, have called the referendum the "people's veto."
10. Peter H Aranson, "Procedural and Substantive Constitutional Protection of Economic Liberties," *Cato Journal*, Fall 1987, p 350.
11. Pieter le Roux, "The case for a social democratic compromise," in N Natrass and E Ardington, eds, *The Political Economy of South Africa* (Cape Town: Oxford University Press, 1990), p 35.

8. The environment: The state versus the environment

1. "A Dirty Inheritance," *Newsweek*, January 22, 1990. See also "Darkness

at Noon," *Time*, April 9, 1990.

2. *Newsweek*, January 22, 1990.

3. Paul Craig Roberts and Karen LaFollette, *Meltdown: Inside the Soviet Economy* (Washington: Cato Institute, 1990), pp 32, 33.

4. *Newsweek*, January 22, 1990.

5. Roberts & LaFollette, p 34.

6. *Ibid*, p 33.

7. *Ibid*, pp 34, 35.

8. Private ownership does not necessarily mean individual ownership. Private property can be owned by individuals, cooperatives, or companies. So government-owned land in South Africa could be privatised in many ways. The land could be divided into plots and given (or sold) to individuals. Or large tracts of land could be left intact but shares issued to joint shareholders (individuals in a tribe or community), who could control the land and buy and sell individual shares as they wish.

9. Robert J Smith, "Earth's Resources: Private Ownership versus Public Waste," *The Individualist*, Vol 12 No 6, p 10.

10. Terry L Anderson and Donald R Leal, *Free Market Environmentalism* (Boulder, Colorado: Westview Press, 1991), pp 56, 57.

11. John Baden, "The Environment and Economic Progress," *Critical Issues, Protecting the Environment: A Free Market Strategy* (Washington: The Heritage Foundation, 1986), p 30.

12. *Report of the Three Committees of the President's Council on a National Environmental Management System* (Pretoria: Government Printer, President's Council 1/1991), pp 25, 34.

13. Mark Laing, "Jekyll-and-Hyde Herbicides," *Rotating the Cube*, (Durban: University of Natal, April 1990), pp 41-45.

14. *Ibid*, p 44.

15. Bruce Corbett, "Development for People and the Planet," *Rotating the Cube*, pp 105-107.

16. Jeremy Ridl, "Of Mines & Mine," *Rotating the Cube*, pp 77-81.

17. See Leon Louw, "Privatisation for Preservation," *The Individualist*, Vol 15 No 2, 1990.

18. *Newsweek*, May 1, 1989. Quoted in Walter Block, ed, *Economics and the Environment: A Reconciliation* (Vancouver: The Fraser Institute, 1990), p 330.

19. Jacklyn Cock and Eddie Koch, eds, *Going Green: People , Politics, and the Environment in South Africa* (Cape Town: Oxford University Press, 1991), p 221.

20. Block, pp 288, 289. Privatising *all* land, water, and air does, of course, pose practical challenges. For how free-market environmentalists are confronting the issues, see Anderson and Leal, *Free Market Environmentalism*, particularly Chapters 3 ("From Free Grass to Fences"), 8 ("Going with the Flow: Expanding Water Markets"), 9 ("Homesteading the Oceans"), and 11 ("Tackling the Tougher Problems"). See also Block,

Economics and the Environment.
21. See President's Council Report on the environment, pp 30, 19, 33, 178, 179, 274, 73, 207, 230.

9. Rights: Making sense of a constitution and bill of rights

1. Paul Craig Roberts, "Seven Days that Shook the World," *National Review*, October 15, 1990.
2. Sammy Adelman, "Capitalising on a New Constitution," *Work in Progress*, August 1990, p 34.
3. Donald Leyshon, "After the Fall," *Leadership*, December 1990/January 1991.
4. Albie Sachs, *Protecting Human Rights in a New South Africa* (Cape Town: Oxford University Press, 1990), p 18.
5. *Ibid*, p 19.
6. Frederic Bastiat, *The Law* (Irvington-on-Hudson, New York: The Foundation for Economic Education, 1987), p 67.
7. *Ibid*, p 6.
8. The right to vote is often included under first-generation rights, but it should be put, with the right of recall and referendum, into a distinct category of "political rights" or "democratic rights." Such rights (or powers or privileges) are *conferred* on citizens and are not discussed here. They are not inherent rights, but rather "procedural political rights" that a society collectively agrees to.
9. "After the Fall," *Leadership*, December 1990/January 1991.
10. Sachs, p 20.
11. *Ibid*, pp 43, 44.
12. *Ibid*, p 25.
13. *Ibid*, pp 25 - 26.
14. *Ibid*, p 163.
15. Sachs also writes:

> The...question of rights of sexual preference could also be tackled as one essentially of privacy and choice. On the one hand, there should be no discrimination against lesbian women and gay men because of their homosexuality (the right to be the same). On the other hand, their private behaviour is a matter for them alone and not for the state (the right to be different).

The sentiment is nice. But consider how singularly nonuniversal Sachs' "rights" are. If there is a "right to be different," why don't people who wish to disassociate themselves from gays — for example, conservative Christians — have that right? Sachs will not grant them the right to be different because they might exercise it. Once again, you have the right to differ only so long as you don't offend Sachs.

I do not approve of businesses and institutions that discriminate against gays. But I don't believe that gives me the right to force them to stop. They have the right. To see the *principle*, reverse the roles. Should gays be able to discriminate against straight people? Sure. They might open gay bars or run gay-staffed businesses. They might lead crippling boycotts against gay-bashing businesses — that is, they might discriminate against straights. If an antidiscrimination law is in place, a gay business person could be forced by law to hire a homophobic, gay-hating employee. I don't believe that Sachs would support such a law. His antidiscrimination clause would be selective.

16. Sachs, p 21.
17. *Weekly Mail*, December 19, 1991 to January 2, 1992.

10. The African National Congress: The ANC's authoritarian roots

1. *Business Day*, February 19, 1990. *Business Day*, February 22, 1990.
2. Reports in both the local and overseas press regularly show little scepticism of ANC proposals.
3. Tom Lodge, "The Lusaka Amendments," *Leadership*, Vol 7 No 4, 1988.
4. "The gentle revenge at the end of apartheid," *Index on Censorship*, 4/90.
5. *Weekly Mail*, October 7, 1988.
6. Article 4 of the Soviet constitution defined democratic centralism as "the obligation of lower bodies to observe the decisions of higher ones" and said it requires "central leadership."
7. *Business Day*, November 28, 1990.
8. *South African Journal on Human Rights*, Vol 5 Part 2, 1989, p 138.
9. Kelsey Stuart, *The Newspaperman's Guide to the Law* (Durban: Butterworths, 1990), p 124.
10. The preamble to the ANC's guidelines is also in line with thought control: it calls on the constitution to "promote the habits of nonracial and nonsexist thinking...and the acquisition of genuinely shared patriotic consciousness." A liberal-democratic constitution does not try to determine people's habits of thinking.
11. This is supported by Werner Viljoen, who, as head of the University of Pretoria branch of the student group Jeugkrag, met with an ANC Youth League delegation in Botswana in January 1990. The ANC delegation was led by Jackie Selebe, a member of the movement's national executive committee. "They said the guidelines exclude some political ideologies," Viljoen said. "They specifically said they would ban the NP, the CP, the AWB, the PAC, and Inkatha. Some took a hard line and said they would add other names to the list. But, in their defence, some of the younger delegates were clearly uncomfortable with this. I'd say there was general agreement on the need for banning, but there was not

specific agreement on which groups would be banned." On media restrictions, he says: "They were definitely in favour of government control of the press. We said we believed in a free, open press and they said, 'Yes, but if the press goes against the regime, the regime must control the philosophy of the press.' It really felt like you were talking to the Conservative Party." *Frontline*, May/June 1990, p 6.

12. Don Caldwell, "The joke is on us," *Frontline*, September 1990.
13. *Ibid*. See also Pierre du Toit and Willie Esterhuyse, eds, *The Myth Makers* (Halfway House: Southern Book Publishers, 1990).
14. This was ironic, coming from a leader aligned to a *communist* party.
15. *Angola Peace Monitor*, Vol 2 No 5, May 22, 1990. This is published by the International Freedom Foundation.
16. *The Washington Post* , June 27, 1990.
17. Don Caldwell, "The Underside of the ANC," *The New Republic*, July 9 & 16, 1990, p 16.
18. *The Washington Post*, July 28, 1991.
19. *The Star*, December 12, 1991.
20. *The Star*, February 10, 1990. Quoted in "In Mandela's Own Words. Statements by the Deputy President of the ANC since his release from prison on February 11, 1990." Prepared by the International Freedom Foundation, June 18, 1990.
21. *The New Republic*, July 9 & 16, 1990, p 17.
22. *Saturday Star*, December 14, 1991.
23. *Sunday Star* estimate from *Sunday Star*, July 14, 1991. International Freedom Foundation estimate supplied to author in February 1992.
24. "Political Report — Presented by Joe Slovo, General Secretary of the SACP," December 5, 1991. Mimeo, p 3.
25. *Saturday Star*, July 13, 1991.
26. These are just some of the publicly known Communist Party members. Many others have been identified as SACP members by foreign governments, intelligence agencies, analysts, academics, and journalists. In its May 4, 1990, issue, *Africa Confidential* commented:

In effect, the Party and the ANC have ceased to be two allied organisations and have become one body with two heads. All Party members are also members of the ANC. The Party uses the ANC as a pool in which to recruit the best and the brightest for Party membership.... If the Party were compelled to reveal its membership, it would reveal many of the same faces who have become known as ANC members.

27. *New Era*, Winter 1990, p 40.
28. Jeremy Baskin, *Striking Back* (Johannesburg: Ravan Press, 1991), p 215.
29. *The Citizen*, March 8, 1990.
30. *New Nation*, January 17-23, 1992.
31. *Daily Mail*, August 15, 1990.
32. *The Washington Post*, April 4, 1990.

33. *New Era*, October 1989, p 22.
34. *Work in Progress*, November/December 1989, p 13. Sisulu, named ANC vice president in 1991, reiterated the call in his speech to the SACP congress on December 5, 1991, with this glowing language:

> That the Communist Party survived 40 years of persecution is also due, in no small measure, to the rock-solid bond between the party and the national liberation movement. This bond between the ANC and the Party is a product of the struggle; it is a bond forged and tempered in the crucible of a common resolve to rid our people of institutionalised racism, national oppression, and exploitation; it is also a crucial part of our present and future struggle....It is therefore with deep pride and great joy that the ANC extends to you warm and fraternal greetings on this most important occasion. ("Address of Comrade Walter Sisulu, deputy president of the African National Congress, to the national congress of the South African Communist Party, Johannesburg, 5 December 1991." Mimeo.)

35. *Advance to National Democracy* (Johannesburg: Report on the ANC National Consultative Conference, December 14-16, 1990), p 11.
36. *The Independent Monthly*, September 1990, p 33.
37. Joe Slovo, Mimeo. p 3.
38. Transcript of interview on WHMM-TV's "Evening Exchange." Washington, April 22, 1991.

11. An ANC bill of rights: The new battleground

1. *Constitutional Principles and Structures for a Democratic South Africa* (Johannesburg: ANC, 1991), pp 10, 11, 13.
2. This is not very convincing. The document goes on to reiterate the 1988 position that the central government will *delegate* authority to lower tiers of government; it does *not* state that lower levels can pass laws in conflict with the central state: "Local and regional government will exercise delegated powers but will have wide discretion in regard to the priorities to be pursued at these levels, provided always that such policies do not conflict with national policies." (p 26.)
3. Under proportional representation, the percentage of seats a party gets in parliament (or, say, a regional parliament or a city council) is equal to its share of the total votes cast. For example, if there are 100 seats in parliament, a party that obtains 52 percent of the vote would get 52 seats, a party that obtains 7 percent of the vote would get 7 seats, and so on — even if the votes are concentrated in one area. Though the ANC document supports proportional representation, the movement's lingering intolerance of small parties is again apparent. The document calls for proportional representation to apply only to parties receiving 5 percent or more of the vote, to exclude what it calls "fringe parties." But a group that musters 2 percent or 3 percent or 4,9 percent of the

vote in South Africa represents hundreds of thousands of people and surely deserves representation, especially when the document recognises that proportional representation "is more satisfactory than forcing political or subversive activity outside parliament." So-called fringe parties could be a moderating influence on the big parties, forcing them to take a broader look at issues. If a conservative white party, radical black party, or green party holds 4 percent of the seats, let the other parties make concessions to it to win support. Saths Cooper of the University of the Western Cape, former national director of the Institute for Multiparty Democracy, correctly calls for *very* multiparty democracy — "anyone with more than half a percent support must have a seat, so they can be involved in the committee work and the parliamentary ethos and you don't have martyred groups emerging." (*Sunday Star Review*, June 23, 1991.)

4. The draft bill also calls for capital punishment to be abolished. Another option, which I prefer (though I oppose capital punishment), is to permit local communities or regions to vote on whether to allow the death penalty in their jurisdictions. It is debatable whether freedom from capital punishment is a right in a liberal-democratic society. The argument is complex, and a constitutional ban is one option. I also believe the issue of abortion — an unrelated but equally emotional issue — can best be settled by voters in local referendums, rather than being dictated to the whole country by a national statute or constitutional amendment.

5. The ANC's latest calls for censorship were immediately applauded. Nicholas Smith, a Wits law lecturer, commented favourably on the bill's proposal to restrict speech by putting the media and other "social institutions" under the duty to discourage sexual and other types of stereotyping: "It is not clear what exactly the duty would entail but there is a lot to be said for the idea that commitment to the liberal value of free speech does not imply a commitment to tolerate the abuse of this right involving an attack on the dignity of a group of people, in this case women." (Nicholas Smith, "Sachs, the ANC's Draft Bill, and Democracy," *Monitor: The Journal of the Human Rights Trust*, December 1990, p 75.)

6. Contrast this to the first amendment of the US constitution: "Congress shall make no law...abridging the freedom of speech, or of the press."

7. It prohibits private discrimination in property ownership on grounds of race, gender, religion, or language, which would prevent likeminded conservative whites, segregationist blacks, Jews, and other groups from peaceably separating themselves from others. This violates classical-liberal notions of private property. It also seems politically unwise in a diverse society. It essentially tells scared minorities that there's no place to hide. Banning state discrimination promotes equality before the law, a liberal goal. Banning private discrimination

violates an individual's freedom of association and contract.

8. All rulings on compensation shall take into account "the need to establish an equitable balance between the public interest and the interest of those affected."

9. *The Star*, November 9, 1976.

10. *Ibid*.

Index

A World Apart
  reasons for banning 83
Adelman, Sammy
  liberal reforms and bill of rights 133
Affirmative action
  ANC 62
  apartheid parallels 65
  Beckett, Denis 69
  definitions 62-63
  group differences are norm 66
  is brown black? 65
  not nonracial 60-62
  Nafcoc proposals for black
    directors 74
  preferential policies 62
  "proportional society" 68
  punitive policies 64
  race classification 59
  race classification brought back 73
  role models 68
  Sachs, Albie 61
  Slovo, Joe 66
  Steele, Shelby 68
  Sowell, Thomas 63
  victim mentality 70-73
Albania
  assault on civil society 18
ANC (African National Congress)
  affirmative action 62
  authoritarian policies and
    history 151-162
  banning fascism, racism 154, 157
  bill of rights 165-172
  censorship 78, 154, 157
  constitutional guidelines versus

liberalism 153
constitutional principles 165
controlling civil society 153, 156
development bank 51
dictatorial friends 158-160
devolution of power 153-154
economic parallels with
  apartheid 36
environment 119
illiberal approach to
  constitutions 152-157
Mandela and Cuba 158
mobilise youth 31
monopoly over civil society 20-23
outlawing opposition 155
"right of the state" 169-172
SACP influence 159-163
view of socialism 160
Apartheid. *See also* Apartheid
  economics
  anticapitalist laws 28-31
  as socialism 27-37
  assault on enterprise 29-30
  labels matter 35
  opposition to by liberal
    capitalists 35
  parallels with affirmative action 65
  parallels with ANC economics 36
  socialist views of architects 31
  spirit 31-32
Apartheid economics/socialism
  assault on enterprise and
    hawkers 29-30
  Cosatu 34
  Gelb, Stephen 34

Jordan, Pallo 27
Naidoo, Jay 34
PAC 28
Slovo, Joe 27, 34
WOSA 27
Aranson, Peter
    interest groups 113
Ash, Timothy Garton
    civil society in eastern Europe 24

Banda, Hastings
    cult of women 19
    speaks for nation 17
Barry, Dave
    control government spending 53
Bass, Cecil
    civic theatre 101
Bastiat, Frederic
    rights and role of state 134
Beckett, Denis
    affirmative action 69
    press freedom 78
    "racist" 81
Bill of rights. See also Rights
    ANC draft bill 165-172
    generations of rights 135
Blackmun, Harry
    affirmative action 62
Blasphemy
    Louis Pienaar 82
Block, Walter
    nappies and environment 126
Booysen, Susan
    resocialisation 79
Botha, PW
    warning to business on free
        speech 85
Botha, Stoffel
    scientific censorship 82
Broederbond
    call for nationalisation 31
Building Industries Federation
    housing spending 44

Caldwell, Don
    criticism of Uprooting Poverty 42
Campaign Bulletin. See Cosatu
Canada
    affirmative action 64

Capitalism. See also Free enterprise
    definition 32-33
    environmentalism 118-120, 124-127
    government discovers free
        enterprise 34
    HNP and CP oppose 32
    "outdated term" 35
    rights in capitalist society 28
    versus socialism 35
Capitalism and Apartheid. See Lipton,
        Merle
Carolus, Cheryl
    ANC-SACP member 159
CCB (Civilian Cooperation Bureau)
    scandal unfolds 90-95
Ceausescu, Nicolae
    assault on civil society 15-16
Censorship. See Free speech
Cheh, Mary
    scrap censorship 84
Chiang and Mao — China 1919-1949
    banned book 80
Civil society
    Africa 17
    ANC and SACP monopoly
        attitude 20-23
    building of 20
    Ceausescu 15-16
    Cosatu 21
    definition 16
    mobilise youth 21
    "political society" 16
    private sector and social
        engineers 18
    propaganda 17
    protection through diversity 20
    Romania 15-16
    South Africa 19-22
    voluntary organisations 16
    war of position 23-24
    women 18
Claims
    versus rights 136
Coetzee, Dirk
    CCB allegations 90
Conscientising
    students 79
Constitutions. See also Rights
    ANC versus liberal constitution 153
    liberal vision 131-132
    role and features 152-157
    South Africa's illiberal past 132

Content of our Character, The. See Steele, Shelby
Corbett, Bruce
   government control of environment 123
Cosatu
   Campaign Bulletin 34
   capitalism 34
   civil society 21
Crane, Ed
   eastern Europe revolutions 24
Cuba
   assault on civil society 18
   Mandela 158
   mobilise youth 22

Daniel Arap Moi
   assault on civil society 17
Decentralisation. *See* Devolution of power
Democracy. *See also* Devolution of power; Referendums
   definition 130
   liberal conception 130
Democratic Party
   eight to 12 states 108
Department of Louise
   alternative to referendum 53
Desai, Barney
   SACP influence in ANC 161
Devolution of power
   application to South Africa 107-109
   central world parliament 105-107
   issues to tackle locally 109
   Switzerland 109
Direct democracy. *See* Referendums
Diversity
   civil society 20
Divider effect
   versus multiplier effect 46
Doornaert, Mia
   restrict racist speech 82
D'Souza, Dinesh
   affirmative action 69
   low expectations of students 70
Du Toit, Pierre
   ANC guidelines are illiberal 156

Eastern Europe
   civil society 15-17, 24

   environmental degradation 117-118
Economics of the Colour Bar, The. See Hutt, William
Environment
   ANC 119
   authoritarian approach 123
   capitalist solutions 119-120, 124-125
   central planning 127
   eastern Europe 117-118
   economics and ecology 119-120, 124-125
   elephants in Namibia 125
   government is the enemy 120-123
   National Environmental Management System 127
   nappies 126
   pockets of socialism 119
   poor people 124
   President's Council report 127
   private property 118
   wildlife 125

Federalism. *See* Devolution of power
Free enterprise. *See also* Capitalism
   CP and HNP oppose 32
   government suppression of 33
   Meyer, Piet 33
   never existed in South Africa 36
   Sachs, Albie 36
   Slovo, Joe 27, 36
Free society
   definition 28
Free speech and censorship
   ANC censorship clauses 78
   Azapo 78
   censorship around the world 84-85
   fascism versus communism 80
   left-wing censorship 77-81
   Meyerson, Denise 81
   PAC 78
   "progressive censorship" 79
   right of free speech 140
   Suttner, Raymond 80
   threats to black journalists 85-86
   what is racist speech? 81-83
   Woods, Donald 83

Gelb, Stephen
   "apartheid is capitalism" 34

Generations of rights. *See also* Rights
definition 135
Gramsci, Antonio
war of position 23
Group differences
affirmative action 66
Growth
and pollution 120
Gwala, Harry
ANC-SACP member 160

Hani, Chris
ANC-SACP member 159
"communist future" for South
Africa 162
on lapsed SACP members 159
Harms Commission
CCB 90
Hawkers
anticapitalist restrictions 30
Haysom, Nicholas
ban racist speech 78
Herstigte Nasionale Party
opposition to capitalism 32
Hitler
right-wing socialism 32
Hofmeyr, Stroebel
"Squeejee" affair 100
Hutt, William
apartheid versus free market 33
apartheid was totalitarian 31

Idasa
press-freedom conference 77
study of student views 79
Illiberal Education. *See* D'Souza, Dinesh
Individual rights. *See also* Rights
versus group claims 141
Indonesia
affirmative action 64
Initiative. *See also* Referendums
definition 112

Jordan, Pallo
failure of capitalism 27
socialism's promise 160

Kaffir Boy. See Mathabane, Mark
Kathrada, Ahmed
ANC-SACP member 160
Kendall, Frances
devolution of power 109
Khmer Rouge
assault on civil society 18

Laing, Mark
control of chemicals 122
Le Roux, Pieter
direct democracy and devolution 114
Learn and Teach
interview with Joe Slovo 34
Lekota, Patrick
nationalisation 36
Leyshon, Donald
liberal reforms and bill of rights 133
right of disassocation "bizarre" 143
Liberal capitalists
opposition to apartheid 35
Lipton, Merle
agriculture 33
race classification 74
Local government. *See* Devolution of
power
Lodge, Tom
ANC constitutional guidelines 152
Louw, Leon
devolution of power 109

Madlala, Nozizwe
ANC-SACP member 160
Majority rule
mathematics of 115
Malan, Daniel Francois
praise for socialism 31
Malawi
assault on civil society 18
Malaysia
affirmative action 64
Mandela, Nelson
economic parallels with apartheid 36
praise for Cuba 158
praise for militant youth 21-22
praise for Tanzania 160
Marcus, Gill
ANC-SACP member 160

Marshall, Thurgood
    affirmative action 65
Mass Democratic Movement
    war of position 23-24
Mathabane, Mark
    victim mentality 73
Mazwai, Thami
    threats to black journalists 85
Mbeki, Thabo
    lapsed SACP member 159
McLachlan, John
    post office palace 101
Meltdown
    Soviet environment 118
Meyer, Piet
    against free enterprise 33
Meyerson, Denise
    free speech 81
Miami
    race riots 65
Mobutu Sese Seko
    what he calls himself 17
Mokaba, Peter
    mobilise youth 21
Molusi, Connie
    censorship by liberators 86
Mothsekga, Mathole
    ban racist speech 78
Moulder, James
    sterile economic debate 35
Mufamadi, Sidney
    ANC-SACP member 160
Mugabe, Robert
    "other son of God" 17
    Women's League 19
Mulder, Connie
    right of the state 171

Naidoo, Jay
    "apartheid is capitalism" 28, 34
Nationalisation
    Broederbond 31
    Lekota, Patrick 36
    Mandela, Nelson 36
    Ossewa Brandwag 32
Ncube, Don
    affirmative action and victimology 73
    foreword to the book 9
Netshitenze, Joel
    ANC-SACP member 160

Nefolovhodhwe, Phandelani
    ban racist speech 78
Nyatsumba, Kaizer
    No More Martyrs poem 6
    threats to black journalists 85
    tired of being portrayed as victim 71
Nkadimeng, John
    ANC-SACP member 160

Ossewa Brandwag
    state control of economy 32
Owen, Ken
    criticism of *Uprooting Poverty* 42
    Mandela's release 151

PAC
    "apartheid is capitalism" 28
Pienaar, Louis
    blasphemy 82
Pillay, Vella
    parallels with apartheid economics 36
Pol Pot
    assault on civil society 18
Political Economy of South Africa, The
    Francis Wilson on redistribution 42
Political society
    civil society 16
Pollution. *See* Environment
Pool tax
    soaking the rich 45
Popov, Gavril
    private property and freedom 132
Population Registration Act
    race classification 59
Preferential policies. *See* Affirmative
    action
Press freedom. *See* Free speech and
    censorship
Private property
    environment 118-119
    Popov, Gavril 132
    rights 136, 138-141
Prohibition of Political Interference Act
    outlawed multiracial parties 80
Propaganda
    civil society 17
*Protecting Human Rights in a New South
    Africa. See* Sachs, Albie

Publications Act
  reasons for outlawing publications 79

Race. *See* Affirmative action
Race classification
  in South Africa 59
  required for affirmative action 73
Ramphele, Mamphela
  promises of redistribution 41
Recall
  accountability of top officials 98
  benefits of 97-101
  CCB scandal 90-95
  definition and how it works 95-96
  left-wing support 101
  pay and pension abuses 98-99
  policing the police 97
  President's Council opposition 102
  United States 89-90
Redistribution
  "NP did it," says Slovo 36
  paying for 39-56
  promises by Cosatu 47
  promises by Sachs 39-40
  promises by Wilson and Ramphele 41
  promising something for nothing 40
Referendums and initiatives
  benefits 113-114
  definitions 113
  initiatives 112
  taxes 52-53
Regulation
  of economy by NP 28-31
Reznick, Maurice
  Johannesburg shopowner 99
Ridl, Jeremy
  environment 123
Rights
  assault on 134-135
  association 143
  Bastiat 134
  bill of rights turned on its head 134
  classical-liberal principles 136
  definitions 136
  discrimination 146
  feel-good conception of rights 144-147
  generations of rights 135
  group rights versus group
    claims 141-142
  handicapped 142

  in capitalist society 28
  public policy versus rights 147-148
  restricting state power 131
  shouting "fire" 140-141
  smoking 139-140
  versus claims 136-137
  what governments do that you
    may not 129
  women 142
Role models
  affirmative action 68
Romania
  assault on civil society 15-16
Rotating the Cube
  chemicals and environment 122

SA National Council for Child and
  Family Welfare
  welfare spending 44
Sachs, Albie
  affirmative action 61-62
  ANC constitutional guidelines 152
  definition of rights 146
  enterprise in South Africa was
    never free 36
  feel-good rights 144-147
  flip-flopping 61-62
  racist speech 78, 82
  redistribution and taxes 39-40, 45-46
  religion 144
  socialist vision 160
Saloojee, Cassim
  ANC constitutional guidelines 152
Schoeman, Ben
  wage control 31
Simonson, Archie
  recall 89
Sisulu, Walter
  one person, one vote 108
  praise for SACP 161
  "scientific socialist" 160
Sithole, Nokwanda
  victim mentality 72
Skweyiya, "Squeejee"
  barred from athletics meeting 99
Skweyiya, Zola
  centralised unitary state 153
  civil society 167
Slovo, Joe
  ANC-SACP alliance 161-162

"apartheid is capitalism" 27
"apartheid not capitalism" 36
civil society 23
NP used affirmative action 66
NP used redistribution 36
socialism will work 34
Slovo, Shawn
  banning of book 83
Smith, Robert J
  environment 119
Smoking
  rights 138
Socialism. *See also* Apartheid
  apartheid 27-37
  architects of apartheid 31
  confusion with capitalism 33
  definition of 32-33
  Malan praises 31
  results 30
  right-wing socialism 32
Somalia
  assault on civil society 18
South Africa: The Solution
  devolution of power 109
South African Journal on Human Rights
  Cheh on censorship 84
  van der Vyver on role of
    constitution 154
South African Labour Bulletin
  SACP 23
South African Trust for Equity and
  Development
  ANC's proposed development
    bank 51
Sowell, Thomas
  group differences are the norm 66
  preferential policies 63
Sparks, Allister
  sterile economic debate 35
Sri Lanka
  affirmative action 64
Suttner, Raymond
  ANC-SACP member 159
  racist speech 80
Switzerland
  size and number of cantons 109
Systemisation
  in Romania 15

Taxes
  ANC proposals 49

decentralising 54
democratising 52-56
divider effect 46-50
hidden taxes 48, 52, 55
petrol tax 43-46
redistribution 39-56
referendums on taxes 52-53
shifting burden to corporations 48
VAT 43-46, 50-52, 53, 55
Tefu, Philemon
  ban racist speech 78
Totalitarianism
  environmentalists' temptation 127
Transvaal Indian Congress
  ANC guidelines 152
Treurnicht, Andries
  opposes free markets 32
Tulip, Matthew
  secret council meetings 100

United States
  affirmative action at universities 63
  affirmative action for whites 64
  recall 89
Uprooting Poverty. See also Wilson, Francis,
  and Ramphele, Mamphela
  criticisms of by Caldwell, Owen 42

Van der Vyver, Johan
  role of constitution 154
Van Tonder, Robert
  bill of rights 148
VAT
  increasing 43-46
  decreasing 50-52
  radio advertisements 53, 55
Venter, Rina
  opposes private hospitals 30
Victim mentality
  Mathabane, Mark 73
  Ncube, Don 73
  Nyatsumba, Kaizer 71
  Sithole, Nokwanda 72
Vietnam
  assault on civil society 18
Voluntary organisations
  civil society 16
Von Holdt, Karl
  SACP and Gramsci 23

Wage control
    Schoeman, Ben 31
War of position
    definition 23
    Mass Democratic Movement 24
Wilson, Francis
    promises of redistribution 41
Wolpe, Howard
    communists not majority in ANC 161
Women
    civil society 18
    rights 142
Woods, Donald
    ban racist speech 83
WOSA
    "apartheid is capitalism" 27

Yengeni, Tony
    ANC-SACP member 160

Abbreviations

ANC — *African National Congress*
AWB — *Afrikaner Weerstandsbeweging*
Azapo — *Azanian People's Organisation*
Cosatu — *Congress of South African Trade Unions*
CP — *Conservative Party*
DP — *Democratic Party*
Eskom — *Electricity Supply Commission*
Frelimo — *Front for the Liberation of Mozambique*
GST — *General sales tax*
Idasa — *Institute for a Democratic Alternative for South Africa*
MDM — *Mass Democratic Movement*
MP — *Member of Parliament*
MPLA — *Popular Movement for the Liberation of Angola*
Nafcoc — *National African Federated Chambers of Commerce and Industry*
NEC — *National Executive Committee*
NP — *National Party*
PAC — *Pan Africanist Congress*
PFP — *Progressive Federal Party*
SAA — *South African Airways*
SACP — *South African Communist Party*
SADF — *South African Defence Force*
SAPA — *South African Press Association*
Sayco — *South African Youth Congress*
UDF — *United Democratic Front*
VAT — *Value-added tax*
Wits — *University of the Witwatersrand*
ZANU — *Zimbabwe Africa National Union*
ZAPU — *Zimbabwe African People's Union*

Acknowledgements

Thanks to my brilliant team of Theresa Griessel, Estelle van der Westhuizen, and Ingrid Bezu, whose hard work and assistance made *No More Martyrs Now* possible.

Thanks also to Libby Husemeyer for her sharp editing; Nancy Seijas and Gary Moore for their invaluable input; Maureen Sullivan, John Koppisch, Richard Grant, Marc Swanepoel, and Dan Leach for their useful comments on earlier drafts; Frances Kendall and Leon Louw for their personal encouragement and pioneering work in democratic liberalism; Marie Grey for her undying enthusiasm; Mark Heaton for his commitment to excellence in production; and Ed Emary, Philip Moore, Michael O'Dowd, Robert van Zyl, and Ann Cluver Weinberg for their support and encouragement.

About the foreword

Don Ncube is an alternate director of the Anglo American Corporation and is the company's group industrial-relations consultant.

He is a member of the Anglo American and De Beers Chairman's Fund and serves on the management committee of the Institute for Multiparty Democracy.

About the author

Don Caldwell is a professional speaker on politics, economics, business, and customer service and is the author of the books *South Africa: The New Revolution*, *The Customer is Always Wrong!*, and *No More Martyrs Now*.

He has contributed to a wide range of South African publications and has worked as managing editor of *Frontline* magazine and as associate economics editor of the *Financial Mail*. He is a frequent guest on radio and TV.

Conferences and training

Don Caldwell's speaking and training is managed exclusively by Marie Grey of Marie Grey & Associates. Don's topics include customer service, affirmative action, politics, economics, redistribution, privatisation, South African scenarios, the environment, team building, leadership, and motivation.

Contact Marie Grey for more information on having Don tailor an address to your organisation — whether for a conference, customer-service workshop, business breakfast, or management seminar.

■ Telephone: (011) 728-3202.
■ Fax: (011) 728-3195.
■ Post: Marie Grey & Associates, Box 30683, Braamfontein 2017.